Ideas for Teachers
from Teachers

Ideas for Teachers from Teachers

Elementary Language Arts

National Council of Teachers of English
1111 Kenyon Road, Urbana, Illinois 61801

NCTE Editorial Board: Arthur Applebee, Thomas L. Clark,
Julie Jensen, Elisabeth McPherson, Zora Rashkis,
John C. Maxwell, *ex officio*, Paul O'Dea, *ex officio*

Staff Editor: Audrey Hodgins

Book Design: Tom Kovacs for TGK Design

NCTE Stock Number 22469

Library of Congress Cataloging in Publication Data

Main entry under title:

Ideas for teachers from teachers.

 1. Language arts (Elementary) 2. English language—
Study and teaching (Elementary) I. National Council of
Teachers of English.
LB1576.I3   1983   372.6′044   83-4175
ISBN 0-8141-2246-9

Contents

Foreword

Teachers are course designers and curriculum builders, but teachers are also strategists who recognize that successful courses and curricula ultimately stand on six challenging and stimulating classroom hours every day. Ideas that deliver content in a lively fashion, however, are consumed at an astonishing rate, and teachers are perennially alert for new ones to adapt to their own teaching styles and goals.

The Idea Exchange at the annual convention of the National Council of Teachers of English is one place where many teachers have found such ideas. For the past seven years, hundreds of teachers have queued up at the Exchange, turning in teaching tips that work for them and receiving in return copies of the ideas submitted by their colleagues. Thus have fresh and useful ideas made their way from classroom to classroom and from coast to coast.

The Idea Exchange has been so popular that the NCTE Executive Committee decided some of this material should be available to a wider audience, in a more permanent form. This collection for elementary teachers, assembled at headquarters, provides a sampling of ideas from recent conventions. Although not all of the ideas submitted are included here, the book does suggest the range and variety of contributions. In addition, some ideas come from teachers who attended a workshop taught by Professor Thomas L. Clark at the University of Nevada. As he put it, "I was so impressed with the Idea Exchange that I stole the idea."

As teachers would have predicted, the largest number of contributions were concerned with the teaching of writing and reading. Smaller categories included getting to know each other in the classroom, making and using dictionaries, punctuation and grammar, and observing and evaluating. Some teachers were concerned with rationale and behavioral objectives; others responded with a no-fail writing assignment or a surefire activity for achieving attention during the first five minutes of class—or the last. All of this we have tried to represent in over one hundred activities arranged in nine chapters. Inclusive we could not be, but we hope we have captured the character and spirit of the Idea Exchange—its camaraderie and good-natured pragmatism and its unselfish professionalism.

In a book like this one, it is appropriate to conclude the opening remarks with a word from one of its many contributors, Belinda Ann Bair of Bohemia Manor High School, Chesapeake City, Maryland:

> On my desk in an unobtrusive metal file box is the rescuer of the late-afternoon, just-before-holiday, harried teacher. In it are the little games as well as the more complex activities I have gleaned from NCTE Idea Exchanges through the years, from professional journals, and from the occasional wild inspiration that strikes. Some take only five or ten minutes but all are fun and practical. Begin your own collection now, a box you or your substitute can turn to when time is longer than lessons.

We have, then, taken Ms. Bair's idea and in the same spirit of sharing offer this book from our members to our members. We hope it will get new teachers off to a start on their idea collections while adding to the contents of well-worn boxes on the desks of old hands.

1 Getting to Know Each Other

Getting to know one another is a learning task that faces teachers and students alike every September, and it's often one that continues throughout the school year. Included in this section are games to help you and your students learn each other's names, directions for a neighborhood map, and instructions for assembling a directory of who's who at school. There's a writing assignment that asks older elementary students to revert to the good old days of show and tell, and others in which youngsters prepare a lifeline, assemble a peer biography, and create a family portrait. There are silhouettes to make—and to use in a variety of autobiographical assignments—and an interest inventory that will teach you a lot more about your students than their names.

People Bingo

This beginning-of-the-year activity helps students get acquainted and learn each other's names. In advance, mimeograph bingo sheets with a grid containing four rows and four columns, for a total of sixteen squares. You'll also need paper clips, cardboard squares, or other bingo markers. Finally, write the name of each student on an individual slip of paper.

Distribute the bingo sheets and ask each student to write his or her name in the square at the top left corner. Students then walk around the classroom, introducing themselves to other students and obtaining signatures from fifteen of them for the remaining squares. When the sheets are filled, one name to a square, students return to their seats.

You (or a designated student) choose one of the name slips at random and call out the name. The student whose name has been called raises his or her hand. The other students take note of that student's identity. Students who have that name on their sheets cover it with a marker. Proceed as in any bingo game. When a player calls "bingo," he or she must be able to match the four names in the horizontal, vertical, or diagonal row with the four correct people. By the end of the period everyone will have made new acquaintances and members of the class will be able to address one another by name. It's a beginning.

Karen Rezendes, Danbury, Connecticut

Icebreaker

Here's a get-acquainted game that helps to build a friendly feeling in the classroom. One student begins by giving his or her first name preceded by a word that begins with the same letter as the name: Curious Carol. The next student says, "You are Curious Carol and I am Just Jack." The game continues until all students have joined the chain, each student repeating in turn the names of those who preceded. To really break the ice, elect to be the last person in the chain and repeat all names correctly. You'll never forget them if you do!

Karen Rugerio, Orange County Administration Center, Orlando, Florida

Class Tree

At the beginning of the school year I put the outline of a large tree on the bulletin board. Each child cuts out a leaf and prints his or her name on it. We have a little discussion about the meanings of names. I print each child's name on the chalkboard. We look up each name in dictionaries of personal names, writing the meaning beside the name. Students then copy the meaning of their names on their leaves. We conclude by putting the leaves on the class tree.

Julie Anne Arnold, Rose Warren Elementary School, Las Vegas, Nevada

Lifeline

This assignment works well with fourth- through sixth-graders and helps youngsters recognize that we all experience certain predictable events (learning to walk, entering school, celebrating birthdays) as well as certain unpredictable events (accidents, family relocations).

Explain that each student will make a lifeline of his or her very own by plotting the dates of important events. For example,

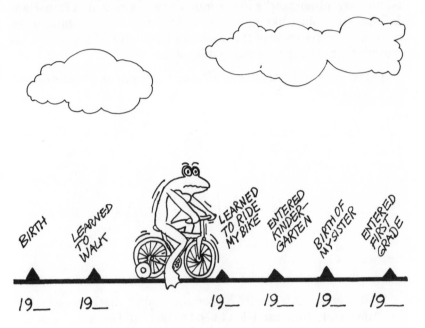

Provide long strips of paper or tagboard and have students draft their lifelines in pencil, including events they remember or have heard that seem important to them. Encourage them to talk to each other and to share ideas.

Assemble in a group and ask students to note events that all or most of them have recorded on their lifelines and events that seem unique to one person. Help them to conclude that we have much in common with each other and much that is unique.

When students are confident that they have thought of all important lifeline events and put them in the correct order, they complete and illustrate their lifelines with crayons or felt-tip markers.

As follow-up activities, ask students to use their lifelines to complete in writing sentences like the following: The happiest (saddest, scariest, funniest, angriest) memory I have is ... Allow students to add to their lifelines when they remember something that now seems important to them. Ask students to write down what they predict will be on all of their lifelines in the future. What events do they hope to find recorded?

Mary Jane Hanson, Harrison Open School, Minneapolis, Minnesota

Name Brain Drain

Names are important! Fitting into a new classroom is important. My students and I like to begin the school year by examining our names. Here are some of the activities I use with fifth-graders, but most of them are fun for youngsters of any age.

1. Students write their initials and names in new and different ways.

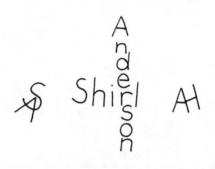

2. Students write positive thoughts using the letters in their names. Letters used don't need to be initial ones.

3. Students look up the meanings of their first and middle names and last names where possible. Baby books and special dictionaries of names are helpful resources.

4. Students design logos for themselves or for each other.

5. Students print their names on a sheet of paper in as many different styles as possible. Have on hand books that illustrate typefaces to get this activity started.

6. Distribute gummed paper. Students make name labels in different sizes and shapes. These can be stuck on many items —for identification or for fun.

7. Post a class picture on the bulletin board. Each student creates a name label to post under the picture.

8. Students write their names in code for classmates to decode. They will have no trouble inventing codes!

9. Students use their names or initials to create a picture or mobile or other art project.

10. Provide stencils, rubber stamps and ink pads, label makers, colored pens, cut-out letters, old magazines, fabric scraps, yarn. Declare a name brain drain during which each student creates "something" based on his or her name.

Shirl Anderson, Myrtle Tate Elementary School, Las Vegas, Nevada

Class Map

If your school is located in a city, you'll need a city map. If you teach in a rural area, you'll need a township or county map. You'll also need map pins and yarn. Tack the map to a large bulletin board. Help students find the streets or roads on which they live and approximately where their homes are located. Mark the spot with a map pin. Attach yarn to the pin and stretch the yarn to a point on the bulletin board outside the boundary of the map. Fasten it with a second pin. Each student then draws a picture of his or her home and family and places it at the point where the yarn ends. Paragraphs of introduction or description may also be added.

Belinda Davis, Andrew Mitchell Elementary School, Boulder City, Nevada

Who's Who at School

When students first come to school, they don't know the people who make up the "system." I suggest that a directory be made for them. For the first-grader it might include principal, secretary, librarian, teacher aides, classroom teachers, special education teachers, and custodian. Directories for students in higher grades might include the superintendent, assistant superintendent, board members, and others who make up the school system. These directories also help parents understand who's who at school.

Ann Redemann, Halle Hewetson Elementary School, Las Vegas, Nevada

What's in a Name?

Ask each student to print his or her name on a sheet of unlined paper. Students then page through magazines to find pictures of objects that begin with the letters in their names. For example, S (sandwich), A (apple), M (money). These pictures are cut out and pasted beside the appropriate letters of the child's name. Encourage youngsters to help each other, especially with longer names or more difficult letter-picture matches. Finally, each child makes up a sentence using the words found to represent the letters in his or her name. For example, Sam spent money for an apple and a sandwich.

The Kindergarten at Sunrise Acres Elementary School, Las Vegas, Nevada

My second-graders think up or look up words that begin with each letter in their names. They can choose which name—first, middle, or last—they want to use or use each in turn. Then they write one sentence about themselves—or about anything—using the words they have found. The words must, however, follow the order of the letters in their names. For example: Sarah—Sarah *a*te *r*ipe *a*pples *h*ungrily.

Sammie McCraw, C. H. Decker Elementary School, Las Vegas, Nevada

I begin this activity by talking with my fourth-graders about how they got their names, whether or not they like them, and what their names mean. Students then write their first names coupled with two adjectives (encourage positive ones) that begin with the same letter: Smiling, Sensitive Samantha. Next I ask them to use their dictionaries to find five (six? seven?) other appropriate adjectives to make the list even longer. I also introduce the term *alliteration*.

To conclude the activity, each student picks the one adjective he or she likes best and chooses an animal whose name begins with the same letter. The student then uses the three words together—adjective, name, animal—Smiling Samantha Skunk—as the name for a cartoon character that he or she invents, illustrates, and posts on our bulletin board.

P.S. Don't throw away those other adjectives. They can be used for mobiles, in poetry lessons, for alphabetizing exercises.

Hope Goffstein, Laura Dearing Elementary School, Las Vegas, Nevada

Roses by Other Names

Children are fascinated by names—their names, their parents' names, the names of their pets. The name a person or object has often influences the way we see that person or object. Children are also fascinated by cartoons. How would the image of Superman, for example, change if his name were Greatman? Does Charlie Brown's name have special significance? Would Snoopy be Snoopy if we called him Ranger? Encourage youngsters to come up with new names for favorite cartoon characters. Do the names change the characters? Bring in books with pictures of creatures, real and fanciful, and ask the class to provide names for them. Ask students to draw their own creatures and name them appropriately.

Nancy Hest, Lois Craig Elementary School, North Las Vegas, Nevada

Begin by reading *Liza Lou* by Mercer Mayer because nicknames are used. Go on to discuss nicknames, how and why we acquire them. Ask students to choose nicknames for themselves and to explain their choices. If there's time, ask them to provide nicknames for each other—and for you—and to explain them.

Rosemary Holmes-Gull, Paul E. Culley Elementary School, Las Vegas, Nevada

Show and Tell—and Write

As part of an autobiography unit, our students revert to the good old days of Show and Tell. Each student brings an object that he or she valued as a young child. After sharing stories about these objects in class, students begin to write. We distribute the pre-writing guide that follows:

> Here are questions about your special object for you to answer in writing. Thinking about these questions and answering them as completely as you can will help you to write about your object in a special way.
>
> 1. Write at least three phrases to describe it.
> 2. Does it have a name? If so, why/how was its name selected?
> 3. Was it something you had wanted? Explain.
> 4. How does it make you feel?
> 5. What did you do with it when you first got it?
> 6. Do you use it now? How?
> 7. Where do you keep it now? Why do you keep it there?
> 8. Is it different now from when you first got it? If so, how is it different or why is it different?
> 9. What do you especially like or enjoy about it?
> 10. Can you tell a story in which your object is important?

And here is a sample paragraph written by one of our students.

> My teddy bear was very important to me because he was my real friend. Since I had always wanted a real animal, I treated him like one. I respected him. I never threw him around. I always played gently with him. When I slept in my crib, he slept next to me. However, since I tossed and turned during the night, he was never there in the morning. When I realized that he was gone, I cried because I had lost my best friend. Then my mother picked him up. Ahhh! Happiness was finding my friend again.

Eileen Morris and Carol Seldin, University of Chicago Lab Schools, Chicago, Illinois

Silhouette Stimulus

You will need large (18″ × 24″) sheets of black construction paper, masking tape, scissors, and a bright light source such as a film or overhead projector. Depending upon the manual dexterity of students, you may want to use scrap paper for some trial-and-error experimentation.

Process

1. Divide the class into groups of three—one student to pose, one to hold, and one to trace. While every student will be positive that he or she can sit still for the few moments it takes to trace the outline of his or her head, in fact, the silhouettes will be better if a student stands behind the poser and holds the head.

2. Have the poser sit close to the wall and about two or three feet from the light source. Position the paper and tape it to the wall. You'll discover that it's easier to move the paper than the student.

3. Have the tracer outline the shadow in pencil so that the shiny line shows later on the black construction paper. Hair is especially important in making a silhouette look like the poser. Be sure students do not cut off the necks of their silhouettes or they won't be happy with the results.

4. After three students have posed, held, and drawn, they turn the light over to the next group while they carefully cut out their silhouettes.

Product

These silhouettes can be used as backgounds, covers, or poster art for a number of autobiographical writing assignments. Here are several that my students have enjoyed.

1. Parts of speech: List adjectives (nouns or verbs) that describe you and your interests.

2. Poems of wishes and dreams.

3. Points of view: In one column put words that you would choose to describe yourself; in another put words that parents, teachers, brothers and sisters, friends would choose.

4. Appearance and reality: Use a piece of paper pasted to one side of the silhouette to describe the way you seem to be and another on the other side of the silhouette to describe the way you really are. (I seem to be a frightened tiger kitten. In reality, I'm a raging tiger.)

5. Summary of important events of a week, month, year.

Marj Montgomery, Day Junior High School, Newtonville, Massachusetts

Peer Biographies

This exercise develops interviewing and writing skills. I try to use it soon after the opening of school because it helps students get to know one another.

I begin by discussing with students what biography is and how it differs from autobiography. I read sample passages from anthologies and magazines. Then the class compiles questions students might ask if they were to write a biography of another student.

I assign partners (boy and girl work well) and have them interview one another for the purpose of writing a biography. I try to pair students who don't know one another well. I reserve about fifteen minutes on three or four separate days so there's time for follow-up questions and last-minute bright ideas. If more information is needed, students phone each other.

We share the biographies in class. Sometimes I read them, leaving out the names, and have students try to guess whose biography is being read. Later, students rewrite them on ditto masters and we assemble booklets so that each student has a copy.

Gloria Heisler, South Kingstown Junior High School, Wakefield, Rhode Island

Family Portraits

Assemble a collection of magazines, newspapers, catalogs, maps, travel brochures, picture pamphlets, and the like. You will also need scissors, paste, and colored paper.

Ask students to think for a few minutes about the members of their families: what they like to do; where they come from; foods they enjoy; celebrations they share; hobbies, sports, and just about anything that would describe them to someone else. Give them the opportunity to share their descriptive words and phrases as you write them on the board. Join in with your ideas as well; in fact, this activity is enhanced if you participate at every step—from brainstorming to collage to composition.

Now ask students to list family members (including themselves) across the top of a sheet of paper, one column for each family member. Keep in mind that families differ and be receptive to single-parent families or family units based on guardians or grandparents. Students then list words or phrases from the chalkboard that describe individual members of their families. They may, of course, add to these lists of descriptors as they work.

Students now move to the picture collection, looking for and cutting out pictures that illustrate the descriptors they have chosen to use in their family outlines. If a student finds a picture that illustrates a characteristic not on the outline, the student adds the appropriate word or phrase to the outline. When the picture collections are complete, use yours to demonstrate how to create a family collage. To preserve these collages, spray them with a fixative or cover them with clear plastic.

Students now begin writing about their families from the information on their outlines. Discuss the purpose and audience for this work—to introduce your family to classmates and to the families of classmates. Write your own rough draft at this time, but be available to students who are having difficulties. Allow time for students to read their rough drafts to each other before revising and assist with revision through individual conferences if possible.

Finished compositions can be typed or handwritten on ditto masters. Reproduce a copy for each member of the class. Each student uses his or her family collage as the cover for a booklet that contains a copy of each student's composition. Both students and their families seem to enjoy reading these booklets, and this sharing makes the classroom a warmer, more friendly place.

Charles Williams, Carol Hittleman, Gloria Lang, and Jay Finello, Huntington Public Schools, Huntington, New York

Interest Inventory

An interest inventory identifies general interests as well as reading interests and can be used to initiate and extend informal teacher/student discussions. I administer an inventory similar to the one shown below to students at the beginning of the school year. It's a way to discover and develop their reading and writing interests and it provides an informal analysis and a basis for further exploration.

Name _____   Age _____
1. What do you like to do after school?
2. What do you do indoors when it rains?
3. What hobbies or collections do you have?
4. Do you have a pet? What?

5. What are your favorite television shows?
6. What games or sports do you like best?
7. To what clubs or other groups do you belong?
8. What is your favorite type of movie?
9. Do you have a public library card? If so, how often do you go to the library?
10. Do you own books? What are some of them?
11. What things do you like to read about?
12. Do you subscribe to any magazines at home? Which ones?
13. Name a book you would like to read again. Why?
14. Do you read the newspaper? How often? Which section do you read first?
15. Do you talk to your friends about the books you have read or are reading?
16. Do you use books to help answer questions you have?
17. Do you like to read aloud in class?
18. Where is your favorite place to read?
19. Do you like to write about what you read?
20. Do you think that you are a good reader for your age?

Suzanne Irwin and Nancy A. Wrzesinski, Irving School, Lorain, Ohio

2 Phonics and Syllabication

First-grade teachers can all recall a child like the six-year-old who looked at her first purple-dittoed phonics exercise and sighed, "Now comes the hard part of first grade." Activities in this section, however, are likely to involve more than pencils—alphabet feet and vowel fingers, musical chairs, pictonames, and a three-step staircase. There are board games and card games, target and team games, and even a way of sampling the consonant blends with a food blender.

Alphabet Feet and Vowel Fingers

Cut out fifty-two footprint patterns. On twenty-six, write the capital letters; on the other twenty-six, write the lowercase letters. Children enjoy putting these on the floor, matching capital and lowercase letters to make a path.

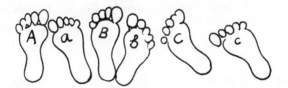

Mark each child's fingers on one hand with either the long or short vowel sounds. Children then point to the correct vowel sound as you pronounce specific words.

Roxy Voorhees, Division of Elementary and Secondary Education, Pierre, South Dakota

All the Words That Are Fit to Print

This activity provides first-graders with practice in letter identification and initial consonant sounds. Give each child a newspaper or magazine and ask the child to cut out words that begin with a given letter, *F* for example. After the words are cut out, they may be pasted on a sheet of paper. Choose a word from each child's collection, look it up in the dictionary, and explain its meaning. Ask the class to help you use it in a variety of sentences.

Lisa Hahn, Halle Hewetson Elementary School, Las Vegas, Nevada

Pen Pin Pan Pun

Use the familiar circle game Musical Chairs to reinforce listening skills and the ability to recognize rhyming words or to identify initial or final consonant sounds or medial vowels. Arrange all student chairs but one in a circle facing out. Announce, "Merry-go-round, go!" Youngsters march around the chairs while you call off words from a list compiled for the designated skill. When students hear a word that does not belong on the list, they sit down. The child who does not get a chair goes to the center of the circle. One chair is removed before the game resumes.

Marcia Eggers, Crestwood Elementary School, Las Vegas, Nevada

Pictonames

Ask students to print their names on sheets of newsprint. Above each letter sketch a familiar object that begins with that letter. For example: bat, egg, toe, and hen.

Your sketch demonstrates that every letter in the student's name is a "take-off" for another word. Now ask the youngster to draw pictures below each letter. For example: boy, elephant, top, and hat.

Cut or fold the newsprint so that only the "pictonames" show and ask the children to "read" each other's names. If there's time, write the names of your students on slips of paper. Each student draws a slip and makes a picture representation for that name. Hold these up one at a time and ask the class to decode each name. If this activity is done early in the year, pictonames can be put on tagboard and hung as name tags from students' desks.

Ann Redemann, Halle Hewetson Elementary School, and Marie E. Meehan, J.M. Ullom Elementary School, Las Vegas, Nevada

Three-Step Staircase

You'll need a collection of picture rhymes (bat, hat, and cat; tree, bee, and knee) for this game, a flannel board, and yarn. Use a piece of yarn to make a three-step staircase on the flannel board. On two of the steps place pictures that rhyme (tree and bee); on a third put one that does not (cat). The child goes up the stairs, naming each picture and deciding which words rhyme and which word does not. The child then picks the next player. Three-step staircase can also be used with antonyms or synonyms or with long and short vowel sounds or initial consonants.

Lisa Hahn, Halle Hewetson Elementary School, Las Vegas, Nevada

The Long and the Short of It

This game provides practice in discriminating between the long and short sounds of the letter *a* and can be extended to other vowel sounds. It may be played as an individual sorting game or by teams as described below.

Cut two tagboard rectangles about 8″ × 14″. Designate with a word and a picture cue which is the short *a* playing board and which the long. Outline nine 1½″ × 2″ rectangles on each playing board. Like this.

Now make twenty-six 1½″ × 2″ word cards, thirteen with short *a* words and thirteen with long *a* words.

Divide the group into two teams and give each team a playing board. Each team should review the vowel sound it will monitor. Mix the word cards and spread them facedown in the center of the table. Play alternates between the two teams, with each player in turn selecting a word card and turning it over so that all may see the word. The player then pronounces the word aloud, for example, "made," and decides whether the sound of *a* in that word matches the sound on the team's playing board. If it does, the player places the word card on one of the rectangles. If the sounds do not match, the student turns the card over and mixes it with the others on the table. When a student places a card on the board incorrectly, the card is awarded to the opposing team. The game ends when one team fills the nine boxes on its playing board.

The game may be varied by adding a third team card, such as the one shown below. Cards for other vowel sounds may also be made: two cards for the sounds of *oo*, two for the sounds of *ow*, one card for the *oi* and *oy* sound as in *oil* and *boy*, one for the *ou* and *ow* sound as in *out* and *cow*.

Carolyn Lyles, Woerther Elementary School, Ballwin, Missouri

Follow the Yellow Brick Road

Draw a zigzag road on a ditto sheet and divide the road into sections. Reproduce a number of these sheets and use them to make review games for short and long vowel sounds. For example, fill in the sections with short *a* words as shown below. You might end with a short *a* "story."

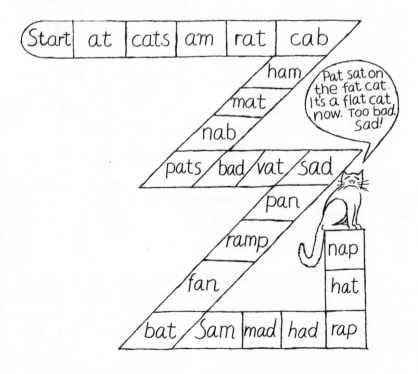

Students play with a partner and need a die and two markers—paper clips will do. The first player throws the die and moves the clip the number of spaces shown. However, the player must read each word correctly as the marker passes, including the word on which the marker lands. If the student misses a word, the marker is placed on the last word correctly pronounced. The first student to reach the end of the road wins.

Marie E. Meehan, J.M. Ullom Elementary School, Las Vegas, Nevada

Consonant Kangaroo

You'll need file folders, index cards, and library book pockets for this activity. Paste eight pockets inside each folder. Print a consonant letter your first-graders have studied on each pocket. Like this:

Now cut from magazines and catalogs pictures of familiar objects the names of which begin with the consonants you have chosen. Paste each picture on a card cut to fit the pocket. More advanced students will enjoy making these cards for you if you set up a consonant corner for them to work in when they have free time.

To play the game a student picks a card, identifies the picture, and puts it into the correct pocket, matching initial consonant sounds.

Julie Anne Arnold, Rose Warren Elementary School, Las Vegas, Nevada

Sampling the Consonant Blends

When I introduce the blends to first-graders, I bring a blender and several oranges and bananas from home. We talk about orange juice and how it tastes. Then we talk about bananas and their taste. After blending orange juice and bananas together, everyone gets a drink. We discuss the new taste—noting that you still get a taste of orange juice and a taste of banana. Then I relate this experience to the blends—you can still hear a trace of each letter but the blend has a brand new sound. A puzzle game is the follow-up.

Cut from magazines and old workbooks pictures of familiar objects the names of which begin with blends and paste each one on a small rectangle of tagboard. Use a felt-tip pen to print each name *across its picture.* Cut each rectangle apart with the blend on one piece and the rest of the word on the other. The pictures help youngsters put the puzzles together correctly as they sound out words like *drapes, truck, plate, grapes,* and *flower.*

Marge Chilton, Doris Hancock Elementary School, Las Vegas, Nevada

Viwol Chengos

I ask my second-graders to print their first and last names on a sheet of paper, for example, Barbara Johnson. Students then change the vowels in their names and write their new names on a large index card, for example, Berbiro Jehnsin. I hold each card up for the class to read—and to guess whose name it is. When a name is guessed, that student stands up. This activity helps us to get acquainted at the beginning of the school year—and to review the vowel sounds.

Margie Ripplinger, Doris French Elementary School, Las Vegas, Nevada

Consonant Chains

Students strengthen their perception of beginning and ending consonant sounds by playing that old favorite "I'm Going on a Trip." Students divide into groups of five or six and sit in a circle on the floor. One student begins by saying, "I'm going on a trip and I'll take a _(cat)_ ." The next student in the circle responds by repeating the first item and adding a second that begins with the ending sound of the first: "I'm going on a trip and I will take a cat and a __(top)__ ." Play continues around the circle in this manner with the consonant chain growing until no child can repeat it without error. "Going on a Trip" is also good for developing listening and memory skills.

Nancy Hest, Lois Craig Elementary School, North Las Vegas, Nevada

Syllable Race

Write syllables from the following word list or from a list of your own on large file cards or cards made from tagboard.

hap	sur	air	gar	but
py	prise	plane	bage	ter
bit	sum	hid	doc	tur
ter	mer	den	tor	key
fun	wind	rab	cor	scis
ny	mill	bit	ner	sors

Use this deck in an individual activity by asking the child to use the syllable cards to make as many words as possible. The game can be made self-correcting by coding the back of each card. Alternately, the deck can be used to play a pairing game following the format of Old Maid. Finally, the game can be played as a relay. The first player on each team comes to a line about ten feet from the chalkboard. Display on the chalk rack four of the syllable cards: two of these must form a word; the other two are distractors and cannot be used to form a word. Players race to arrange the syllable cards to form a word. The first player to do so scores a point for his or her team. Continue until all players have had at least one turn. Three-, four-, and more-syllable words may be used for older players and a more difficult game.

Merrily P. Hansen, New York, New York

Targeting Syllables

Here is an activity that involves coordination and fast thinking and is enjoyed by my fourth-graders. It may be played by teams or individuals.

Make a target from construction paper or tagboard similar to the one shown below. Make three or four if you want the entire class to play without restless waiting.

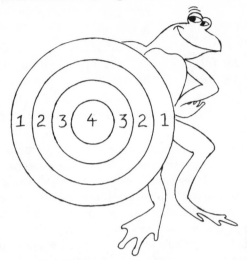

Lay the target on the floor and play the game by tossing tokens or coins. If a token lands in number 4, the student must give a four-syllable word; for this he or she scores four points. The student gives a three-syllable word if the token lands in number 3, scoring three points, and so on. The same word may not be used twice during the game. After a specified time, the team or individual with the most points wins.

If you like, offer a bonus point for the correct spelling of words that you declare "spelling monsters."

Diane Ng, Helen Marie Smith Elementary School, Las Vegas, Nevada

Syl' lable Stress

Teaching syllable stress or accent has always been a difficult task for me, probably because so many students (and teachers?) don't hear or feel this stress naturally. I think I'm having more success since I began to attack the problem with more diverse "weapons." After covering the basic textbook lessons, I try these tricks.

1. Create syllable-stress categories into which all one-, two-, and three-syllable words will fall. For example:

Ten	*Sev'* en	Ju *ly'*
plant	*par'* ty	be *gin'*
yes	*ta'* ble	for *give'*
cold	*end'* ing	ga *rage'*
Sev' en ty	E *lev'* en	Twen ty *one'*
gath' er ing	per *for'* mance	un der *stand'*
won' der ful	at *ten'* tion	dis ap *point'*
quar' ter back	un *cov'* er	rec om *mend'*

Test these categories with students by using whatever words come to mind. Use first and last names of students and other friendly words.

2. Build syllable stress strings. Students write one-, two-, and three-syllable words on 2″ × 2″ tags, categorize them (first as a class, then in small groups, then individually), and staple them to the appropriate syllable stress string (one string for each category). Encourage daily contributions, and check them at the end of class for accuracy. Buzz out bloopers—odd words that don't fit seem to pop out when a list is read orally and words are heard in rapid succession.

3. Perhaps a syllable stress string race is in order. Each team draws a category and seeks to surpass the strings of the other teams, or the whole class may rise to the challenge of keeping the strings *equal* in length. Lagging and sagging strings can be announced and word-nominees sought.

Lynn Genter, Woodbury Elementary School, Woodbury, Minnesota

3 Sight Words and Reading

Sight-word flowers and caterpillars to take home and card games to play at school are among the suggestions for the review and mastery of basic vocabulary. "Reading" brand names is offered as a way for beginning readers to achieve instant success. There's a scheme for organizing reading groups within the classroom to ensure that each youngster works once with the teacher, once independently, and once at an activity center. Storytelling pencils and illuminated letters help to involve young readers in a personal way with their story favorites. There's an exercise for skimming and one for the intensive reading of a four-inch square on a road map. Projects are described for an annual balloon day patterned after Carolyn Haywood's *Away Went the Balloons*, for a week of Tomten secrets based on Astrid Lindgren's Tomten books, for a Super Bowl reading runoff, and for a school- or communitywide children's author day.

Brand Name Bonus

Children want very much to "learn to read" on the first day of first grade. Most of them already recognize brand names from advertising. List on tagboard or at the chalkboard products well known to children such as Kool-aid, Cocoa Puffs, Dr. Pepper, Hershey, Campbell's for those who recognize them to "read." Then match empty boxes, bottles, and cans to each brand name so that all children will be able to "read" the list. They will go home on the first day announcing proudly, "I can read!"

Marge Chilton, Doris Hancock Elementary School, Las Vegas, Nevada

Say It with Flowers

As kindergarten and first-graders are introduced to their first reading books, keep track of the new words they master by creating a word garden on your bulletin board. I use this title at the top: "Watch our flowers grow." And this text at the bottom: "The more you read, the more you know."

Each child begins with the center of a flower on which I write the child's name and the title of the book he or she is reading. Each new word mastered is written on a petal which the child pins around the flower's center. When seven or eight words are mastered, the child glues the petals in place and the flower is complete. When the book is finished, the child takes home the corresponding flowers.

This activity can also be done with word caterpillars. On the head, write the child's name and the title of the book. Write each word mastered on a segment of the body. Flowers and caterpillars are an easy way to review sight vocabulary in the classroom and you can be virtually certain that parents will ask for a reading at home.

Angela Stervinou, Port Royal School, Southhampton, Bermuda

If You're Happy and You Know It, Then Your Face Will Surely Show It

You'll need a deck of at least twenty-five cards containing basic sight words for a group of three or four youngsters. In addition, make five cards with a sad face on each. Shuffle the cards and place them facedown on the table. Each child in turn picks up a card and pronounces the word shown there. The child continues to draw cards until he or she misses a word or draws a sad face. The object is to call out as many words as possible before drawing a sad face or missing a word.

If you make several decks covering a basic one- or two-hundred words, groups may exchange decks and the whole class can play at the same time.

Debra J. Williams, Walter Bracken Elementary School, Las Vegas, Nevada

Word Card Rummy

This card game can be played by a group of four or five children, so you may want to make enough decks so that everyone in your class can play at the same time.

To make a thirty-card deck, draw three pictures of each of the following on cards: apple, flower, bird, house, tree, ball, wagon, cat, dog, and hat. The pictures need not be identical. Now print a different word on each card. Choose these from a basic word list for the grade you are teaching or from current reading material your students are mastering.

The cards are shuffled and each child receives three cards. The remainder of the deck is placed facedown on the table. The object of the game is to collect a set of three cards (three trees, for example) *and to read the words printed on the cards as well.* To play the game, the first child asks another if he or she has a given picture—a flower, for example. If the child has, he or she gives it to the child who requested it. The child receiving the card must pronounce the word correctly or forfeit the card. The child then draws one card from the pile. The next child in turn asks for a picture he or she needs to complete a set of three, and the game continues until one child is out of cards or until all cards are matched.

Betty Moore, Gordon McCaw Elementary School, Henderson, Nevada

As the Wheel Turns

I have reading groups on three levels in my second-grade classroom and use a rotation system based on two wheels that are easily interpreted by youngsters. The first wheel, shown below, is moved three times during the daily reading period. By the end of the period, students in each of the three groups (Pooh, Tigger, and

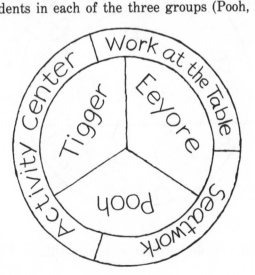

Eeyore) have worked once at the table with me, once at the activity center, and once at their desks.

When a reading group moves to the activity center, it is subdivided into five groups (A through E), as shown on the chart below. Five activities are available at the center and each youngster completes the activity scheduled that day on the activity wheel for his or her letter group. The wheel at the activity center is turned each day. By the end of the week, each child has had an opportunity to complete all five activities. Each week the five activities are changed.

GROUP	A	B	C	D	E
Pooh	John Carol	Lisa Sherry	Shane Ned	Mike Debbie	Tony Jennifer
Tigger					
Eeyore					

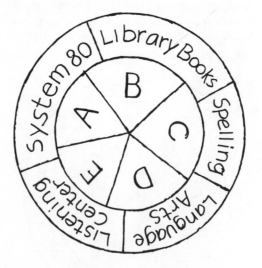

Jeanne Fridell, Lincoln Elementary School, Ottawa, Kansas

Storytelling Pencils

This activity helps to involve youngsters from kindergarten through third grade in your storytelling. You'll need a copy of Wanda Gag's classic, *Millions of Cats,*, an overhead projector, grease pencils, and 8½" × 11" transparencies. Heavyweight transparencies work better with younger children.

Begin by asking about all the different kinds of cats the children have had and have seen. Try for as many descriptive details as possible. Go on to encourage a wide range of imaginative responses —striped cats, polka-dot cats, fat cats, skinny cats, cats on roller skates.

Introduce the grease pencils and transparencies and demonstrate how to use them. Have each child draw as many different kinds of cats on a transparency as he or she wishes. Collect the drawings.

Tell the story of *Millions of Cats*, using the children's drawings. To emphasize "hundreds of cats, thousands of cats, millions and billions and trillions of cats," layer the transparencies one on top of the other; move them around for the fight scene.

Any cumulative folktale *(Henny Penny, The Little Red Hen, This Is the House That Jack Built)* is suitable for this technique as are these books:

> Burningham, J., *Mr. Grumpy's Outing* (progression of animals)
>
> Burton, V.L., *The Little House* (buildings grow into a city)
>
> Eastman, P., *Are You My Mother?* (various machines)
>
> Geisel, T.S., *And to Think I Saw It on Mulberry Street* (students add to the parade)
>
> Lionni, L., *The Biggest House in the World* (larger and larger houses)
>
> Lionni, L., *Little Blue and Little Yellow* (overlays of blue and yellow to make green)

Dolly Cinquino, Glen Rock Public Schools, Glen Rock, New Jersey

Illuminating

Bring to class examples of illuminated letters—medieval and modern. Then ask students to select a favorite book and design an illuminated letter for the first word in a favorite chapter. One illumination that I particularly remember was a monkey-laden *H* designed by a fourth-grader for the Howler monkey chapter of *Wonders of the Monkey World* by Jacquelyn Berrill. This is an activity that should appeal to students from elementary school right through junior and senior high school and might be done with English and art teachers cooperating.

Bill Bissell, George E. Harris Elementary School, Las Vegas, Nevada

Skimmers

This game helps my fifth-graders learn to skim for detail. Laminate grocery ads onto 8" × 10" cards or tack them on a bulletin board. Devise ten questions on the items and their prices and write them on another card. Assign partners.

One student scans the ad and writes down the appropriate sale prices or other information requested on the card. The time taken to complete this task is recorded in seconds by the other student. Then the process is reversed, and time and accuracy compared. The skimming game can be repeated for several rounds if you devise several question cards.

Jeanne Hartmans, Paul E. Culley Elementary School, Las Vegas, Nevada

Exploring Four Inches

You'll need several road maps for this activity. Students may work alone or with partners. Outline a four-inch square on a road map for each player or twosome. At least two or three squares may be drawn on each map. Spread the maps out on the floor and ask students to list all the information they can find within their designated squares. Keep a list of items found and discuss the results of these mini-explorations.

Debra J. Williams, Walter Bracken Elementary School, Las Vegas, Nevada

Up, Up, and Away: Balloon Day at White Bear Lake

Second-graders at our school recently took part in a first annual balloon day patterned after the book *Away Went the Balloons* by

Carolyn Haywood. After the successful launching, we are sure our youngsters will always remember this title and author.

In preparation for the event, I read aloud the first chapter of the book to each class during its weekly time in the media center. Classroom teachers finished reading the book with their individual classes before the big day. We asked our PTO for funds to pay for the helium and the balloons (special balloons are available at McDonald's at nominal cost), and room mothers came to fill them. Each student wrote a note to attach to the string of his or her balloon, including the school address and the launcher's name. We hoped, as in the book, that people would find our balloons and write back.

Balloon day dawned cold, but with a steady, strong wind. In the afternoon everyone gathered on the athletic field and counted down in unison. Suddenly eighty yellow balloons filled the sky and were carried up and away in a southeasterly direction. A photographer from the *White Bear Press* took pictures for the paper.

The balloon that traveled farthest was found near Rochester by a tenth-grade boy who wrote a letter to the youngster who had launched it. As students got responses, these became part of a hallway display that told the school the story of the second-grade balloon day.

Clare Hibbard, Lincoln School, White Bear Lake, Minnesota

Tomten Secrets

Youngsters in grades two through four are almost certain to enjoy this activity. Begin by reading aloud *The Tomten* or *The Tomten and the Fox* by Astrid Lindgren. The Tomten, a delightful gnome-like creature, then becomes the motivating force in the following activity that emphasizes writing and group interaction.

December is a perfect month for Tomtens, but they can appear at any season. I usually have youngsters draw names on Friday, then I set up a schedule something like this. On Monday, everyone receives a letter that gives a hint about his or her secret Tomten; on Tuesday, a poem; on Wednesday, a postcard; on Thursday, a riddle or other clue to Tomten identity; and on Friday, an item made by Tomten. You may want to schedule class time to talk about the various writing projects and about the thoughtfulness of Tomtens who don't forget. Writing may be completed at school, but Tomten identities are more likely to be kept secret when writing is done at home. I provide a basket for collecting Tomten communications each day, and I schedule a time for passing them out. On the final day we gather together to make guesses about the identities of our secret Tomtens.

Lois Schoeneck, Damon Runyon School, Littleton, Colorado

Not Only the Names Have Been Changed

This activity helps elementary school students appreciate the interdependence of character, plot, and setting and also generates some highly creative story variations. Each child may write or tell a story or students may work together in small groups.

Select with youngsters one or more characters and a setting— these will remain constant in everyone's story. The variation will be "a package." Change the characteristics of this package for each child or small group and discover how the plots change as the packages change. Suggested packages: plain brown wrapper, crated, outer wrapping battered and torn, holes for a living creature, package marked "Return to sender" or "Do not open" or "Open with care" or "Do not open until Christmas." Other changes can have to do with size, shape, method of delivery.

The activity may be repeated, keeping two other aspects constant but changing a third. For example, cut a picture from the *National Geographic* to serve as the setting for everyone's story but change the age, sex, or personality of the main character for each child. Or keep the characters constant and give each child a picture of a different setting.

Marilyn Lathrop, Ella Canavan School, Medina, Ohio

Super Bowl Readers

To encourage independent reading I run a football read-off from September to the Super Bowl in January, at which time I award small prizes to high scorers.

Set aside a bulletin board on which you lay out a football field. Get help from the class for a more creative design than you might invent: yard lines laid out with string or paper strips, end zones in vivid yellow, astroturf from indoor/outdoor carpeting! Each student needs a paper football labeled with his or her name. You'll also need a supply of book-check cards to verify that students have read the books that enable them to gain yards for a touchdown. I generally ask for title, author, setting, major characters, brief re-telling of the part liked least or the part liked best, but card requirements vary from one week or month to the next.

For each book read, the student fills out a book-check card. When you are satisfied that the student has completed the book, put his or her football on the ten-yard line. Each time the student hands in an acceptable card, he or she advances another ten yards. If you like, grant bonus yards for especially well-done cards. Keep track of all touchdowns as students advance down the field. In January, declare your Super Bowl readers. Paperbacks make good trophies.

Nancy Y. Ottman, T. Edwards Junior High School, South Windsor, Connecticut

Author! Author!

Author Day is an exciting way to motivate students to read and write enthusiastically. On such a day young people meet a con-temporary author. Students plan the program during the previous month in English classes. Their preparation includes the following:

1. Reading books by the author
2. Preparing questions to ask the author
3. Finding biographical information about the author and re-views or critical material on his or her writing
4. Writing an introduction of the author
5. Writing invitations to administrators, librarians, and other interested persons
6. Writing publicity for local and school newspapers
7. Creating art work and book displays for Author Day

Following the program, students write thank-you letters to the author, and many have received letters back. Another follow-up activity is to report on the event for local newspapers.

Why do we hold Author Day?

1. Enthusiasm is contagious. When other schools hear of our program, they ask to be included. A project of this kind brings together administrators, parents, teachers, librarians, and students.

2. The motivation for reading is authentic. When students know they will meet and talk to the author, they read with attention. They read with a purpose when they read to discover what questions they might ask the author.

3. The experience of writing for real audiences is a new one for most students. Correctness and clarity suddenly matter when you are writing for publication and to adults.

How do you organize an Author Day?

1. Convince administrators that it is a good idea. You will need their help (and financing).

2. Select an author. When you call, clearly state the age and interests of the audience. Define what you expect. How long should he or she plan to speak? Is the format to be a lecture, a panel, an informal question-and-answer session, or a combination? Discuss fees.

3. Compile a list of books by the author. Decide which ones you want students to read. Get help from your community and school libraries. Sometimes an author's publisher will help.

4. Make a reading schedule for students. Better readers may complete several books. You may want to read some material aloud to ensure the involvement of all students. As students read and listen, have them write questions they would like to ask the author on file cards.

5. Set up student committees to divide the work. Assign chairpersons and set deadlines. Typical committees include writers (publicity, invitations); artists (publicity, library and bulletin board displays, program design); reception (greeting guests, ushering); typing and mimeographing; refreshments (set-up and clean-up); questioners.

Two weeks before Author Day you and your classes should be ready to do the following:

1. Submit publicity to local papers.

2. Send invitations.

3. Print programs.

4. Send a letter to the author to confirm time and place. Include a map or directions to your school.

5. Ask students who will make introductions to rehearse before the class.

6. Organize the question period. Know who will ask what. Have a planned order of questioning to ensure that all those who prepared get a chance to ask questions. This procedure also avoids duplication of questions.

7. You may wish to videotape the event, make a tape recording, or take slides and photographs of students and author.

Our school has found that Author Day develops specific skills in an integrated way and with much enthusiasm. It is obvious to the entire community that students are developing reading, writing, and speaking skills. Public interest in Author Day helps to develop good school and community relations.

I have a videotape of Author Day in 1977 that includes four authors talking about their books and writing: Jane Langton, Betty Cavanna, Georgess McHargue, and Michael Roberts. I also have a list of over a hundred authors and illustrators and their addresses. You can reach me at the address below, just add the ZIP 01773. Of course librarians in your school and community are able to help you locate authors in your area.

Helen M. Greenhow, Brooks Junior High School, Lincoln, Massachusetts

4 Word Study, Vocabulary Development, and Spelling

Although many of the activities in this section might well have been placed in the preceding section, Sight Words and Reading, or in the subsequent section, Using and Making Dictionaries, they have been brought together here primarily because they encourage youngsters to think about a word as *word*—its configuration, its letter components and patterns, its meanings and uses—rather than merely to retrieve it from a storehouse of recognition words.

The first four activities are word games that may be played individually, in small groups, or with the class as a whole; the emphasis is on the letter combinations and patterns of individual words. **Grid Games** and **PRS Homes** place greater emphasis on meaning, an emphasis that continues for the next six activities. The section ends with suggestions for an individualized—and inexpensive—spelling program.

Playing the X's

This game has been dubbed "Playing the X's" by my third-graders, but students in upper grades will also enjoy it.

Place a sentence on the board, but in place of the letters use only x's. Be sure to leave spaces between the words. Students then take turns guessing a letter in the sentence. If that letter is present, the corresponding x or x's are erased and replaced with the correct letter. A student who has correctly identified a letter is allowed to guess at the entire sentence, but students quickly learn to be careful. Guessing only part of a sentence correctly may give the entire sentence away for another student. This simple little game has more potential than is at first apparent, especially if you give some thought to the sentences you use. It's useful for those extra five or ten minutes before lunch or dismissal.

Candice Bush, C.P. Squires Elementary School, North Las Vegas, Nevada

The Die Is Cast

Youngsters play this word game in groups of three or four. [E]ach
player in turn throws a die and tries to come up with a w[ord]
containing the number of letters corresponding to the numbe[r]
shown on the die. The group decides if a word does not qualify.
Accepted words are listed on a sheet of paper, and the group
scores a point for each correct word. The winner is the group with
the most points at the end of a stipulated time.

Vary the game by asking students to provide the number of
rhyming words shown on the die or to supply words that contain
the number of vowels shown.

Cardon Allred, J.E. Manch School, Las Vegas, Nevada

Word Scramble Ramble Amble

My sixth-graders enjoy finding words in words, but this game can
be adapted to almost any level. It's certain to spark a new interest
in words.

Write a word on the board from which students can make a new
word by moving the letters around. All letters may be used or
some may be left over. Then give a definition orally for the new
word to be discovered. For example, write the word *now* on the
board and give the definition "past tense of win." I have students
write the new word on a piece of paper because we play the game
as a contest, but students can respond orally or you can play the
game as a team relay. For younger children use words like *pin*
(nip), *team* (meat, tea, eat, mat, tam). For older youngsters try
words like *members* (embers, sere), *learn* (near, lean, are), *example*
(peel, peal, lax, ample).

Sherry Wilkie, Madison School, Las Vegas, Nevada

Spill and Spell Revised

This spelling game is appropriate for any grade level and works
well near the end of a class period or when you want to work with
an individual student or small group.

Appoint a secretary to write at the chalkboard. Using Spill and
Spell cubes, "spill" one letter and have the secretary write it on the

any word that contains that letter. "Spill" a
...e it recorded on the board; students now
...rd, one that contains both letters. "Spill" a
... third word containing all three letters.
...r until the class is stumped. Advanced
...d job when they come up with a word
...lled" letters.

... once a word has been said, it may not be
...stipulation keeps students from yelling out words
... being called upon since their word has then been used and
may not be used again.

Marti Swanson, Grant Community High School, Fox Lake, Illinois

Grid Game

Here's a game that emphasizes vocabulary brainstorming. Write a
word or phrase vertically on the left side of a grid. The size of the
grid will be determined by the word or phrase you choose. The
word can be seasonal, as shown below, but it does not have to be.
Across the top of the grid write category labels: nouns, verbs,
television shows, foods, plants, automobiles, ice-cream flavors. Students try to fill in each box with a word that begins with the letter
on the left and also conforms to the category label at the top of the
column.

	noun	boy's name	TV show	Plant	verb
S	ship				
P	pond				praise
r				radish	
i		Irving			
n					
g				geranium	

The grid game can be played by individuals for extra credit or just for fun, but we usually play with teams earning moves on a Chutes and Ladders board for filling the spaces correctly. Grids can be put on the chalkboard, on dittos, or on an overhead projector. Here are suggestions for the school year, but you'll come up with others that have special meaning for your students.

September—Welcome back, School daze
October—Halloween, pumpkin, ghoulish
November—Thanksgiving, turkey
December—Hanukkah, Christmas, mistletoe
January—New Year, resolution
February—Valentine, Washington, Lincoln
March—Leprechaun
April—Springtime, April showers
May—Vacation

Hope Goffstein, Laura Dearing Elementary School, Las Vegas, Nevada

PRS Homes

This manipulative activity can replace a more traditional worksheet to review prefixes, roots, and suffixes. Cut a number of squares from tagboard. The size depends on the age level you teach. Write a suffix on each. Cut an equal number of triangles, sized proportionately, and write a root word on each. Finally, prepare small rectangles with a prefix on each. For example:

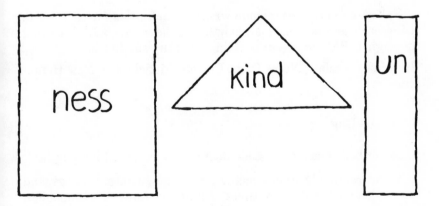

Students construct as many houses as possible, using one prefix, root, and suffix. You'll want to prepare an answer key so that students can correct their own work, and remember that alternatives are possible—*unkindness* or *unkindly,* for example.

Houses will resemble the one below, and I've included a short word list appropriate for intermediate grades to get you started.

en tangle ment   un kind ness
re fill able   dis courage ment
un time ly   un self ish
un sight ly   dis card ed
pre record ed   en camp ment

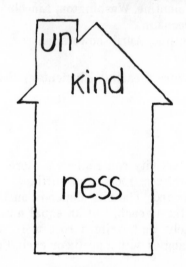

Follow-up activities include writing a definition for each word, using each in a sentence, alphabetizing the words, and designing an original PRS home—or building an entire subdivision.

Sr. Louise Auclair, Notre Dame College, Manchester, New Hampshire

It's in the Bag

Make, or better still have students make, word-matching puzzles.

1. Cut relatively simple pictures from magazines, catalogs, and calendars or draw outlines of animals, flowers, automobiles, trees, geometric shapes, and the like.

2. Draw lines to divide each picture into several sections. These lines may intersect or go in any direction.

3. Print words to be matched above and below the same dividing lines. Puzzles can be made with synonyms, antonyms, homonyms, rhyming words, words matched to meanings, words matched to pronunciation respellings, words that go together (*bat* and *ball*), words that make compound words (*basket* and *ball*). Your puzzle should resemble the one sketched below.

4. Mount the picture on tagboard and laminate it if you like.

5. Cut along the dividing lines and store each puzzle in a labeled Ziploc bag. Since these puzzles are self-correcting, you'll find many opportunities to use them.

6. If you like, put the words for another puzzle on the back of a picture puzzle. This puzzle will be more difficult to complete, for there will be no picture clues.

Beth Whipple, Myrtle Tate Elementary School, Las Vegas, Nevada

Word of the Week

A section of my bulletin board looks like this:

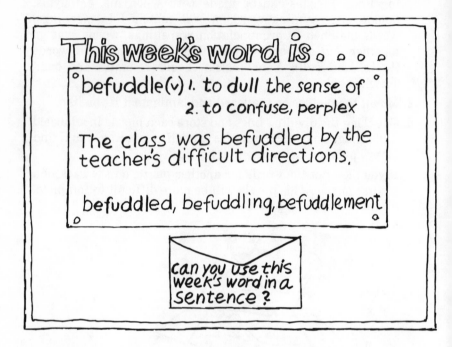

1. On Monday we discuss the word and its derivatives.
2. During the week we use the word in class in various situations and students insert original sentences using the word or its derivatives in the envelope.
3. On Friday we share their sentences and nominate "Word-of-the-Week Winners." Selected sentences can also be used as a dictation exercise.

Kathleen Pszenny, Ralph B. O'Maley School, Gloucester, Massachusetts

Pictures Worth at Least Twenty-Five Words

Students can work in groups to make these puzzles for each other, but you will probably want to make several yourself to serve as models.

1. Draw and color a picture of a general subject that can be used to generate useful vocabulary words, for example, a forest scene with wildlife.
2. Mark off squares on the back of the picture and write a vocabulary word generated by the picture into each square: *forest, grove, leaf, leaves, hoof, hooves, trail, herd, feather*, for example.
3. Rule an identical sheet of paper into matching squares and write a definition for each word in the corresponding square.
4. Cut the picture apart, following the lines of the squares.

Students exchange puzzles and reassemble the pictures by placing each word facedown on top of the square containing its definition. These self-correcting puzzles may also be made by cutting up a poster or large picture from a magazine or calendar. You'll be surprised at the interesting and useful vocabulary that students "find" in pictures. It's also fun to send puzzles as "gifts" to another classroom, to trade puzzles with another class, or to send one to a member of the class confined at home or in the hospital.

Margie Ripplinger, Doris French Elementary School, and Mary Barbara Gnatovich, George E. Harris Elementary School, Las Vegas, Nevada

Concentration: Direction of Attention to a Single Object

Compile a vocabulary list appropriate to the level of your students, especially one that is related to a unit of work underway. If your list is long enough, you can have several games of Concentration underway at the same time.

Divide the class into groups of three or four students and divide the vocabulary list equally among groups. Give each group two 3″ × 5″ cards for each vocabulary word it has. On one card a member of the group neatly writes a vocabulary word. On another, a member neatly copies the pronunciation respelling and the definition of that word.

When all the groups are finished, collect and shuffle the cards. Place them facedown on the table in rows and columns as for Concentration. Each student in turn picks up two cards, hoping to make a match between word and definition. The dictionary can resolve disputes. If the cards match, the student keeps both cards but must first use the word correctly in a sentence. If the cards do not match, the student returns them to their original positions on the table. The winner is the student with the most cards.

Linda Gregg, William E. Ferron Elementary School, Las Vegas, Nevada

Sloganizing

Here's an exercise that makes a point in an advertising or word study unit. Ask each student to clip a picture/slogan ad from a magazine. The student then cuts the slogan from the chosen ad, being careful to keep it intact, and pastes it on a separate sheet of paper. The picture portion of the ad is pasted on another piece of paper. Later, in class, students pass slogans in one direction, pictures in the other. The class then tries to match slogans with products. The exercise demonstrates vividly the sameness of the terms used by advertisers to influence buyers.

Verus Young, Lois Craig Elementary School, North Las Vegas, Nevada

Blue Books and Pens: An Individualized Spelling Program

Each week, usually on Monday, I give each student a blue book with ten words written in it. I have taken the words from the student's writing during the previous week and from a paragraph that I dictated. I choose this paragraph for its interest level and because it offers a variety of spelling challenges. The dictation emphasizes listening skills as well as spelling and handwriting.

During the week students study their own lists and write an interesting complete sentence for each word. I give a small prize each week to the student who has written the most interesting, thoughtful, or amusing sentences. The use of the word from the spelling list must, of course, be correct.

Near the end of the week students pair off, exchange blue books, and quiz each other. I try to keep pairs relatively equal so students have no difficulty reading each other's lists.

This spelling program combines penmanship, sentence writing, creative thinking, peer interaction, and challenging individualized word lists for each student. Best of all, it costs no more than a set of blue books.

Rosalys B. Wilson, Dedham Junior High School, Dedham, Massachusetts

5 Making and Using Dictionaries

"To make dictionaries is dull work," noted Samuel Johnson in the preface to his dictionary. But your students are likely to disagree when they've tried their hands at the cut-and-paste dictionary, the tired word dictionary, the homonym dictionary, the dictionary of superstitions, and the dictionary of things to do. There are also activities to introduce alphabetizing, the use of guide words, and the decoding of diacritical markings.

Dachshund ABC

Cut the dog ends and alphabet cards shown below from tagboard. Then have the children put the cards in alphabetical order to form the body of the dog.

For more advanced students, write words to be alphabetized on the body segments. Get tricky: use only words beginning with the same letter—aunt, age, after, any, angel, ape, apple.

Kathy Huse-Inman, Division of Elementary and Secondary Education, Pierre, South Dakota

43

Alphabet Shuffle

After first-graders have learned their ABC's, divide the alphabet into three sections labeled beginning, middle, and end. Make a tagboard label for each section (or use the chalkboard) as shown below.

Choose three students whose first names begin with letters that represent the three categories. Ask each youngster in turn what letter comes first in his or her first name. Then ask the student to move to the appropriate section of the alphabet. After this demonstration, categorize the class by first names. When everyone is in a beginning, middle, or end category, reshuffle by using last names. If there's time, use middle names, names of pets, or street names.

Now teach for transfer. Hold up a dictionary and explain that it is divided into three sections, too. Demonstrate by asking for words and categorizing them first with the beginning, middle, end labels and then showing in which third of the dictionary they are found. As time goes on, students will open the dictionary to the correct third without starting their word search at the first page.

Ann Redemann, Halle Hewetson Elementary School, Las Vegas, Nevada

Guide Words Were Made to Be Used

Students so often ignore the time-saving guide words in the dictionary. Here is an activity that helps them understand how to use them. You'll need tongue depressors, index cards, and a dictionary. Write pairs of guide words on three or four depressors. Then use the index cards to make a set of a dozen or so words that can be sorted according to the guide words and later alphabetized. If you code the answers on the backs of the cards, the exercise is self-correcting. For example:

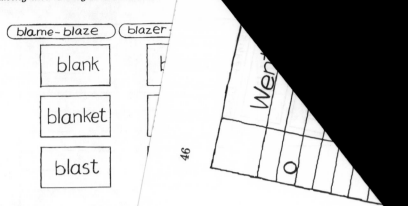

Diane Ng, Helen Marie
Nevada

Cut-and-Paste Dictionary

My first-graders enjoy making picture dictionaries. Collect in advance newspapers (especially the Sunday comics), magazines, coloring books, catalogs, junk mail—any disposable illustrative material. Each youngster finds and cuts out the letters of the alphabet, gluing each to a page. Both upper- and lowercase letters may be shown. Several pictures may then be used to illustrate a given letter. Sometimes students create category dictionaries—animals, foods, clothing, toys and games.

Larry Pilon, Marion F. Cahlan Elementary School, North Las Vegas, Nevada

Tired Word Dictionary

Youngsters enjoy making books. When we are beginning creative writing, we make a dictionary of "tired" words. I write an overused word on the board, and students contribute words they could use instead. For example, *went* in "Mike went down the road." When we have run out of ideas, we create the "went" page for our tired word dictionary by listing the fresh, new words in alphabetical order. A sample page follows.

ambled
boogied
crawled
hobbled
jogged
marched
raced
ran
shuffled
skipped
stagger
strolled

We keep the pages, arranged alphabetically, in a notebook and when we discover another tired word, we create a fresh page. In effect, we are making our own thesaurus. This activity helps in creative writing, but it also expands the young child's vocabulary.

Nancy Hest, Lois Craig Elementary School, North Las Vegas, Nevada

Dictionary Builders

Instead of using standard vocabulary lists, I sometimes ask students to create their own dictionaries. Each student chooses a book from his or her independent reading and selects a given number of words from it. After I've checked their lists, students look up the words in the dictionary and copy syllabication, definition, and part of speech. They also write sentences for an agreed-upon number of words.

Now they are ready to make dictionaries. With the usual supply of fabric, wallpaper, and cardboard, we make books and copy the dictionary work into them. Students copy their work onto the pages before binding them to avoid dismantling the books when mistakes are made. Many students make dictionaries in sizes and shapes that suggest the books from which they took the words. I have had books shaped like baseballs, ice-cream cones, and haunted houses. Most youngsters enjoy illustrating their dictionaries, but those shy about drawing find pictures in magazines and neatly cut and paste them into their dictionaries.

I have found that when students are allowed to pick a book with which they are comfortable, they take great pride in their work. This project provides practice in using the dictionary, expands vocabularies, and is a pleasant experience for those who enjoy making books but are not particularly strong in creative writing.

Susanne Whitbeck, Andover Elementary School, Andover, New Hampshire

From Black Cats to Sidewalk Cracks

Around Halloween my students compile a dictionary of superstitions. We collect all the superstitions they have ever heard, including their meanings and origins if possible. We add to the collection through interviewing people and from books. Illustrations are the last step in producing a fascinating and attractive book.

Ruth A. Mills, C.V.T. Gilbert School, North Las Vegas, Nevada

Dictionary of Things to Do

Help students to compile a *Just for Kids* dictionary that lists the child-oriented facilities within the community or immediate area. This dictionary may include a "fun for free" section as well as businesses such as video arcades, skating rinks, and theaters. Students may provide directions for each listing, a map on which all listings are located, expenses, business hours, phone numbers, and

the like. My fifth-graders enjoy this activity but the type of information will, of course, vary with the grade level of the compilers.

Shana Turner, George E. Harris Elementary School, Las Vegas,
Nevada

Homonym Helper

Some youngsters have difficulty using and spelling homonyms
correctly, but almost all of them enjoy collecting and considering
them. So I came up with the idea of a homonym dictionary. I pass
out unlined, three-hole notebook paper and brads to hold the booklet together. Students design covers appropriate to the contents
and to their own personalities. I explain that the booklets must be
brought to class daily for the next few weeks because they will be
used daily.

Every day when students come into my room they find on the
chalkboard that day's set of homonyms, for example, *great* and
grate. These are the words that they enter into their booklets that
day, providing an interesting sentence and illustration for each.
Dictionaries are available for verifying meanings about which
students are uncertain. I have noticed that many students are
curious to see what each day's homonyms will be and look for them
almost immediately as they enter the room. They especially enjoy
relatively unfamiliar pairs. Of course they know *plum* but many
do not know *plumb*; *done* is familiar but *dun* will send them to
the dictionary.

Besides enjoying the challenge of compiling interesting entries
for each homonym, students are creating a personal resource for
tricky words, and I encourage them to take care with the spelling
and punctuation.

Judy Cromett, Lewiston High School, Lewiston, Minnesota

Diacritical Diagnoses

Many students have genuine difficulty decoding diacritical marks.
I have found this nonthreatening activity to be a help to many.
You need several dictionaries, preferably a class set, with a pro-
nunciation key that is easy to interpret.

Begin by reviewing the use of the pronunciation key, giving
examples of words that contain the sounds represented by the
diacritical marks. Introduce the activity by writing a sentence on

the chalkboard, spelling the words according to the pronunciation key given in the dictionary the class is using. Now ask each student to write a sentence, spelling each word in the manner of the pronunciation key. Students should write the words first with only the help of the key; then they may check them against the individual entries in the dictionary.

After students have worked out their sentences, they copy them neatly on strips of paper. Sometimes I make a quiz game from the sentences by numbering them and posting them on the bulletin board. Students try to transcribe each sentence, this time spelling all words correctly. Sometimes I ask each student in turn to hold up a sentence and call for volunteers to read it correctly.

Students seem to have fun working out the pronunciation of words they may not have known prior to decoding their classmates' sentences, and they discover that dictionaries really are useful tools. Perhaps the biggest benefit is that the fear of mispronouncing words is reduced as students learn to make accurate diacritical diagnoses.

Kim M. McLaughlin, St. Austin's Grade School, Minneapolis, Minnesota

Mathemadness

Sometimes new subject-matter terms, especially in math, intimidate youngsters. I suggest, therefore, that we make a dictionary of such words in language arts class.

Begin by having students alphabetize a preselected list of terms, or add to the dictionary throughout the semester. Students and teacher together then create daffynitions for each word. Allow your imaginations to run rampant. The field work begins when you amass the true definition. Your labors are now ready for the printed page. I use the following format, with terms in alphabetical order:

> Unfamiliar term.   1. Daffynition   2. Definition

Here are two examples from a dictionary produced by my fifthgraders.

> **octagon.**   1. October's gone.   2. A polygon having eight angles and eight sides.
> **parallel lines.**   1. A pair of Lell lions.   2. Two lines lying evenly in the same direction but never meeting.

Donald Grosenick, Halle Hewetson Elementary School, Las Vegas, Nevada

6 Writing

Activities in this section suggest ways to motivate young writers and engage them at the prewriting stage. There is a relaxed and spontaneous approach, time for talk, opportunity for sensory exploration, room for verbal experimentation. Many of these assignments might later be reworked, revised, and edited to create fuller and more complex treatments.

The four activities that conclude this section are certain to take the groans out of poetry assignments. There are six-foot poems, poems that bubble out of Bromo-Seltzer tablets, and cinquain in the first grade.

Cliff-Hangers in the Classroom

Elementary students enjoy these two writing assignments, which seem to produce stories that everyone enjoys sharing.

For the first, you will need a supply of coat hangers and long pieces of paper. I give instructions that go something like this: "Write the beginning of an exciting story on the piece of paper. Don't finish the story! Stop right at the exciting part. Now fasten the piece of paper on a coat hanger and hang your story in a place where someone else can finish it. You finish another person's cliff-hanger."

You'll need to prepare for the second when students are out of the room. Tape a trail of large, three-toed footprints on the floor, over tables, up the wall, across the ceiling—be imaginative. End the trail at an open window. Then leave a few clues—an empty milk carton, candy bar wrappers, orange peelings—or clues of your own sinister devising. When students return, ask them to be detectives and observe the footprints and other clues. Then they write stories using as many clues as they can find. Encourage them to describe the intruder, to tell why it was in the classroom, to decide where it went.

Douglas E. Knight, Dike-Newell School, Bath, Maine

Jabberjabberjabber

I find these three exercises useful in creative dramatics, but I suspect they'd prove fun in almost any language arts class at almost any grade level and might serve as useful prewriting activities.

Hold up an object—almost any object; everyone must talk about it nonstop and simultaneously. After several seconds, replace it immediately with another—and the talk goes on. Only one rule: Students may not stop talking about the object before them.

Divide the class into groups of four to six and sit in small circles. Announce a topic. Person A in each circle begins to talk to the others nonstop on the topic. When you give a signal, person B immediately begins talking. When each member of the circle has had a turn, announce a new topic and repeat the activity. Again, only one rule: Don't stop talking. Suggested topics: corners, little things, big things, buildings, butterflies, dirty socks, grandma's house, Jello.

Create a think wheel by asking students to sit in a circle. Dim the lights if you wish and ask students to close their eyes and relax. Pronounce a word—*morning*, for example. Each student in turn says the first word that comes to mind, continuing for a full turn of the wheel. Other words to try: friends, love, beauty, scary, childhood, magical, darkness.

Jeff McLaughlin, Intermediate Unit 13 School, East Petersburg, Pennsylvania

Vegetable Vagaries

In the fall about the time of our first hard frost, I ask my fourth-graders to bring in a vegetable from their gardens. Youngsters whose families do not have gardens can usually find a potato, a carrot, or an onion at home or use an extra vegetable brought by a friend.

The day the vegetables arrive, our attention centers on our harvest. Each child spends time carefully examining his or her vegetable—color, texture, shape, size. Does it resemble anything else? How does it grow? How is it cooked? Do you like to eat it? After thinking about these questions, each child writes a biography of the vegetable. The personality and adventures developed for each vegetable are limited only by the child's imagination.

Ann F. Smith, Comiskey School, Northfield, Vermont

Put Yourself in My Shoes

Provide an opportunity for students to project themselves into another's shoes, to be someone else for a few minutes. I draw outlines of a variety of shoes for my students to use to write stories on—sneakers, ballet slippers, football cleats, ice skates, hiking boots, bunny slippers. One of my drawings happens to be a cowboy boot, and on top of the boot I write, "If I wore this boot my name would be . . . And I would . . ." Students may complete as many shoes as they wish.

When the shoe fantasies are complete, I post them on the bulletin board, and we sometimes have a little discussion about these new personalities in our classroom. If you prefer, students may draw their own shoes for this assignment.

Sherry Wilkie, Madison School, Las Vegas, Nevada

Don't Fence Them In

Take to the outdoors to help students refine skills of observation and descriptive writing. I've had success with these on-the-spot assignments.

1. Can you hear a scene? Visit a place in your neighborhood and jot down as many words as you can that will help us hear that place.
2. Can you feel a place? Fit yourself into a nook or cranny, indoors or out. Tell us in at least three sentences what it feels like to be there.
3. Find a natural object that speaks to you with beauty. Write a description that makes clear this object's significance to you.
4. Find two items outdoors and compare/contrast them: a stone and a leaf, a thistle and a bird, a candy wrapper and an acorn, a cat and a car, a telephone pole and a matchstick. How are they alike? How are they different? Now find a partner. Decide on two objects together. One of you writes the comparison—how the objects are alike; the other writes the contrast—how they differ.

Lois Schoeneck, Damon Runyon School, Littleton, Colorado

Brown Bagging It

I use this exercise to emphasize the difference between objective and subjective description, but it's a suitable assignment for descriptive writers at almost any grade level.

Place in a brown bag for each student a variety of everyday items: an onion, a mothball, a piece of sponge, a burnt piece of toast, a shoestring, a feather. Distribute the bags and instruct students not to remove the objects from the bags or show them to anyone. Each student then writes a brief objective description of each item in his or her brown bag, a description in which the item is not named. To see how successful students have been, we take turns reading our descriptions to the class without, of course, opening the bags until all guesses have been made.

In the second part of the exercise, students adopt the viewpoint of one of the objects in their bags and describe a typical day in its life: A Day in the Life of an Onion, Burnt Toast Biography, Shoestring Saga.

Elizabeth Pedicord, Canton South High School, Canton, Ohio

Sound Assignment

Records of sound effects (an individual sound effect usually lasts from ten to sixty seconds) are available at local libraries, but you can also record your own onto cassette tapes—sirens, squeaking doors, ticking clocks, tolling bells, chirping birds, an unnerving scream. Play *one* sound effect for the class. Ask students to listen carefully the first time it is played and to imagine the scene that produced that sound. In short, students should create in their minds a picture, a setting, and eventually a story. Ask them to concentrate on that scene and who is involved. Play the sound effect a second time. Now students write the story or vignette they have imagined. I usually allow about twenty minutes, but you may find students asking for more time as they begin to work out their ideas.

Debbie Rub, Audubon Junior High School, Los Angeles, California

Beginning with Dialogue

I use this assignment with eighth-graders before they begin writing stories, but it is appropriate for a wide range of grade levels. As a result of this assignment, I think students include more and better dialogue and more accurately punctuated dialogue than had classes in previous years.

Each student chooses a person he or she wants to be—living or dead, real or imaginary, perhaps a character from a story or television show. Pair these "characters" in any way you choose. Each pair then carries on a written conversation, passing a sheet of paper back and forth, each student writing his or her line in the conversation instead of speaking it. Students get to play out a role as well as to practice writing and punctuating dialogue. Some of these conversations are later developed into stories; some merely serve as practice.

Anne M. Topp, LeSueur High School, LeSueur, Minnesota

I Am a Camera

I find this activity useful in helping students identify main idea or theme, write descriptive detail, and sequence ideas. These are the instructions I give.

> *Step one.* Select a fairly large picture, color or black and white, that shows a scene that you like or dislike. Your theme is (the city at night, restaurant rush hour, mountain sunset, lonely beach, crowded beach).
>
> *Step two.* Make a "camera" with a strip of colored paper 2" wide and 4" long. Fold this paper in half crosswise and cut out a rectangle 1½" × 1". Your camera frame should be a small rectangle centered within a larger rectangle as shown below.
>
> *Step three.* Move your camera frame over your picture. Put yourself in the position of a photographer filming a story. Catch the sequence of your story so that a viewer will clearly understand what your story is about. When you are satisfied with the "shots" you have chosen, use a pencil to mark them out by positioning the camera frame over the picture and tracing the rectangle. You must have a minimum of five frames.
>
> *Step four.* Cut out these frames and paste them on a piece of unlined paper provided in class. Put them in a straight line and as close together as they would be found in a filmstrip.
>
> *Step five.* Describe each frame of your film in specific detail. Number those descriptions to correspond to the frames.

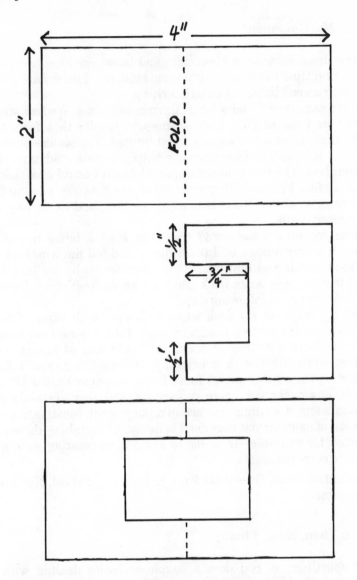

Step six. Now put your descriptions together. Add words and phrases so that your viewer knows exactly what you are trying to describe by the narration you have written. Recopy this "script" neatly.

Step seven. On "film day" each of you will have an opportunity to display your film and the accompanying text.

Marianna Lawler, Schalmont Middle School, Schenectady, New York

Dear Ms. Dohrman

Many times because of class sizes and busy schedules, we simply don't find time to listen to individual students. I have found a way of being a good listener through writing.

This past year I had a large third-grade class. We had studied letter writing, and students seemed to handle that form well. Talk time, however, always seemed limited. Youngsters clustered around my desk before school, wanting to talk and talk about themselves. The bell would ring, and I found I could give them no time. Before I knew it, they were off to other classes, passing from one room to another, one teacher to another, and never any time for personal talk.

One morning I suggested that they start a letter to me and place it on my desk. I told them they could tell me whatever was on their minds and that what they wrote would be confidential. I said that I would write back and they would find letters from me on their desks the following day.

To my surprise, my desk was overflowing with letters. I found out so many interesting things through those letters. I got to know how students felt, their concerns at home and at school. Their letters were filled with everything and anything, and I found many expressed themselves more freely on paper than orally. All in all, our exchanges were rewarding, and they certainly gave students lots of writing practice in a purposeful, constructive way. A word of caution: you may need to devise a timetable—three days' leeway, for example—in order to avoid disappointing your more prolific correspondents.

Joanne Dohrman, Greenvale Park Elementary School, Northfield, Minnesota

First, Then, Next, Finally

Our fourth-grade pod does a couple activities dealing with sequence and clarity in writing that have proved to be fun and valuable.

In the first, we ask each student to write down the steps in making a peanut butter and jelly sandwich. The next day, we provide bread, peanut butter, jelly, and a knife. Each student gets to make a sandwich, step by step, according to another child's directions. For the sake of making a point, we require that they follow directions literally. If the paper says "spread peanut butter on bread" but fails to mention using a knife, they can't use a knife. The kids have a good time and also see the importance of giving clear, exact directions.

Another day, we set up a small town in our room. Desks are pushed together to make "blocks." Certain desks are labeled bank, school, grocery store, town hall, etc. Streets are named and street signs posted. Each student then writes a set of directions explaining how to go from one place to another. We exchange papers, and every child walks through the town following the directions he or she received. The kids always think it's going to be so easy, and they are amazed at the care and concentration required to do it right.

Sandra L. Horn, Columbus Elementary School, Forest Lake, Minnesota

Popcorn Sale

If the teacher fails to provide opportunities for writing that result in purposeful communication, students tend to find writing a hollow experience and remain uninvolved. Many classroom activities, however, can be organized to include purposive writing. Here is how a popcorn sale provided opportunities for written communication in a fifth-grade classroom.

1. A class discussion on how to raise money for a particular class project led to the decision to hold a popcorn sale. Our first writing task was to compose a letter to the principal requesting permission to hold the sale, outlining the reasons for the sale, and detailing how the sale would be organized.

2. Then we needed to develop forms to be completed by class members with information indicating the contributions they would make to the sale.

3. Next we wrote up the results of an experiment conducted to determine the quantity of unpopped corn needed to produce a given quantity of popped corn.

4. A report outlining materials needed and estimates of quantities, expenses, and proposed selling prices was next.

5. Clear and accurate records of expenses and receipts were ongoing.

6. Advertisements, announcements, and notices to be displayed in school were another major writing project.

7. Finally, we produced a class book, *The Popcorn Sale*.

8. And a creative follow-up: Look for an opportunity to discuss the sensory impressions students have of popcorn. This could occur shortly after students have popped corn in the classroom to determine quantities. Discuss sensory appeals: hearing (the sound popcorn makes popping and being chewed), smell, touch (the way it feels in mouth and hand), taste, sight. List at the chalkboard words suggested by students that evoke the sensory aspects of popcorn, but give them freedom to choose the form their writing will take. For example, haiku:

> The sound of popcorn
> Rattles, crackles, spits with heat
> Edible battle

Diane Bewell, Child Guidance Clinic of Greater Winnipeg, Winnipeg, Manitoba

Cereal Crunch

You'll need a collection of empty cereal boxes for this activity. Ask neighbors, students, and parents for help in advance. List the names of the cereals on the board. Pronounce and discuss them, encouraging youngsters to consider why cereals are named as they are. Ask them to suggest new names for cereals and to explain their choices.

Each student then covers a cereal box with construction paper and creates a new cereal name and an appropriately designed box. If there's time, assign partners and share cereal inventions through television commercials written and enacted by students.

Phyllis M. Gies, M.E. Cahlan Elementary School, North Las Vegas, Nevada

Once upon a Name

You'll need reference books that explain name derivations; for example, Basil Cottle's *Penguin Dictionary of Surnames*, Elsdon C. Smith's *New Dictionary of American Family Names*, or George R.

Stewart's *American Given Names: Their Origin and History*. Each student studies the history of his or her name—given names and surnames when possible. Using these ideas, the child makes up a story of how that meaning came to be. This can be written as a personal tale, a myth, or other narrative form. When stories are complete, students make them into books complete with illustrations and laminated covers. These make lovely gifts for parents on a special occasion.

Jeanne Hartmans, Paul E. Culley Elementary School, Las Vegas, Nevada

Mail Call

This ongoing classroom project helps students master correct letter forms and provides a variety of experiences in writing and evaluating friendly and business letters.

Decorate a large cardboard box to resemble a U.S. mailbox. Introduce correct letter forms and post models of both friendly and business letters near the "mailbox."

Each student writes a letter, folds it, and correctly addresses the folded letter, which is then dropped into the mailbox. On stipulated days I appoint a letter carrier, who removes the letters and delivers one to each student who has mailed one. The receiver reads and evaluates content and letter form. The reader may also make comments to the writer—or write a letter in return—and the most interesting letters are often shared with the class.

Sometimes I use this assignment weekly; sometimes less frequently. Letters may also be assigned as homework, as may responses. Only the instruction by the teacher, the delivery of the letters, and the sharing of comments and contents need take place in class.

Lots of practice is necessary if students are to master letter forms, but I have also found that students write more interesting letters when they know their readers will be other students rather than a teacher. Letters also involve descriptive, narrative, expository, and persuasive writing—all forms of writing that students in the upper elementary grades need to begin using.

Finally, here are suggestions for letters that have proved successful in my classes. You and your students will, I know, come up with many others.

Write a letter
1. to your teacher, suggesting that students be allowed to celebrate "Labor Day" each month
2. to a friend, describing what you saw or how you felt (or what happened to you) on a five-mile bike ride
3. from one character in a novel or short story to another, discussing a problem related to the story
4. to a friend in the East, telling about striking it rich in the California Gold Rush
5. to Christopher Columbus, asking to sail with him to India
6. to the Walt Disney Studios, describing a cartoon character you have created and want them to buy
7. to a witch, inviting her to your Halloween party
8. from Big Foot, ordering a new pair of shoes
9. to Smokey the Bear, congratulating him for his good forestry work
10. to Jack Frost, complaining about the trouble his last visit caused
11. to Santa Claus, asking him to visit an old person who needs many things
12. from the Old Year, bragging about how he or she handled problems during his or her term in office
13. from a prophet, telling what he or she thinks will happen during the coming year
14. to a space hero, asking to go along on the next mission
15. to a parent or relative, describing the view from a balloon
16. to Cinderella's stepmother, applying for Cinderella's job after the wedding
17. from the tiger in one cage to the tigers in another cage
18. from a fish, requesting the mayor to clean up the lake water
19. to a former United States president, commenting on an action that he took during his term
20. to a scientist, asking for help on a problem you are having with your new invention
21. from a leprechaun in America, telling his Irish cousin about the unlucky things Americans do
22. to a museum curator, asking for an identification of a bone you have found
23. to the author, telling how his or her book might have been improved (should have ended)
24. from your pet (or younger brother or sister), asking for better treatment
25. to Peter Pan, requesting permission to live in Never-Never Land

26. to Mr. Webster, telling of a word you have made up to go in the dictionary

27. to your teacher, describing a perfect summer vacation

Polly Duncan, Tanglewood Middle School, Greenville, South Carolina

Pictures *and* a Thousand Words

Fourth- through sixth-graders enjoy writing stories and assembling books inspired by magazine pictures. My instructions go something like this:

> Page through several magazines, tearing out a collection of pictures that appeal to you. Next, spread out these pictures, letting them suggest characters, settings, plots—ways they might fit together to tell a story. Discard or add pictures if you want. Now write the story suggested to you by your pictures. Proofread and revise until the story pleases you.
>
> Now comes the bookmaking fun. Decide on the color of paper you want to use for your book, its format, the kind of script, the placement of writing and pictures on each page. I'll be giving some special instructions as we assemble our books together in class.

Results are delightful, creative, surprise-on-the-next-page books that can be shared through the library or by loaning them to other rooms.

Dorothy Wood, Highlands School, Edina, Minnesota

Young Authors Write for Younger Readers

One of the best experiences I have had with seventh-graders was the writing of stories to be shared with second-graders, but I think fifth- and sixth-graders would also enjoy this project. This assignment was made in December and so Christmas stories were popular, but stories about other family traditions would be equally appropriate. I stipulated that stories must be original but could be written as prose or poetry. We also talked about appeals to the senses, all five of them.

Prior to writing, students brought in favorite stories from early childhood, and I secured stories recommended by a second-grade teacher. For several periods, we shared these stories, talking about the level of the writing and appeals to the senses. We also examined the illustrations. We read "Twas the Night before Christmas." To illustrate how one piece of writing can be used as a pattern for another, I read aloud two takeoffs that followed Moore's form and rhyme scheme but changed the content. Then we began writing.

I was amazed at the enthusiasm. Not one student complained, "I can't think of anything to write about!" Students wrote in class during the first week. During the next, they revised and illustrated their stories. Scraps of fabric, fur, old greeting cards, magazine cutouts, and paper of all kinds appeared as students created visual and tactile images. These illustrations made some of the duller and less successful stories fun to read, and weaker writers achieved a sense of accomplishment. Finished products varied widely, with stories about lonely children who received cuddly animals for Christmas, families reunited, holiday travels to grandparents, and some very original ideas like *Big Foot Has Christmas, Too.*

A second-grade teacher read all of the stories and selected those most appropriate for her class. My young authors then went to her room and read these stories aloud. It was, indeed, a successful writing experience for my students and for me. I teach in high school now, but I remember with fondness the joy and delight of this special group of seventh-graders.

Viva Sewell, Borger High School, Borger, Texas

About six weeks before school closes, my sixth-graders write books for the first-graders in our school. This is the plan I recommend.

1. Ask the first-grade teacher for the spelling or vocabulary words she has used with her class during the entire year. Reproduce a copy for each student.

2. Ask your librarian for about twenty-five picture books for the sixth-graders to examine and discuss.

3. Schedule a time when you will have at least one hour for the project on three consecutive days.

4. Begin by handing out the word lists and discussing the picture books. Then distribute a large sheet of paper to each student. Students rule off the paper into ten or twelve squares —each square will become a page in their rough drafts. (I require books of at least ten pages.) Students then block out their stories in large, dark printing and active pictures. I encourage them to use words from the first-grade lists as

often as possible. I help them with editing, and each student goes on to produce a finished book that includes cover, title page, and numbered pages.

5. When the project is complete, we make an appointment with the first-grade teacher and my sixth-graders visit her room and read their books aloud.

Myra MacLeish, Oakwood School, Minneapolis, Minnesota

In addition to designing and completing their own children's books and sharing them with younger children, my students come to realize the elements of successful children's fiction: easy-to-follow plot, quick action, understandable characters, appropriate language, and colorful illustrations.

Here is a summary of how we proceed.

Day one. Discuss children's fiction; ask students to recall some of their favorite stories. Each student reads four children's books, either from the selection in class (I get about fifty books from an elementary school librarian for this purpose) or from their home libraries. Students then complete an evaluation sheet of about ten questions for each book; points covered include plot, characters, language, illustrations.

Day two. Reading and evaluating children's books continue. The four evaluations are due on day three.

Day three. Discuss what children have discovered about the books they read. Summarize the elements of good children's fiction. Collect the evaluations. Students begin writing their stories, which will be suitable for younger children. Drafts are to be completed as homework and brought to class on day four.

Day four. Demonstrate how to use a storyboard to organize the story and its illustrations. Emphasize that the pictures are merely sketches of what will eventually be the illustrations. The storyboard is only a rough draft, as shown below.

Day five. Students complete their storyboards, bringing them to me when they think they have them letter perfect. I encourage them to ask fellow students to read their work before discussing it with me.

Days six, seven (eight if they need it). Students write their stories in book form and illustrate them in color. Allow plenty of time because good pictures require it.

Day eight or nine. Discuss the information found on a title page and book cover. Students complete title pages and covers for their books. If necessary, books are completed as homework. They are to be turned in the following day.

Day nine or ten. Students read their books aloud, and the class votes for its favorites. Authors of books selected arrange with elementary teachers to share their books with younger children. A public library might also have a reading hour where students could share their books.

Additional observations. I don't require all students to do their own illustrations. They may ask another, better artist to sketch drawings for them to color. This tactic relieves students who hate to draw and encourages family and friends to participate in the project. Also, I don't allow alphabet books because they take too long to illustrate and are usually boring.

I hope this project works as well for you and your students as it does for us. After including it in my curriculum for several years, I now have parents and former students endorsing the experience.

Jill Tammen, Hudson Middle School, Hudson, Wisconsin

Garfield Scores Again

I've set up a creative writing center to show students that there are many forms of creative writing besides the dreaded "write a story." In this center are twelve task cards to complete each month. I try to focus them around a monthly theme. For September I concentrated on Garfield the cat. One task card, for example, read, "Cat Chow, Inc., is going out of business. Invent a new variety of cat food that will save them from bankruptcy. Design and label the can, including the kinds of information usually found on cans." I saved empty cat food cans so that each student had a can to work with.

At the end of the month, we share these projects with the class. You'd be surprised how much these sixth-graders enjoy creative writing now.

Sherry Wilkie, Madison School, Las Vegas, Nevada

Six-Foot Poems

You'll need felt-tip pens, slips of paper about 1" × 3", and a long, long sheet of paper. Use shelf paper or tape together large sheets of paper.

Begin by choosing with your students a subject for the poem. If you've been studying the circus, for example, one of the animals or a special act might be appropriate. Then gather together on the floor in a circle.

Ask each youngster to think of a word that tells about the subject. Encourage them to think of "neat," exciting words—describing words or action words. When a child offers a word, write it on one of the slips of paper and give it to the child as his or her own word. Keep this part of the activity lively and ensure that everyone gives three or four words so that each child has a little collection of slips. Interrupt this step several times and ask each child to read his or her words to the group.

Tell the youngsters that they're going to glue their words onto the long paper to make a poem, *but first* . . . Ask a child to hand you one of his or her words. The group now thinks of a few words to go with that word. The new words are friends who go before or after the chosen word, so encourage students to put the chosen word sometimes at the beginning, sometimes in the middle, and sometimes near the end. For example:

Topic: elephants

Word: wrinkled

Phrases or word friends: wrinkled gray ears (beginning); funny wrinkled skin (middle); like a huge prune, wrinkled (end)

Try to limit the phrases to three or four words.

Beginning at the top of the long paper, write the phrase in big letters. When you are ready to write the chosen word, ask the "owner" to glue it to the paper in its proper position. Repeat for each word, gluing it to the long paper as you write the rest of the phrase. After two or three phrases, ask students to read the emerging poem. Stretch out the words and phrases to cover the length of the paper. Vary the colors used in writing if that seems appropriate to the topic. Finally, hang the six-foot poem on the wall. Youngsters may want to provide illustrations for it.

Don Howard, Miles Laboratory School, Tucson, Arizona

Kaleidoscopic

This writing activity can be adapted for any level of instruction and for a variety of end products, especially poetry. You'll need Bromo-Seltzer, food coloring (in drop bottles), water, a clear pie pan, an overhead projector and screen, a record player, and a few favorite records.

Ask students to jot down words and images that convey what they see and feel as they watch the screen. Place the pie pan on the overhead projector and pour some water into it. Add drops of various colors of food coloring. Every now and then slip a few Bromo-Seltzer tablets into the swirls of color. These create bomb-like explosions. Use your favorite record as background music and change the water often.

Jeanne Gerlach, West Liberty State College, West Liberty, West Virginia

Cinquain in the First Grade

First-graders enjoy poetry, but when they write original verse, their expression is often thwarted because of concern for rhythm and rhyme. Cinquain is a structured form of verse that keeps poetic thoughts and feelings moving without fretting over rhythm and rhyme.

A cinquain has five lines. Although there are several variations, I follow this pattern:

First line: one word that states the title

Second line: two words that describe the title

Third line: three words that express action

Fourth line: four words that express feeling

Fifth line: one word that is a synonym for the title

Initially, we write a cinquain cooperatively. Then each child writes a verse following the same steps. I ask students to work quickly without regard for spelling and spacing and invite them to help each other. When the cinquains are completed, the children are delighted with their own work and with the work of their classmates. I share this work with pride and pleasure.

Tonia
Eyes, face
Looking, thinking, guessing
Mixed-up, happy, ornery, curious
Me

—Tonia, age 7

Jaws
Mouth, teeth
Swimming, hunting, eating
Lonely, jealous, angry, mean
Shark

—Jason, age 7

Babies
Soft, cute
Playing, sleeping, eating
Hungry, cranky, content, happy
Kids

—Serena, age 6

Sandra Walker, Byron Elementary School, Byron, Minnesota

Twelve Days of Halloween

I use this activity just before Halloween, but it can be adapted to other occasions. I begin by playing a record of "The Twelve Days of Christmas" and showing an overhead transparency. Of course an oral reading can suffice and a nicely illustrated text can be substituted for the transparency. We then talk about alliteration and repetition, noting the pattern of nouns and the verb endings. We also list together at the chalkboard some of the words commonly—and not so commonly—associated with Halloween. Students then write their own poems following the "Twelve Days" model. Here is an excerpt from the kind of poem your students will produce.

> On the twelfth day of Halloween,
> An old witch gave to me
> Twelve cats a-clawing,
> Eleven fairies floating,
> Ten goblins ghouling,
> Nine spiders spinning,
> Eight phantoms prowling,
> Seven skeletons shaking,
> Six Draculas drooling,
> Five glowing ghosts,
> Four calling kids,
> Three mean men,
> Two big "Boo's,"
> And a bagful of candy for me!

Eleanor McLaughlin, George Street Junior High School, Fredericton, New Brunswick

Loverly

A story in the *Minneapolis Tribune* was the inspiration for this activity.

> She [Mrs. Jo Culnane] wanted people to know that eighth-graders have beautiful thoughts. So she asked them to write down the things they love. . . . Mrs. Culnane asked them to list up to 50 things they love in this world. Then she had them narrow it to 10. "The result was almost like a photo of each child," she said. "You could almost identify them by what they wrote."

Naturally we had to try this, too.

The Things I Love

Brand new puppies frolicking around,
The smell of baby powder,
The perfume Helen wears almost every day,
Going to the Y-deals knowing I probably won't get asked to dance,
But going anyway,
Playing with small kids when they get a big kick out of a piggyback ride,
The pen names when you can write a story and no one knows who wrote,
Almost.

—Squimp

Susan Rietz, substitute teacher, St. Peter, Minnesota

7 Grammar, Usage, and Punctuation

Reassembling cut-up sentences and signaling correct and incorrect usage patterns with red and green cards are two of the sentence-sense activities for younger elementary students. Older students will enjoy **Plus Fours**, a game that encourages them to expand sentences as well as to become familiar with the functions of nouns and adjectives, verbs and adverbs. Punctuation pins allow younger children to handle—literally—punctuation while dialogue transcriptions provide opportunities for older students to practice punctuation skills. Punctuation pictures are enjoyed by students of any age—and by parents and teachers.

Sentence Sense

Ask each youngster to make up a sentence and copy it onto a strip of tagboard, leaving space between each word. Next, the child cuts the tagboard strip between each word, including the period as a separate card, and scrambles the individual cards. Youngsters first reassemble their own sentence puzzles and then exchange puzzles with classmates. For very young children, cut zigzag lines between words, as in a jigsaw puzzle, so children have visual as well as logical clues in reassembling sentences.

Sister Jacqueline R. Verville, Notre Dame College, Manchester, New Hampshire

Signal Cards

Children enjoy responding physically to questions. I use "flip-ups" when my first-graders practice usage patterns, but the technique can be used in many other ways and at more advanced grade levels. Give each child one green and one red card. I begin by reading a sentence such as "He gots my toy." If the sentence sounds right, students flip up their green cards, signaling that I should go on to the next sentence. If the sentence sounds wrong, they flip up the red card, which tells me to stop; something in the sentence needs to be changed. At this point we find the error and correct it. Caution: agree that you will give a signal for flipping up the cards so that students take time to think about the sentence before responding.

Nancy Hest, Lois Craig Elementary School, North Las Vegas, Nevada

Punctuation Pins

Create a set of punctuation pins by putting the marks of punctuation on clip-on clothespins. You'll need multiples. Print sentences without their punctuation marks on strips of tagboard. Students pick a sentence at random and punctuate it with the correct pins.

Kathy Huse-Inman, Division of Elementary and Secondary Education, Pierre, South Dakota

Question Bee

Practice using tricky word pairs with a question and answer technique. If, for example, students are drilling on the words *isn't* and *aren't*, tell the first youngster to ask a question using the word *isn't*. The student who answers it must use the word *aren't*. Like this:

> First student: "Isn't John coming?"
> Second student: "No, he's staying home because his friends aren't coming."

Vary the game by reversing the order: the first student provides a statement using one of the pair of tricky words; the second student asks a question that might have elicited that answer. This switch calls for some thought.

Betty Moore, Gordon McCaw Elementary School, Henderson, Nevada

A Few of My Favorite Things

Middle-schoolers and older elementary students enjoy this worksheet, and it brings up more punctuation and capitalization snags than at first seem apparent.

> Here is an opportunity to apply some of what you know about punctuation, capitalization, and spelling. Indicate your personal favorite in each category and write a sentence about each of your choices. Use the first item as an example.
>
> 1. car   Buick
>   Our family hopes that Dad will trade in our old car on a new Buick.

2. department store	15. month
3. musical group	16. chewing gum
4. beverage	17. toy
5. holiday	18. baseball team
6. season	19. shopping mall
7. poem	20. athlete
8. television program	21. ice cream
9. song	22. newspaper
10. short story	23. magazine
11. movie star	24. movie
12. girl's name	25. cheese
13. state	26. city
14. game	27. theme amusement park

28. sandwich	40. sneakers
29. comic strip	41. musical instrument
30. vegetable	42. color
31. bird	43. animal
32. author	44. Muppet
33. snack food	45. pen
34. flower	46. singer
35. restaurant	47. cookie
36. candy bar	48. boy's name
37. cereal	49. shampoo
38. school subject	50. college team
39. jeans	

Judith K. Smith, Largo Middle School, Largo, Florida

Picture Talk

Pictures of people cut from magazines can spark ideas when students write character sketches and simple narratives. Here is a warm-up exercise that provides an opportunity for punctuation review. Ask each student to bring to class at least one picture of a person cut from a magazine. Assign partners and ask each pair to "join" pictures by creating dialogue. Each student speaks for the picture he or she supplied. Students transcribe this dialogue, using correct punctuation. Encourage partners to work together to achieve the best possible job of punctuation.

Kay Cornelius, Grissom High School, Huntsville, Alabama

Halloween Handout

Here's an October sentence-sense exercise that students enjoy.

> Improve this story by breaking it into shorter sentences. You may add or cross out a few words. Punctuate all sentences carefully.

> One night when the moon was full a wicked witch and her black cat took off in search of the ingredients for a very special stew but her broom was not working very well that night and she knew she was in trouble when it began to buck and jump and she especially knew she was in trouble when her cat, whose mind she could read, started to think about jumping, because the cat knew the broom needed a new set of spark plugs and would conk out completely before long, but the witch couldn't do much about it except try to get down safely, which she did, but when she pointed the broom down,

it picked up more and more speed and she didn't know if she could pull out of the dive if her engine quit but then she ran into this strand of thin rope hanging over the side of a cliff and the rope wrapped itself around the broom and stopped it but the witch and the cat both fell off and landed on top of a haystack, but that broke their fall and after they went into town and bought some spark plugs they were able to continue on their way, which they did, and they found their ingredients and made their stew and the witch put the cat into the stew and changed him into a prince who was every bit as ugly as the witch was.

Robert K. Williams, North View Junior High School, Brooklyn Park, Minnesota

Punctuation: Prelude and Finale

Lure unsuspecting students into studying punctuation by asking them to create pictures using only punctuation marks cut from construction paper. On an 8½″ × 11″ sheet of construction paper students paste cutouts of punctuation marks of any size to make a pattern or design; person, place, or thing. Over the semesters students have turned out some very clever punctuation pictures: a Model T Ford, a pirate, Popeye, Snoopy, a girl with pigtails, Mickey Mouse, the flag, a flower garden.

I've successfully used this assignment as a contest during an open house for parents, asking them to vote to determine the winning punctuation picture. At least three things were accomplished: my room was decorated; I was spared the difficult task of choosing a winner; parents had a pleasant memory of the English classroom and a topic to talk about with their sons and daughters.

To enliven punctuation review, ask the class to collaborate in the writing of a story. Students then tape the story with punctuation sound effects a la Victor Borge. You'll hear some highly imaginative sounds for periods, commas, exclamation points, dashes, apostrophes, and so forth—and students won't overlook a single opportunity to punctuate.

Virginia McCormick, Allen High School, Allentown, Pennsylvania

Plus Fours

I use the following game when my fifth-graders are learning the parts of speech. It also helps them learn how to expand sentences.

Label four paper bags or other containers: *noun, verb, adjective,* and *adverb.* Give each youngster four slips of paper on which to write a noun, a verb, an adjective, and an adverb. Place each slip in the correct bag.

Divide the class into teams. A player from each team picks one word from each bag and constructs a complete sentence that uses the four words. The sentence is written on the chalkboard. The next player from each team chooses four more words and tries to add them to the sentence. The expanded sentence must make sense, although there is some latitude for whimsy and humor. For each correct addition a player makes, the team earns one point. Unused words are set aside.

When the class has run out of words, the game is over and the points for each team are totaled. If you like and if there are several words in the discard pile, run a final double-point round. A player from each team in turn has an opportunity to draw one of the discarded words and add it to the team's sentence. If the addition makes sense, the team scores two points.

Judith Fields, Elbert B. Edwards Elementary School, Las Vegas, Nevada

8 Observing and Evaluating

Observation is often a more accurate way of evaluating the language arts skills of youngsters than traditional testing. **Projected Patterns, Learning Center for the Lazy,** and **Discussion Catalyst** are three activities that bring that principle into practice. Teachers have always known that when students review, important learning goes on—synthesis and generalization as well as mastery. A half dozen games—**I Have, Who Has, Tic-Tac-Toe, Bingo, Fishing, Kickball,** and **Baseball**—provide lively formats for the review of almost any kind of material. The section ends with a plan for a gala all-school problem-solving day.

Projected Patterns

You'll need duplicate sets of identical objects for this activity: scissors, ruler, pencil, eraser, key, paper clip, for example. Arrange one set of these objects on an overhead projector and project their image on the screen. Give the class a minute to study the arrangement. Turn off the projector. Now ask several children to arrange duplicate sets of objects in exactly the same positions as the set they saw on the screen. Reduce the number of objects if the task is too difficult at first. Vary the objects and their placement, and give each child several turns. You sometimes discover youngsters who have difficulty with visual memory or spatial relationships.

Rosemary Holmes-Gull, Paul E. Culley Elementary School, Las Vegas, Nevada

Learning Center for the Lazy

Write activities on large sheets of construction paper or tagboard or cut out and mount pages from leftover workbooks and sample copies of texts. Arrange these on the wall (bulletin board, chalkboard—even the floor) and cover the whole thing with clear plastic.

It's sold in twelve-foot widths at hardware stores for about fifteen cents a linear foot.

Give youngsters overhead pens, plastic markers, or markers for white "blackboards" and let them tackle the activities. Work can be erased with an old mitten, towel, or sponge. Our class has sock puppets to do the job and an ear syringe to squirt a little water for pens.

You'll find that this scheme provides an excellent opportunity for you to observe a child's attack skills. The child's back is to you and he or she is unaware of observation.

Norma K. Smith, Ravena Elementary School, Ravena, New York

Discussion Catalyst

Ask students to prepare one to three questions they have after reading an assignment. Have them write these questions on the chalkboards prior to a discussion of the assignment. You should literally be surrounded by student questions. You'll find that this practice improves the quality and value of the discussion because you can quickly judge the depth of student understanding and the influence their attitudes have had on their perceptions.

William Speiser, Rumson-Fair Haven School, Rumson, New Jersey

Time Enough with Tapes

A tape recorder allows you to "clone around" in class. Record oral tests, drills, dictation exercises, lectures, and class discussions and you have an instant replay for absentees, for individual remediation and review—and for repetition of a quiz or exercise in other classes. Using the tape recorder helps you find the class time to help students individually, to keep records, to read student drafts. I find that I have fewer sore throats and that students' listening skills improve.

Susan Howard, Paxon Junior High School, Jacksonville, Florida

Fishing for the Questions

This simple format can be adapted for usage practice, spelling review, vocabulary study—almost any topic. Make at least one fish for each youngster in the room. Write a question to be answered, a word to be spelled, a usage pattern to be incorporated into the child's own sentence, on each fish. Attach a paper clip and place the fish in a box. Children fish with a stick that has a magnet attached to one end. One child at a time lands a fish and answers the question printed on it. If the question is missed, the fish can be returned to the pond. Keep individual scores if you wish and declare a winner when all the fish have been caught.

Julie Anne Arnold, Rose Warren Elementary School, Las Vegas, Nevada

I Have, Who Has

I borrowed this activity from a math teacher. It can be used to reinforce skills in any subject. Its greatest value lies in the fact that although each student holds only one card, he or she must listen carefully and think through every problem in order to be able to respond at the correct time. I have used the game successfully for grammar, vocabulary, and story content review.

The basic card design is shown below; as a simple example I am using verb forms. Notice that the "Who has" question on one card is answered by the "I have" statement of the next card.

I *Have* Eat	I *Have* Tore	I *Have* Had Run
Who *Has* the Past Tense of Tear?	Who *Has* the Past Participle Of Run?	Who *Has* the Present Tense of Eat?

To make the cards, set up the design sheet shown below. Decide on the size of the deck. Beginning with the "Who has" column, write your first question after number 1. Write the answer in the "I have" column after number 2. Write the next question in the "Who has" column after number 2 and its answer in the "I have" column after number 3. Continue in this manner until you have enough questions for the size deck you need. The "Who has" question on the last line is answered in the "I have" column of number 1. Now copy the number 1 "I have" statement and the number 1 "Who has" statement onto the same card. Repeat for each card until the deck is complete.

GAME DESIGN SHEET

I have...

1.
2. I have tore.
3 I have had run.
.
.
24.
25.

Who has...

1. Who has the past tense of tear?
2. Who has the past participle of run?
3.
.
24.
25.

I h... has jumped.

To play the game, shuffle the cards and deal them out, one to each student until the deck is exhausted. (Two cards per student is sometimes more effective.) Choose a student to begin. That student reads the "I have" statement on his or her card, pauses, and reads the "Who has" question. The student holding the answer responds by reading his or her entire card in the same manner. The game continues until the first student answers.

Karen Kutiper, Alief Independent School District, Alief, Texas

Testing with Tic-Tac-Toe

I use this activity to help students master the use of *to, too,* and *two,* but the game can be used with *there, their,* and *they're; its* and *it's; your* and *you're,* and with many other kinds of content. There's no need for answers to come in sets of three.

Draw tic-tac-toe grids on the chalkboard and divide the class into pairs or small teams. One player or team uses the X; the other, the O. Decide which player or team will begin the game. Read a sentence that uses *to, too,* and *two.* The first player chooses the appropriate word. The correct answer gives that student the opportunity to place an X or O in a square of the game grid. If the answer was incorrect, the sentence goes to the other player or team. The winner is determined by the traditional rules of tic-tac-toe.

Diane Ng, Helen Marie Smith Elementary School, Las Vegas, Nevada

Bingo Review

I often use bingo games to review basic grammar, but the game can be adapted to any review for which you can devise a list of at least twenty-five items to be put on the playing cards: grammar and usage patterns, homonyms, synonyms, antonyms, character recognition, vocabulary and definitions.

My students call this game Bonus Bingo because I give bonus points on test day for "bingos" earned on review day. (I keep a tally during the game.) Here is how I use the game to review personal pronouns.

To prepare for the game, fill the squares on each bingo card with twenty-five answers, for example, pronouns: I, my/mine, me, we, us, you, he, she, etc. I've included a sample playing card below. Since cards take time to make, ask students to fill their cards from a list of pronouns on the board. Be sure the cards are filled randomly.

You'll also need to prepare a set of call cards that contain descriptions of each pronoun. Samples are shown below.

When everyone has a playing card, distribute a handful of markers to each student—cardboard squares or paper clips will serve. Call out a description of one of the pronouns from a call card drawn at random. Students who have the corresponding pronoun on their cards, cover that square—if they recognize the match.

When a student calls "bingo," others are asked if they qualify. Students must make this claim before I check the cards, and each bingo must include the *last* pronoun I described. These precautions prevent students from cashing in on someone else's bingo. Of course, students may go ahead and cover pronouns missed earlier as I check the cards. We usually go on for several bingo calls before clearing the cards and beginning again.

Patricia Bjerstedt, Lincoln High School, Gahanna, Ohio

Dual Purpose Kickball

Use a game of kickball to review almost any kind of material— vocabulary from social studies class, the spelling list, factual material from an assigned story. I divide the class into two permanent teams. These teams play a regulation game of kickball, with one exception. Prior to each player's turn to kick, I ask a question from a list I've prepared in advance. If the player answers correctly, he or she may kick. If the question is missed, the student loses the opportunity to kick.

Verus Young, Lois Craig Elementary School, North Las Vegas, Nevada, and Patricia G. Houle, Andover Elementary School, Andover, New Hampshire

Baseball Review

This game can be used to review almost any kind of material from spelling to usage to literature. To begin, write at least fifty questions covering the material to be reviewed. Go through these and star the most difficult.

Next, staple or glue the diamonds and spades (in descending order) from a deck of cards to a sheet of poster board as shown below. Glue a small envelope (book card pockets work nicely) below each card and insert several questions in each envelope. Put the starred questions in the envelopes beneath the Ace, King, Queen, and Jack of each suit.

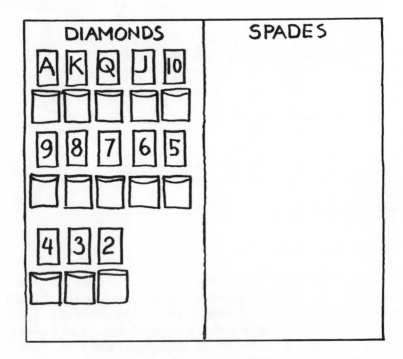

Now outline a baseball diamond on a sheet of poster board. You might decorate it with pictures of baseball players. At each base and at home plate paste two adhesive-backed picture hooks as shown below. Finally, cut about twenty two-inch squares of red and black construction paper and punch a hole in each.

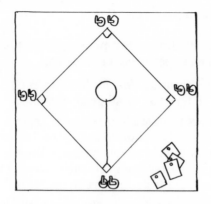

To play the game, divide players into two teams—the red and the black. Place the other half of the deck of cards, divided into hearts and clubs, facedown on the table. Turn up a card from the pile that matches the color of the team at bat (for example, the seven of hearts). Pull a question from the envelope of the corresponding red card on the poster (seven of diamonds). If the student at bat answers the question correctly, his or her team records a base hit by placing a red square on the first base hook. All cards from two through ten score base hits. If you turn a Jack, Queen, King, or Ace, and the student at bat answers correctly, the team scores a home run. A team remains at bat until three students strike out by answering incorrectly. All players on base move when a student scores. For example, if there is a player on first, a player on second, and a player on third, and the batter answers a one-base question correctly, all players advance one base and the player on third comes home. If a student answers a question from the Jack through the Ace correctly, all players on base come home, including the batter.

Two sets of alternate rules change the pace of the game.

1. Teams may alternate in answering instead of switching when the team at bat has struck out three times.

2. Shuffle the hearts and clubs together. The team whose color comes up gets the question. Teams change at bat as the color changes.

Joan Fleischmann, Perkiomen Valley High School, Schwenksville, Pennsylvania

Rather Than Grading Every Paper

These options to grading every paper reduce the paper load but expand the writing experiences of students.

1. Provide opportunities for students to read their writing to classmates in large or small group settings.
2. Find audiences for student writing. Letters should be sent. Editorials should be submitted to school or local newspapers. Display student writing everywhere. Book students as guest authors to give readings of their work in other classes. Arrange for them to go in pairs to reduce intimidation.
3. Use journals as a place for students to explore experiences; later, relate them to more formal written assignments.
4. Intervene in the composing stage of student writing. It is then that the comments you ordinarily write at the end of a finished paper can influence the product you will receive.
5. Write with your students. Complete the assignments you give them. Among other benefits, you will discover unforeseen problems with assignments while there is still time to help students work through them.
6. Give the student the final choice of papers to be graded. Ask students to keep their work in writing folders. After they have written several descriptive paragraphs, for example, allow each student to choose the one that will be graded.

Leslie A. Kent, Longfellow Intermediate School, Falls Church, Virginia

Problem-solving Day

With a firm belief that meeting the needs of the gifted improves the curriculum for all students, I organized Problem-solving Day. I asked social studies, math, and science teachers to come up with problems for students to solve. These could be brainteasers or problems more directly related to subject matter. We designated one day as Problem-solving Day and awarded prizes in such areas as most problems solved, best problem-solver in each subject, most persistent problem-solver. The interdisciplinary crosscurrents were refreshing, and students certainly learned the steps of problem solving.

Materials such as the following were useful: *Mind Benders* edited by Rob Nelson and Robin Smith (Midwest Publications), *Think Tank* by Dianne Draze (Dandy Lion Publications), *Scratching the Surface of Creative Problem Solving* by Ruth B. Noller and Ernest Mauthe (DOK Publishers), and *Making Waves with Creative Problem Solving* by Vaune Ainsworth-Land and Norma Fletcher (DOK Publishers).

Betty Schwermann, Chaska Middle School, Chaska, Minnesota

9 The First Five Minutes— and the Last

Begin a desktop file box of five-minute idea cards with these. Many of the word and letter games in preceding sections also are useful for getting a class to settle down or perk up. Add to your collection from newspapers, magazines, and professional journals. You'll be glad you did on a noisy Friday or a sleepy Monday— and your substitute will be forever grateful.

Classroom Calisthenics

An overhead projector works nicely for daily warm-up exercises. As students enter the room, their attention is focused on the overhead screen where an analogy, thought puzzle, or clozure exercise awaits them. I take attendance and they are ready to check the warm-up and begin class.

Susan Howard, Paxon Junior High School, Jacksonville, Florida

In-group

Here's a deduction activity for an odd moment or two. Put the following columns and heads on the board but give *no* directions:

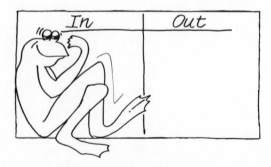

Decide without telling the class what group will be "in" (green vegetables, for example). Begin by writing the name of an object

in that group under "in"; add another from that category. Now put an "out" word in its respective box. As soon as students catch on to what you're doing, they'll begin offering suggestions. Don't tell them what you're looking for; allow them to discover the solution themselves. Other categories I've used—objects through which one can see, students in the room wearing red, and categories appropriate to material we have studied in class.

Beverly Midthun, Rippleside Elementary School, Aitkin, Minnesota

In the Manner of the Adverb

When a few minutes remain at the end of a class period, we sometimes play this game. A student is chosen to be "it" and asked to leave the room. The class then chooses an adverb, *quickly* for example. When "it" returns, he or she asks members of the class to do something specific "in the manner of the adverb." "Erase the board," for example, "in the manner of the adverb." Or, "Smile, in the manner of the adverb." The student who is "it" continues to ask for demonstrations until he or she guesses the adverb.

I think this game gives students an understanding of adverbs as well as practice in getting up in front of the group. It also generates a class spirit since I participate in the game.

Betty Ford, Brecksville High School, Broadview Heights, Ohio

Simile, Metaphor, and Psychoanalysis

Ask students to complete sentences like the following: "Are you more like a VW or a Cadillac?" Their response begins: "I am more like a . . . because . . ." The game taps thinking skills, produces some genuinely creative responses, and generates good humor. Here are a few other questions to try, but you and your students will come up with many others.

Are you more like a baseball or a football?

Are you more like a sneaker or a black leather loafer?

Are you more like disco or country music?

Are you more like Calvin Klein jeans or cutoffs?

Are you more like the sun or the moon?

Are you more like the Rocky Mountains or Daytona Beach?

In a variation, ask students to complete sentences like this one: "If I were a __(flower)__ I would be a __(rose)__ because . . ." Use a variety of topics: If I were a movie, sport, car, song, piece of furniture, item of clothing, food.

Karen Rugerio, Orange County Administration Center, Orlando, Florida

Inflation

Here's a filler for a few leftover minutes or a journal entry: If you were walking down the road and saw a penny, would you *stoop* to pick it up? Why or why not?

Susan Rietz, substitute teacher, St. Peter, Minnesota

Jim Dandy Name Game

Introduce at the chalkboard several names that are also used in other contexts, for example, an Indian drum (tom-tom) or a type of song sung at Christmas (carol). The examples that follow may be put on worksheets or used at the board. After a few minutes, share the answers as a group. Be sure to allow time for students to add to the Jim Dandy list.

1. short prayer said before meals (Grace)
2. absorbent fabric with uncut pile (Terry)
3. winner (Victor)
4. statement of what is owed (Bill)
5. sharp projection or hook (Barb)
6. flower (Iris, Daisy, Rose)
7. award for best movie (Oscar)
8. award for best television show (Emmy)
9. award for best mystery book (Edgar)
10. type of beef roast or steak (Chuck)
11. British policeman (Bobby)
12. wine of Spanish origin (Sherry)
13. sandwich of ground beef, barbecue sauce, and spices (Sloppy Joe)
14. tall grass (Reed)
15. to bring legal action (Sue)
16. quick down-and-up motion (Bob)
17. plant used in cooking as a seasoning (Basil, Rosemary)
18. Mafia leader (Don)
19. beam of light (Ray)
20. precious stone (Opal, Ruby)
21. flowerless, seedless plants with leaflike fronds (Fern)

22. spearlike weapon (Lance)
23. abnormal growth within the shell of some mollusks (Pearl)
24. American flycatcher (Phoebe)
25. forthright and sincere (Frank)
26. thin nail with small head (Brad)
27. notch or chip (Nick)
28. shrub with thick, glossy leaves (Holly)
29. to flatten or shape with light blows of the hand (Pat)
30. pole used for fishing (Rod)
31. state (Virginia)
32. abbreviation for instrument that transmits sound (Mike)
33. legal document to dispose of property (Will)
34. 10,560 feet (Miles)

Sue Jarvis Rauld, Department of Defense School, Panama

Creative Problem Solving

It was Albert Einstein who observed that "imagination is more important than knowledge." Brainstorming is a technique to generate as many alternatives or solutions as possible for a given problem. Do not stop to evaluate; this is done after all suggestions are recorded. (Why fly with the flaps down?) Too often, we encourage students to do things in a prescribed fashion. (Convention is the gravity that imagination must transcend. Encourage students to let their minds soar.) Take or make frequent opportunities for students to see things in new ways. Here are two examples.

1. Ask students to join all points on the grid in four straight lines without raising their pens.

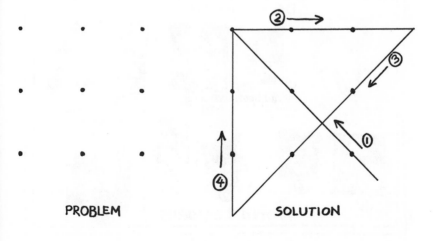

PROBLEM   SOLUTION

2. Challenge the class with an object such as a coat hanger or an ashtray: what uses could you find for this object on a desert island? Each student draws up a long list in competition with others. Alternately, divide the class into groups, each group vying with the others.

After students get the hang of brainstorming, move on to tasks more closely related to specific language arts assignments, again listing solutions, evaluating them, and selecting the best. Assignments such as these lend themselves to brainstorming.

1. What other courses of action could a character in a story have taken?
2. Ask students to revise in several ways an awkward sentence you have written on the board: list, evaluate, choose.
3. How many words can students list that will serve in tired, overworked he said/she said constructions?

Nick Sopinka, Sheridan College, Oakville, Ontario

Window on the World

Clip a dozen or so pictures of prominent leaders/events on the world, national, or local scene that fit a theme: world leaders, sports professionals, television personalities, good citizens in our town. Number each picture but do not identify it and display the collection on the bulletin board with an appropriate title.

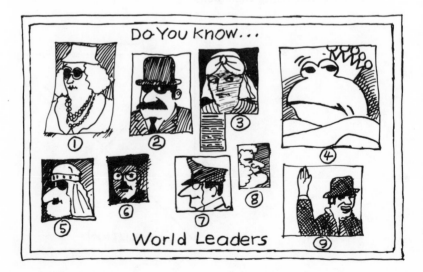

Encourage students during the following week to unravel the mysteries of these pictures, using the resources of newspapers and magazines at home and school and discussion clues from parents and peers. At the end of each week spend fifteen minutes (or longer) identifying the pictures and discussing their significance.

Vary the activity by dividing the class into groups of four or five. Give each group a minute to offer its hypothesis and choose a picture to identify. Continue with each group in turn until all pictures have been identified by the end of the week. Each group earns one point for each correct identification. Members of the group with the highest score are the news sleuths of the week.

Ann B. Holum, Excelsior Elementary School, Excelsior, Minnesota

Title Index

Kuki Gallmann was born near Venice and studied political sciences at the University of Padua. In 1972 she moved to Kenya with her husband and son, who were both to die in tragic circumstances. As a tribute to their memory she founded the Gallmann Memorial Foundation, which promotes and sponsors the education of Kenyans. An environmentalist, poet and writer, she still lives on her ranch in Kenya, Ol ari Nyiro, with her daughter Sveva.

Her other books are a collection of poetry in Italian, *Il Colore del Vento*, *African Nights* and her autobiography, *I Dreamed of Africa*, an international bestseller in eighteen languages and the subject of a forthcoming major film.

NIGHT OF THE LIONS

Africa is a place which retains what most of the world has lost: space, roots, traditions, awesome beauty, true wilderness, rare animals, extraordinary people. In this haunting collection of stories, Kuki Gallmann unveils the Kenya that she knows and loves. She approaches her familiar world with wonder and delight, rejoicing in each new experience, each rediscovery of the mysterious land which has become her home with all its superstitions, its dangers, its colours and scents, its pervasive heat and above all its magic.

Books by Kuki Gallmann
Published by The House of Ulverscroft:

I DREAMED OF AFRICA
AFRICAN NIGHTS

KUKI GALLMANN

NIGHT OF THE LIONS

Complete and Unabridged

CHARNWOOD
Leicester

First published in Great Britain in 1999 by
Viking
London

First Charnwood Edition
published 2001
by arrangement with
Penguin Books Limited
London

British Library CIP Data

Gallmann, Kuki
  Night of the lions.—Large print ed.—
Charnwood library series
1. Gallmann, Kuki—Homes and haunts—Kenya
2. Large type books
3. Kenya—Description and travel
4. Kenya—Social life and customs—20th century
I. Title
967.6′2′042′092

ISBN 0–7089–9234–X

Published by
F. A. Thorpe (Publishing)
Anstey, Leicestershire

Set by Words & Graphics Ltd.
Anstey, Leicestershire
Printed and bound in Great Britain by
T. J. International Ltd., Padstow, Cornwall

This book is printed on acid-free paper

For Makena, a daughter of Africa, and for all my young African friends

Dreams can change your life,
and eventually the world.

FATIMA MERNISSI, *The Harem Within*

Acknowledgements

I would like to thank my African friends at Ol ari Nyiro, for their loyal support, and for holding the fort when I was deep in my writing; my readers, who have taken the time to write that they have fallen in love with Africa by reading my stories, have travelled to Kenya to discover their truth and, having found it, have become the good-will ambassadors this continent needs.

Gilfrid Powys, always; Toby Eady, my 'brother', agent and staunchest ally; Aino Block, who once again enthusiastically read my script; Adrian House, for his advice; the Gallmann Memorial Foundation's patron, team and supporters, for helping the dream. My daughter 'Makena', for her love, her wisdom and her smile.

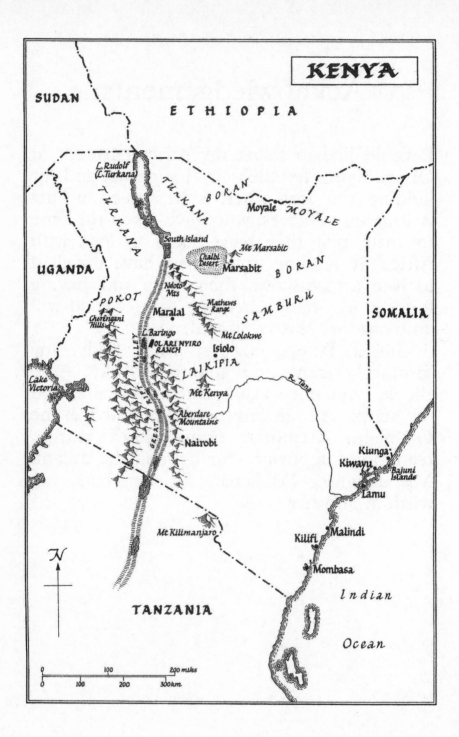

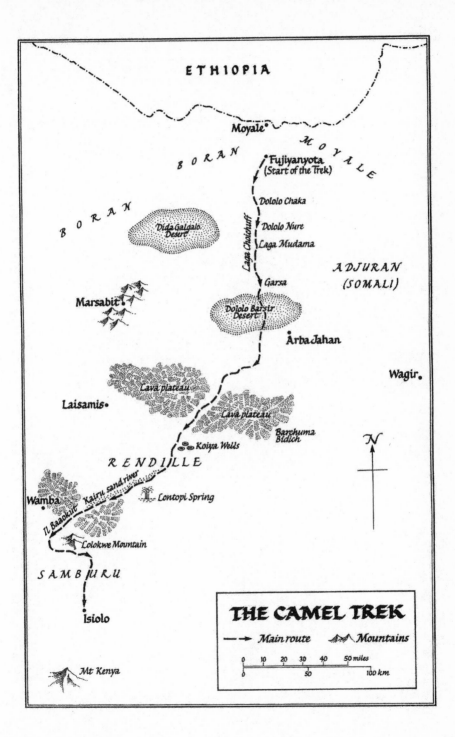

ETHIOPIA

Moyale

MOYALE

BORAN

• Fujiyanyota
(Start of the Trek)

BORAN

Dololo Chaka

Dida Galgalo
Desert

Dololo Nure

Laga Mudama

Laga Chalbuff

ADJURAN
(SOMALI)

Garsa

Marsabit•

Dololo Barsir
Desert

• Arba Jahan

Wagir•

Lava plateau

Laisamis•

Lava plateau

Barchuma
Bidich

Koiya Wells

RENDILLE

Kairu sand river

Wamba

Lontopi Spring

Il Baadut

Lolokwe Mountain

SAMBURU

Isiolo

THE CAMEL TREK

→ Main route   Mountains

0   10   20   30   40   50 miles
0   50   100 km

Mt Kenya

Introduction

When I first came to Africa, the people addressed me as Memsaab; in time, they baptized me Nyawera, The One Who Works Hard. Now, they call me Mama.

Because I have chosen to stay, and because I belong.

Africa is a continent of extremes.

There is an Africa of tragedy and famine, of corruption and war, of blood and hunger and tears, of incurable disease and tribal clashes and political unrest. There are droughts and there are floods. There are crowded cities, glue-sniffing street children, child-prostitutes, bidonvilles where open sewage carries the lurid refuse of a hopeless conglomerate of people with no jobs, no homes, no future, roads littered with potholes and garbage heaps where skinny goats forage.

It is the Africa one reads about today in every paper, the one we daily see in reports on cable television. It is a captive Africa, dependent on the blackmail of foreign aid, constantly judged, constantly criticized and never understood. Here the rich West has imprinted its competitive, frantic image, created alien needs, imposed alien philosophies and financed impossible schemes, unsuited to the true spirit and potential of this troubled and fantastic continent, all too ready to take back that help and sit in judgement of yet another failure.

1

I do not sing that Africa.

There is no need for yet another negative reportage, which would leave a bitter taste and would serve no purpose.

There is a different side to this ancient land. It is the Africa that, since the beginning of time, has evoked in travellers a deep recognition, an inexplicable yearning to return. The place which still has what most of the world has lost. Space. Roots. Traditions. Stunning beauty. True wilderness. Rare animals. Extraordinary people. The land that will always attract those who can still dream.

This Africa, into whose embrace went Paolo and Emanuele, called early to the land of beyond, healed my sorrow and became my life purpose. This maternal, primordial Africa taught me acceptance, endurance and survival. I recognized it as a place where wisdom could be found. A place to end this journey, and begin a new one. A place of renewal and rebirth. A good place to die.

In the very heart of Kenya where I still live, Ol ari Nyiro — The Place of Dark Waters — I walked the hills and the valleys in those dark days of solitude, tiring my body, asking the wind the questions whose answers are the reasons for life. I missed Paolo, a man for all seasons and places, handsome, gifted with irresistible charm, eloquent and brave, happy in the bush and at ease in a palace; I missed his poetry and flair. I missed Emanuele, who taught me first what it means to be a mother, my sensitive, intelligent boy, whose eyes had the sadness and wisdom of

2

ages, who was taken into that good night by one of the snakes he had loved.

Walking alone through the pervading magic of untouched African landscapes, open to growth as one is when at the bottom of pain, I felt quintessentially part of the whole. One evening, looking down at the breathtaking depths of the Mukutan Gorge on the Great Rift Valley, in this living cathedral of the spirit I found peace.

There was Sveve, the daughter Paolo would never know, the radiant girl who was my hope and my future. I was in Africa, and this was my cure.

In memory of Paolo and Emanuele I started the Gallmann Memorial Foundation and devoted the rest of my life to making a positive difference for the African environment.

★   ★   ★

Mine are love stories about Kenya, my Africa.

It is the Africa of sunshine and breathtaking, endless vistas, of roaming herds on the plains, of red dust and galloping giraffe, of forests and snow and prehistoric lakes, of gentle, handsome, intelligent people whose poverty is not of the spirit. People for whom tradition is important, to whom family values still matter, who protect the young and respect the old, care for the sick and feed the hungry, even if it means sharing the little that they have; generous people, ready to smile, and to forgive; people with a song in their heart and a dance in their step; enduring, compassionate and infinitely patient. The people

3

of Kenya, whose antique, proven wisdom I respect. I salute them and I thank them for having allowed me to live amongst them, to bury my men in the soil of my garden, as Africans do, and for allowing me the honour and the choice of becoming a Kenyan like them.

★   ★   ★

I have new stories to tell. I have old stories that I have not yet told.

The elephant, after dark, raid my garden at Kuti as they did a quarter of a century ago; I encounter — now more than ever — buffalo in my car lights; there are still rhino coming to the salt lick below The Nest, and in the moonless nights lions prey on the cattle around the *boma*, as they have since the beginning of lion and cattle in Africa. Butterflies and rare birds bejewel the forests and on the silent lakes millions of pink flamingo forage.

The Pokot herders stand on one leg, a black blanket thrown over a shoulder with supreme elegance, necks bright with beads and an ostrich feather beckoning on their skull cap.

The waves of another tide reach silently along the mangroves, while the fish eagle surveys her hunting grounds somewhere on the north coast, away from the beaten tracks. There are still remote places untouched by man's progress where harmony prevails.

Magic, and the inexplicable, still touch our lives. This is the lyrical, therapeutic Africa that I describe; the one I live every day of my life. The one that it is my life aim to preserve.

Scores of bright young Kenyans visit the Wilderness Education Centre, which I built to honour the memory of my son, and discover in Ol ari Nyiro their Africa. Each of these children is a messenger, who will carry this crusade a step further. Through education and experience the generation of today will realize the importance of their unique environment.

For the world needs beauty and youth needs hope.

It is to these young people, and to my daughter Sveva, whom they call Makena, that I dedicate this book of true stories.

Part One

Tales of the Great Rift Valley

The Summer of the Crayfish

For my father

Looking on the happy Autumn fields,
And thinking of the days that are no more.

TENNYSON, *The Princess*

On the opposite bank, two camels browsed with prehensile lips from the waxy shrubs of rhus. They moved on phlegmatically and in seconds disappeared completely. Harvester ants busily carried grass seeds, zig-zagging in a scattered procession, hurrying down their holes. Crouched on my haunches, the sun hot on the back of my khaki shirt and on my naked legs, I was fishing.

The brown surface of the water broke in a ripple and a large muddy claw emerged, to grab the morsel of rotten meat tied to a string I was holding.

'I got it!' I screamed happily and with a jerk I yanked the creature out of the water.

There it was, on the murram shore of the dam at Ol Maisor, a diminutive monster from the underworld, red and glistening, whiskers sizing up the new environment, legs already tentatively crawling their way backward towards the dam.

On the other bank, five zebra approached. They stood still a moment, looked around, and trotted, head down, to drink while their stallion

9

watched, tail twitching at invisible flies. No breeze interrupted the dreamy heat-waves lifting from the soil, and from the thorny treetops came the joyous, powerful choir of cicadas and African birds at noon.

A dust devil swirled over madly and was soon extinguished.

'The largest crayfish I have seen in a very long time,' approved Paolo. 'Amazing how fast they grow here. I thought they only thrived in a cold climate.'

We collected a bucketful in less than two hours and drove back to Ol ari Nyiro in the evening, pursuing a herd of jumping oryx, facing a wild orange sunset, singing an Italian song, and the savannah grass was tall and streaked with mystery in the fading light.

Next day, I drove to Ngobitu's dam and ceremoniously let all the crayfish go.

'One day I'll catch you again,' I let them know. 'You and all the generations you'll produce in all the years to come.' They disappeared into the murky red water leaving just a few bubbles.

They were early days in Laikipia.

They were days of exploring, of adventure, of love and of bewilderment, when we discovered the new land we had chosen for our home, and ourselves. They were days of youth and fun, when tomorrow was still gilded, when happiness was the morning birds and the evening clouds, turquoise lizards on hot stones, weaver birds building their nests on the fever trees, dung beetles laboriously rolling huge balls, heady perfumes of wild jasmine, and the Pokot women, bare-breasted and in long skin skirts, ambling proudly along the Ol ari Nyiro boundary, head high, minding their cattle.

When I would marvel at buffalo wallowing in the mud baths, at elephant moving silently like shadows through a glade, a few metres away, unaffected by my presence. When I would stand in the night at the bottom of my new garden, almost exactly where the graves now are, a long shawl protecting me from the chill of the eastern breeze, my ears alert to hear the hyena crying on the hills and lion or leopard calling their raucous, rhythmic hunting song.

When my family was still together, and my men with me.

⋆ ⋆ ⋆

In the months and years which followed so much happened that I forgot my crayfish.

It was the summer of 1981, when Paolo had been a year in his grave and the tree that he had become was bearing its first flowers and the baby he had fathered, but never seen, had begun to talk, that I suddenly remembered.

'Shall we try and see if there are any crayfish in Ngobitu's dam?' I asked Emanuele. 'If they did not all die, there should be lots by now. When was it that we put them in? Five, six years ago?' We could not recall. But Emanuele, a long-limbed teenager with serious-mocking eyes, jumped on his new motorbike, carrying some defrosted meat as a bait, and disappeared in a rusty cloud of dust.

'If they are there I'll catch them. Prepare the dill and mayonnaise, Pep!'

I did not really believe we would find any. No dried-out bleached shell had been discovered along the banks — the remnant of a stork's or heron's meal — to announce their presence. Nor, when we went out for tilapia or black bass, did we ever detect the strange shadows lurking clumsily in the shallows.

So I was immensely surprised when Emanuele appeared, triumphant, an hour or so later, carrying in his hands the largest, healthiest crayfish I had ever seen.

'There are zillions of them there,' he announced. 'We must put them on the menu.'

And so I did.

Simon my cook protested weakly, with Turkana pride, at the invasion of weird insects in his kitchen, but finally surrendered when the odd baby lobster, now attractively bright red and crowned with celery and lemon wedges, gained him additional compliments for his already outstanding cuisine.

So it was that it became a feature of hot afternoons on the ranch to go fishing, and no Venetian scampi risotto was ever tastier than the Laikipia crayfish we perfected, with lots of fresh pepper and parsley and a dash of brandy as a final touch.

But it was not just the gourmet satisfaction.

Whenever I see the crayfish at my table, I feel an immediate nostalgia, their appearance and their flavour is an instant joyous memory of other happy days, and I go back in space and season, to the time I was a little girl with pigtails and curious eyes, avidly pursuing excitement and adventure, to the unforgettable Summer of the Crayfish. The first summer I recall with my father.

★ ★ ★

We lived in the country, in Veneto, in a village called Crespano del Grappa, at the foot of mountain slopes covered in pine, chestnuts and *cornioli*,[1] where my grandfather owned the silk factory. There my young father, fresh from the Second World War — where he got some medals, lost most of his friends and his dreams, but not his longing for exploring and discovering — practised medicine at the local hospital.

I was an inquisitive child, full of questions, and those early childhood days spent in the country, with any amount of space and the freedom of a large fascinating garden, a wood, an orchard, a vineyard and a stable, were to mark my life for ever. As for ever would I yearn for the outdoors, the world of imagination, of living things, of leaves and buds, of hidden nests with eggs, of sprouting seeds, of smell of grass and berries and wild shy creatures.

I was never a town girl, content to be surrounded by the noise and glitters of a modern city. On the pavements, crowded with hurrying strangers, in the lifts, speeding to vertiginous heights, in the shopping malls of marble and

---

[1] A type of Italian crab-apple.

fountains, I felt confused and out of place. When, in the years to come, Fate brought me to travel to the world capitals, following the dream and crusade that my destiny had woven for me, I always looked for a window from where I could see the sky; for a place where to walk barefoot; for growing things alive and silent beside the man-made sophisticated junk that stifled me. All this is owed to those early days.

Inside me, bright and keen, there still is a little girl who wants to run, seak the unexplored, who loves the smell of mown grass and campfires, of running water and mountain streams, of low tide and daisies in the sun and cyclamen in marvellous clumps to be discovered in the dense undergrowth.

★ ★ ★

When my mother went to have her clothes made at the house, outside the village, of a farmer's wife called Ines, who had the gift of magic hands for sewing, I often went too.

Ines worked in her kitchen. It was the largest and most comfortable room in her house, high-ceilinged, cool in the summer, when a breeze moved from the front vine pergola to the shady back garden and the vegetable patch, and cosy in the winter, when the cooking stove was crowded with pots constantly bubbling away their appetizing vapours of hearty soups and sauces.

As a result, to her annoyance, my mother's freshly delivered winter clothes all seemed to exude a smell of minestrone. Weather permitting, they had to be hung out for days before she could wear them, and sprayed with lavender and her favourite perfume, 'Fleur de Rocaille' by Caron, a festive bouquet to me exotic, inebriating, irresistible.

I was interested in this strange, different house, and observed its details with immense curiosity.

One corner of a large wooden table was covered with a grey blanket and a clean white sheet: on this Ines cut out her patterns, stencilled out of old newspapers, and stitched them with a black Singer sewing-machine.

On the mantelpiece were sepia photographs of old weddings, all the grooms identical with their heavy moustaches and ill-fitting black coats, strangled in starched collars and bow ties, ears protruding, the only variation the middle or side partings of their brilliantine-sleeked hair. They stood rigid, their hands on a papier mâché column, or on the back of an ornate chair where the brides sat. These were identical too, jowly, black-eyed, trussed up in corsets which could not disguise their florid good health, stolidly staring at the camera with incurious diffidence.

There were oval portraits of long-lost grand-mothers, a faded photograph of Pio X, the *Papa Sarto*, next to vivid depictions of the sacred, bloody heart of Christ, a flame emanating from its middle; a crucifix with a shrivelled olive twig stuck behind it from last Palm Sunday; a doll dressed in pink lace, a few trinkets won at the village fair.

Ines was thin for an Italian woman of her age, with a sallow complexion from lack of sunshine. She wore an apron tucked about with needles, and her permed black hair was streaked with grey.

Chickens sometimes wandered in through the open door, with a blade of sun and dancing midges, and ventured tentatively on the white and black tiles, one foot at a time, observing me sidelong, with red-rimmed eyes.

If the session trailed on too long, I was allowed to go out to explore the sunny fields, provided I stayed within the compound. So it was that one day I ventured to the stream which formed a still pond set in a clump of mulberry trees below the house. I peered into the dark green waters and glimpsed a curious shadow like a long weird insect, hiding below a stone next to my laughing mirrored image.

It was that time of childhood when everything is new and exciting, of vivid physical impressions, smells of new places and animals, tastes of new fruit.

The scent of humid earth, of ferns and cyclamen in the recesses of the wood's undergrowth; the floury sweetness of the first roast chestnut, warm and slightly burned; the surprising variations in the odours of rabbit or goat droppings, chicken coop or geese, pigsty or stable, of horses and cows; the subtle delicious differences in the taste of roast pigeon and duck breast; of fresh raspberry or blackberry, currants or small wild strawberry; of milky new hazelnuts or walnuts, of different types of grapes. The

16

white nuances of jasmine or wild gardenias, tuberose or lily of the valley.

It was a constant joy, living in the unpolluted country with a whole world to explore, and I shall carry with me always memories of 'first times', vivid and fresh of a thousand details.

The intoxicating sharp *corniola* wine, a forbidden sip quickly offered by a laughing maid, Lidia, a relative of Ines's, when she took us once to her parents' farmhouse on an afternoon walk, a blessed diversion which I begged her to repeat. A free new universe unfolded there for me in all its marvels, unknown to my parents. I helped to harvest, picking with my small hands, the heavy sun-warm grapes coated in verdigris, and put them in a wide basket of woven reeds; I watched mesmerized the winy juice spurt purple in the barrels through stamping toes on late September afternoons; I helped with the milking, sitting in the dark stable, pungent cow dung heavy in my nostrils; following Lidia's brothers I climbed haystacks smelling of freshly mown grass, lucerne and wildflowers and, astride a cherry tree's branch, amongst its leaves like a bird, I ate cherries until I felt like bursting; copying the other children, I kept the stones in my cheek and spat them out all at once, trying to hit my friends and laughing with abandon.

Small things were treasures, mysteries, objects of curiosity and investigation: a dead water rat in a mossy hole, with stiff whiskers and bared yellow teeth, a lizard decomposing in the sun by a clump of forget-me-not; drinking reverently from the sacred spring in a shady glade below

17

the hill of Covolo. There — Lidia narrated — the Virgin Mary appeared to a lost, thirsty, pious child shepherdess, and stuck three of her holy burning fingers into the rock, creating three holes from which fresh clean water spurted instantly. Like a minor Lourdes, the springs of *Tre-Busi*[1] had become a place of worship, and a monastery had been built up the hill, destination of many of our afternoon walks. We reached it along a steep, dusty white gravel road, flanked at regular intervals by *capitelli*,[2] filled with votive tributes of flowers and silver hearts, where the story was told in naïve oleographic frescoes.

Oh donna donna
donna lombarda
vieni stasera a ballare con me.
E io si
che vegnaria
ma ho il marito e non e non posso venir . . .[3]

We returned singing old ballads, of love stories and betrayals and honour vindicated, and passion and tears, and stopped halfway for our *merenda*[4] of bread and cheese and raspberry syrup, sitting on the grass in the shade of a

---

[1] 'Three holes' in Venetian dialect.

[2] Shrines.

[3] 'Oh you woman from Lombardia/come tonight and dance with me./ Oh yes oh yes, I would come with thee/but I am married and cannot go.'

[4] Snack.

chestnut tree. There, looking down at the valley, I loved to search out my grandfather's house, disguised by a green clump of Cedars of Lebanon, next to the *filanda*[1] which was always easy to find, marked by its tall, smoky chimney made of old bricks.

In this bucolic contest of magical country delights, the discovery of the quaint, odd fish was intoxicating.

That evening I could not resist the temptation to recount it, and described to my father, with a wealth of details, the mysterious creature that I thought I had seen. My father listened, with the attention he always paid to my stories, and understood; and thus began the magic, exhilarating Summer of the Crayfish.

My father, with the enthusiasm and abandon that destined him to be forever young, forever inspiring, loved to find special gifts of wild morsels, gourmet foods that nature reserved for her followers, the tireless walkers, the early risers, the mountain climbers, the ones who deserved the privilege. He told us stories of handfuls of raspberries picked while running from enemy fire, of *porcini* mushrooms discovered on perilous banks inaccessible to the lazy; and the crayfish discovery coloured those mid-summer days with excitement and anticipation.

'They must be crayfish, so rare in these waters, and quite delicious. We'll go fishing tomorrow night, and you will come too, because it is your

---

[1] Silk factory.

19

discovery and you must guide me.' My father knew how to touch a deep chord of pride in my eager small heart. I was perhaps five, and not normally allowed out after dark: the exception lent my day an unbearable thrill.

We left together in the evening like conspirators, taking with us a packed dinner of sandwiches, torches and blankets and bits of meat and old salami as bait. I brought my father to the pond in the clump of trees. We peered, searching the water with the torch. My heart beat wildly: had it been an illusion? On the gravel of the bottom, amongst the stones and watercress, two grey shapes armed with claws were fighting silently.

'Well done!' approved my father, my hero, and the night glowed with my tumultuous pride.

The imprudent shellfish, attracted by the meat effluvia dissolving in the current and by the torchlight, were easily captured, and put into a tin bucket. I helped, holding the torch, carrying the bucket, and my father taught me how to grab the crayfish, just below their pincers, so they could not nip us. Splattered in mud, wet and shivering, I fell asleep exhausted in my blanket on the way back.

The crayfish were quite elusive. We could only catch a few at the time, not enough for a meal. We decided to store them at home, in one of the tanks at the back of the silk factory, a deep old cement tub where it was exciting to see the ghostly figures disappear in the mossy depths.

We went back almost every night. My father pointed out remote stars and taught me their names, we sang the partisan songs of the last war, and I was elated. The flavour of escapade, the new independence, the sounds of the night appealed to my imagination, and the experience had borders of reverie like a summer tale.

As the season progressed, the shapes became numerous in the silk factory tank.

It was finally September, the time of harvest and of returning to town, where, for the first time, I would go to school. The night of the crayfish dinner arrived.

My father surprised me by not helping with the recapture of the crayfish from their tank: this occasion was tame, and a net was produced.

He only appeared at dinner time, when already a delicious aroma was filling the house, of white wine and olive oil, and herbs and garlic.

I had been worried about eating the creatures I had come to know so well, but when they appeared on the silver platters, crowned with lemon wedges, I was startled to see my old grey friends changed to red glistening jewels. Their transformation took away my guilt. They no longer looked like those little monsters I had observed fighting in the still, silent waters and, following the others, I ate them with glee. Of the flavour, I only remember it was one of the most surprisingly delicious I had ever tasted.

No one knew that secretly, that afternoon, I had taken two couples from the full buckets and put them back furtively in the tank where they had survived so well for a month. By now, a thousand crayfish perhaps fill the tanks and ponds of that forgotten garden.

That evening, while the lamp threw weird patterns on to the white linen table-cloth monogrammed with my grandmother's initials, I looked at my father across the table, pensively sucking a claw, and knew that he already missed the adventure, and would have approved of my secret.

And once more, in his green, short-sighted eyes, I recognized myself.

Remember the Seagulls

For Livio

But Jonathan Livingston Seagull
was not a common bird
. . . more than anything he loved to fly.

RICHARD BACH, *Jonathan Livingston Seagull,*
A Story

During one of my rare visits to Italy a couple of years ago, returning from a delicious lunch of fish and chilled wine in the *valle*[1] of a friend, I found myself driving through the piazza of Jesolo which had been so familiar to me over twenty years earlier, before I came to live in Africa and turned that page of my life for ever.

There was a grey stillness in the early April afternoon, a familiar humidity, and the smell of freshwater seaweeds from the invisible lagoon came through the car window, bringing back memories, and a sudden nostalgia.

On the spur of the moment I turned to my friend Marisa, companion of many expeditions and European peregrinations.

'Shall we go to Cavallino? I haven't been back since 1972. It's only a few miles from here.'

---

[1] A geographical characteristic of the Venetian lagoon.

She turned her red head and the gold-flecked eyes flashed the quick smile which had earned her the nickname 'Fox'.

'Why not? Are you sure you can handle it? It will be changed. Maybe no one is there.' She had been one of our frequent guests in the past.

'Let's try. It will be ages before I come this way again. Perhaps I never will.'

With instant silent agreement she steered her silver-grey Mercedes to the right, and in a few moments we crossed the small bridge, out on to the white gravel of the dirt-road on the canal dyke, and we were on our way.

The slopes were covered in fresh tall grass; a few primroses had begun to sprout, and creamy calla lilies along the banks on the water edge.

I recognized the turns of the track, the narrow, late-nineteenth-century red-brick peasant dwellings on the other side of the canal, small ploughed vegetable patches, a vine twisting into a pergola, fields of asparagus, a row of peach trees. Somehow things looked smaller and the distance was shorter than I recalled.

The road turned sharply right, the view opening out to the sea, the island of Burano in the distance, and there, suddenly, was a courtyard, a gracious brick house covered in green creepers mirrored in the still water of the lagoon, familiar outbuildings. We were there.

Our car came to a halt, skidding on the gravel. There was no other vehicle parked in the drive, and the dark green wooden shutters were closed. It looked as if there was nobody around. After a moment's hesitation, I opened the car door.

24

A muffled noise of voices and of boxes dragged on a cement floor came from a low construction on the right, below which there was a boathouse built straight on to the darkish water. Framed through its porch were a few white egrets in the distance, standing amongst the rushes on the *barena*,[1] which looked as barren and wild as ever. Two large seagulls flew over slowly, and as I followed them with my eyes, I noticed that someone was looking out of the *cavana*.[2] I turned.

There was no reason why he should have known me after twenty-two years, appearing unexpectedly, out of context as I had, but I would have recognized his face anywhere.

He wore waders and an oilcloth windbreaker over a sailor's sweater as he had the last time I had seen him. The woollen cap covered half his face, and kind black eyes lit up amongst the wrinkles dug by years of squinting through autumn fogs, of peering into shallow waters for darting sea-bass spawn. His skin was burned a dark copper even though he had sheltered it with calloused hands while scanning the sky in countless summer suns, trying to spot the first duck migrating back from the north.

It took him only a moment, and all at once his arms lifted in surprise and welcome, his hand was raised to his cap, his mouth opened in the

---

[1] A sandbank or shoal.

[2] Venetian term for boathouse.

widest grin, and, without taking his eyes from my face a moment:

'*Maria, Signor, Gesù varda chi che ghe xe!*' he exclaimed in Venetian dialect. '*La signora la xe tornada. La signora Kuki!*'[1] We moved forward at the same time and almost embraced. We halted, holding each other's hands.

'*Livio! Nol xe cambià. Come falo a recordarse de mi?*'[2] I answered automatically in an idiom I had not used in years. I was overwhelmed. Although I had hoped that I would find him, I had not really expected to do so.

Livio had been Paolo's headman in the *valle*, the head fisherman, the head hunter and the game warden. A typical product of the *valle* where he was born and whose secrets he knew, he was the invaluable collaborator on whom Paolo had relied totally. Competent, honest, of good disposition, he loved his job and excelled at it. Over the years he had become a trusted friend.

Then Paolo went to Africa and never came back. When Paolo died I received a cable: 'We send you and the children our heart-felt condolences for Dr Paolo's sad demise. Famiglia Dalla Mora.'

I had not had contact since.

With instant recognition, he greeted Marisa too; she had not changed much since the old days.

---

[1] 'Mary, Lord, Jesus, look who is here! Signora has come back!'

[2] 'Livio! You haven't changed. How can you still recognize me?'

I wondered at the long memories of people who live in remote spots. It happens always in Africa: one meets someone in some god-forsaken place, and is recognized instantly, as if nothing had happened to fog the memory in the intervening time.

He insisted on giving us a *caffè corretto*,[1] and showing us the house. With trepidation I entered rooms that had been familiar, climbed stairs that had felt Paolo's rapid step, Emanuele's little boy's run.

I looked out at the unchanged expanse of water from the small windows of the altered dining room, where the sound of laughter and popping corks had risen high in days gone by. Only the tall smoky chimney had not been touched.

Cavallino had been Paolo's and his first wife's place. I had never really considered it my home in the three years or so before coming to Africa, when I had often stayed there, while I was still living with my mother in the country. Yet I had felt its spell, the charm of its old stones and sleepy past, the beauty of the lagoon bathed in the mercury and coral of September sunsets, the ancient rhythm of traditions on which the life of a fishing *valle* was based. For Paolo, it had been a consolation while he waited to return to Kenya, the place to which he had discovered he belonged.

We went from room to room and sat finally,

---

[1] Coffee with a measure of strong liqueur added, traditional in Veneto in winter.

sipping our coffee in the dark dining room, where game wardens and *valle*-hands had gathered after long fishing or shooting mornings, to eat their earthy meals of crab soup and grilled eels with *polenta*, and roasted chestnuts washed down by bottles and bottles of new wine.

When we went out I noticed that a lone seagull was flying high above us and Livio followed my eyes.

'Do you remember,' he smiled at me, 'the time I gave you the seagull chicks?'

And memories flew back on still wings.

★ ★ ★

One afternoon, in the uncertain hour of opal before night falls, when the lagoon looks like a fluid mirror, Livio had returned from his daily tour of the locks and docked the boat inside its shelter.

Below his dark woollen beret the weather-beaten fisherman face smiled, and a hundred happy wrinkles marked his red cheeks.

'I have a present for you,' he offered in dialect. 'Come and see.'

On the bottom of the boat, beside a coil of rope on the tar-blackened planks, two brownish, fluffy birds crouched, from whose open beaks came desperate screams of hunger and terror.

'They are *magoghi*,'[1] said Livio proudly, 'just hatched. There were still broken shell pieces stuck to their plumes and all over the nest.'

---

[1] Young seagulls in Venetian dialect.

Perhaps I did not manage to thank him. I felt bewildered and guilty that my love of animals, which was well known, had brought about this unconscious cruelty.

Through my mind darted plans to return the miserable newborn creatures to their marsh, to the beautiful destiny of which they had been for ever robbed: but the sun had set, dissolving into the water in reflections of red and mother of pearl, and there was nothing to do but agree to look after them.

It was a time when I wore long skirts in bright cotton, partly to protect my legs from the damp without wearing trousers which rubbed against the still fresh scars of my femur fracture, partly because I felt they matched the newly found peace, the bucolic pleasures and simplicity of country life in the Venetian *valle*.

I gathered my skirt into a nest and cautiously I lay there the birds. The gaping beaks with the pointed pink tongues, the greedy red-rimmed eyes and the ungainly cackling were far removed from the majestic grace of the adult royal seagulls they would one day become.

With little originality I remembered the story of the Ugly Duckling which like many fairytales is pervaded by the revenge of the small and humble against the wealthy and handsome. Cinderella, Snow White and armies of Thumbelinas had their animal equivalent in the ugly cygnet vindicated by Hans Christian Andersen. So, feeling like a fairy godmother, I set about caring for my wards.

To begin with I looked for an appropriate

container. An old dolls' pram in green plastic looked perfect, and I lined it with wood shavings, small pieces of materials and clean rags.

Emanuele captured small fry from along the shore and presented them to me.

While I prepared their crib I kept the baby seagulls tucked into my skirt, working with one hand without noticing that the chirps had grown weak in the warm darkness of the folds. When I tried to put them in the pram they were asleep. I contemplated them for a while, still in my skirt, soft tiny balls of feathers like a Victorian muffler, one with its head below the other's wing.

When hunger woke them up hours later I was numb with stiffness.

I quietened their shrieks of outrage, forcing the fish that Emanuele handed to me down their wide throats. They devoured it voraciously, with ease born of instinct, pecking my fingers in their greed. That was probably their first meal, and it was thrilling that they accepted me so quickly. When there was no more fish, I covered the pram with a rag, and in the darkness they slept again.

That night I read what I could find about aquatic birds in Paolo's extensive library. So I came to learn of a curious experiment, performed on baby ducklings.

When the eggs were about to hatch, a few were removed from the nest and put into an incubator, a surrogate nest, where, instead of the mother duck, there was a rectangular cardboard box, tied with a string so that it could be pulled along.

The moment they broke out of their shell, the ducklings went immediately to the cardboard shape, nestling under it and moving with it whenever the string jerked it away.

At that stage they returned the ducklings to their real nest, where in the meantime the others had hatched, and were gathered around the mother duck, following her every movement. The experiment-ducklings did not join them. They remained confused, cowering in a corner until the box was placed near them, and they rushed to it with jubilant chirps. Thus was the theory confirmed that birds recognize and are imprinted by the first moving object they see after hatching from their egg.

When I put them on the bank and retreated a few paces to look at them, they rushed towards me with piercing screams, relaxing only when they managed to huddle under my skirt.

I experimented several times, my heart in my mouth, and the result was always the same. They did not follow anyone else, on the contrary they shrank from people, but at my appearance their cries changed as if they definitely recognized me. I realized that something similar to the experiment I had read about had happened to the wretched young seagulls; they had chosen me as their mother substitute.

The revelation that two royal seagull chicks, among the noblest of birds, unsurpassed masters of sea and ocean, dancers of the sky, had chosen me as their mother, humbled me, made me proud and scared me with the responsibility. In my role as mother-seagull I felt awkward and inadequate.

I decided that I must try, at least partially, to fulfil my task by teaching them to swim.

It was May. Already the days were getting longer and the sun warmed the chill water of the *colauro*[1] where captive sea bass fattened, waiting for autumn, and eels the colour of mud slid in the weedy bottom with disquieting movements.

Next day I gently set the seagulls on the grassy slope of the canal, where seaweed and bleached crab legs dried in the sun. I moved with tentative steps into the oily cool water, feeling the mud squirm beneath my toes when they disturbed a flatfish or an eel.

The gulls came to the water edge they did not yet know, and there they stood, uncertain, stumping in the mud with spread claws, crying.

I moved deeper into the water, imitating their sounds like a farmer's wife when she calls her chickens, a comical scene to the uninitiated. But the only spectator was Emanuele, connoisseur and lover of animals and loyal supporter, who was following events from the shore, biting his finger with concentration. He was no more than four years old, and it must have been an extraordinary adventure.

Step by cautious step, shrieking unceasingly, the seagulls followed. Then they launched themselves, leaving behind them a touchingly tiny wake, like frail paper boats obliquely drifting

---

[1] Venetian dialect: part of the canal that links the *valle* to the lagoon.

in the current. They swam towards me with increasing confidence. From the shore Emanuele laughed and clapped.

Finally soothed, in their element, with an instinctive fluid elegance which their former awkward steps had not foreshadowed, the magoghi floated around my head, their tiny eyes for the first time at the same level as mine.

Every day after that first attempt, we swam together and I fed them the small fish that Emanuele managed to capture for them. Ten days or so went by.

The time of the unavoidable first separation found me nervous and uncertain, like a real mother about to leave her own newborn behind in the care of strangers. A certain premonition made me fear that something would happen to them in my absence.

It was the dog which in the night after I left broke into the bathroom where, after having fed them more than usual, I had confined them to keep them safe and comfortable.

It was a pain that I had never experienced before, a sense of failure, as if I had betrayed them, failing the universal rule of caring for the young.

It was a lesson reinforced when later I went to live in Africa, never to encourage the gift of a wild creature, which captivity would kill or make into a slave, a worse fate still.

And I saw a new meaning in the large seagull which followed our attempt at swimming, soaring and gliding in large circles over our heads, calling raucously in vain.

I looked at Livio. The afternoon was drawing on, it was getting late. The grey fog of every evening, with its drifting ghosts, was rising from the water. Time to return.

'The seagulls. Yes, of course. It was sad when they were killed, but perhaps it was as well. As much as I loved them, I could never have taught them how to fly.'

We embraced with promises of writing, keeping in touch. I knew I might never return.

We drove off. I looked back before turning. The house was fading in the mist, silent, with all its past untold and unrevealed.

Livio's figure was silhouetted against the sky, a hand still raised in farewell.

The seagull had disappeared.

A Dance of Spiders

It was as though, in that remote corner of the
world, I had received a sinister hint as to the
existence of certain influences outside the
palpable terrestrial sequences of life.

LLEWELYN POWYS, *Black Laughter*

'A tragic thing has happened. I am terribly
sorry.' The voice was serious, strangely hesitant. I
tightened my grip on the telephone receiver.

A silence, charged with premonition of doom.
'It's Julius.'

$\star \quad \star \quad \star$

The red-haired man swallowed another sip, and
his restless, intelligent eyes became misty behind
his thick glasses. I was glad I had fixed him a
very strong whisky: it looked as if he would need
every drop.

In the candlelight of the sitting room of my
Nairobi house, his face was lustrous with sweat.
His eyelids were red-rimmed, and there was a
slight tremor in the hand which held the glass.
His voice had an inspired intonation, the
emphatic quality of Sunday sermons, the
sternness of Dickensian teachers in young boys'
schools.

'Talk,' I encouraged him. 'I think it would help

you if you could tell me the story from the beginning. How did you meet Julius?'

His freckled face lit up in a smile.

'I will never forget the first time I saw him. Many years ago, when I had just begun teaching at Amani Boys School, I went with a colleague to a Kikuyu village looking for candidates for a scholarship to the school. He stood out amongst all those boys with a presence that struck me instantly. The peasants listening to him hung silently on his lips. Still so small, he was aloof, unreachable. From that moment I loved him.'

A glazed look clouded his eyes.

'He was nine years old.'

* * *

The early afternoon sun brightened the fields of coffee bushes and the red wet earth trampled by many feet. Banana trees, planted in clumps, shaded rows of young maize shoots. A mottled group of cattle, goats and a few hispid, mud-spattered sheep grazed off the long elephant grass that grew green and abundant on the slopes of Kiambu. Grey clouds, just emerging from the horizon, announced the daily evening storm of the short rains. From the country church, a melodious sound flew in waves, young voices singing a lilting hymn that came from distant lands.

Standing in the churchyard, facing an audience of villagers of all ages and both sexes, was the church choir of young boys. They wore long robes of vivid blue, with wide white collars falling over their shoulders. Their eyes in the dark faces were bright, imbued with a strange sense of wonder, and they sang with the rhythm and enthusiasm of innocence and unquestioning faith. Their features were still childish, unformed, smooth, the voices pure and high.

He stood out amongst them. He was not the tallest, and his harmonious voice was not the strongest.

Perhaps it was his beauty. The clear brow, the curling, girlish eyelashes, his smile. It was, perhaps, the way he held himself, radiating pride and confidence.

Perhaps it was the feeling that he was remote and difficult to conquer.

When the singing stopped the boy came forward a few steps, and walked out on to the patch of grass before mounting into the wooden pulpit. His voice was frail and crystalline, yet enhanced by a quaintly powerful authority. He addressed the colourful crowd with his religious exhortations and a spontaneous grace which went beyond prayer.

Anthony looked around, observing his fellow spectators. Old women, their grey heads in scarves, dressed in long skirts and sweaters hand-knitted in bright yarns; young women, carrying invisible sleeping infants well wrapped in pink and green lacy shawls tied to their backs; old men, young men, heads bare, still mostly in their shapeless working clothes. The lazy afternoon insects buzzed in the sun. No one moved. The crowd was spellbound, enraptured by the boy's charm. Standing in the half shade of an avocado tree, Anthony watched to the end. Then he approached.

'Would you like to study in a big school in Nairobi, where there is a great choir, and music matters?'

The boy looked up: large, liquid eyes with impossibly long, silky eyelashes. The boy smiled, a dazzling flash of even teeth like matching macadamia nuts, a warmth of honeycomb in the hazel eyes, which seemed to touch and melt something in Anthony's chest, and his legs were reduced to wax.

'Yes, I would.'

'Do you think your father will let you?'

'I have no father. He died two years ago.' A shadow drifted across his brow like a curtain which was soon lifted again. 'He drank. I have four brothers. I am the eldest.'

Anthony swallowed.

'And your mother?'

The little boy shrugged.

'She would not mind. She has much to do. There is no money and she works in the *shamba*. She also helps in the church.' His face hardened and his eyes clouded over. 'After church, she goes to the *muganga*.'

'I could look after you. I teach there. Would you like that?'

'Perhaps,' said the boy with an adult smile, 'you will let me read your books? I like to learn about animals and nature. I have no books of my own.'

Again the sudden white of even teeth.

'My name is Julius.'

'My name is Julius.'

The handsome face smiled at me and I noticed the eyes which seemed to take over most of his face.

'A good-looking young man,' I thought. He wore a pair of clean new jeans, a striped blue and white cotton shirt. A plastic watch, new and brightly coloured, was fastened round his slim wrist. I looked at his feet: good leather moccasins, a blue pullover slung around his shoulders. His skin was an amber brown, unblemished. Short curly hair and fine hands with clean short nails. On his upper lip a shadow of a moustache. He was slim, with narrow hips. Slightly effeminate? There was a distinctive radiance about him which could not be missed.

'It is very kind of you to ask me to dinner,' he said carefully in good English. He looked up at my tall *makuti* roof, around at the polished furniture, the gleaming copper and brass vases. As on every night, a candle trembled in front of the silver frame with Emanuele's photograph. A fine blue smoke drifted from the incense holder. My eight dogs slept on the carpets in various poses of abandoned contentment. Two servants in starched white uniforms were preparing the table, laying red hibiscus flowers. The fire crackled vivaciously in the vast fireplace.

There was a candid wonder in his eyes.

'I have never been in a place like this before.'

A few weeks earlier I had received a letter, signed by Anthony S., his teacher, sponsor and protector, who asked if we could host in our research camp one of his most brilliant students, the head prefect of Amani, who needed first-hand experience in the outdoor environment in order to write a descriptive essay which would allow him to run for a scholarship to Cambridge university.

Amani was well known for its high standards of education and for making available superior academic training to students of underprivileged background but with good minds; it was known to instil discipline and a sense of responsibility. In the firmament of Kenyan schools, Amani was a shining star, unique. There were well over a thousand students there. Whoever managed to become head prefect must have been rather unusually gifted with leadership and intelligence. But even so, Cambridge university was still as far from Amani as a distant planet.

I had been intrigued and had immediately agreed to host this boy for a month or so.

Looking at him now, I felt that I wanted to help his ambition to materialize, and that I would see more and more of him over the years. There was something special about him, which I could detect immediately, but not describe.

'I understand that you would like to read geography at Cambridge. A really ambitious plan.'

Not for a moment was there hesitation in his tone:

'I have been fortunate. I want to give back to my country what I have received over the years. Cambridge. I am sure I will enjoy it there.'

I opened my bar cabinet.

'Would you like a glass of wine?'

For a moment only, he looked lost, then he grinned.

'I would rather have a Coke, if it is all right with you. I am not used to wine.'

★　★　★

'We can't find Julius.'

Anthony's voice sounded tight and strangled on the phone. 'He has disappeared. Gone. I can't locate him anywhere. He is meant to leave for Cambridge in two days time. I was hoping you might have heard from him.'

His emphatic preacher's tone became a whine.

'What are we going to do?'

I answered with the calm that always prevails in me when others around me lose theirs.

'Take it easy. He is practically a man, remember? Why should he always report where he goes? He has to be able to cope on his own in England. I am sure there is a perfectly ordinary explanation. Do you have any reason to think otherwise? Perhaps he has gone to say his farewells to some friends.'

'That is exactly what I fear,' Anthony whispered.

★　★　★

The noise of a car engine was followed by the slamming of a door, then of another. Footsteps descended the stairs to my front door. Someone knocked. I went to open.

Julius stood forlorn on my doorstep, in a dejected attitude, head bent and the collar of his wind jacket open on his thin neck. The change from the secure, radiant boy who looked me always straight in the eyes struck me like a blow.

'Julius. Are you all right?' No answer.

'Julius, for God's sake. Come on. Come in. Tell me what's happened. It can't be as bad as that.'

A movement behind Julius, the leaves of the gardenia bush swayed. From the shadows, another shape emerged. The suddenness of the movement startled me. I caught my breath.

'Get in,' said Anthony, as if talking to a rebellious little boy who had thrown a tantrum. I noticed his eyes were enlarged. He pushed him in.

'You must confess to Kuki what has happened.'

Julius sat on my white sofa in the soft light like a culprit ready to confess a crime. The absurdity of the situation annoyed me.

'What is it?' I probed gently. 'There is nothing at all that you 'have' to tell me. Your life is your life. You look fine to me. Can I help you in any way?'

'Tell her,' urged Anthony.

I braced myself for the worst, and yet I felt there was really nothing the boy could have done so tragic as to justify such attitude.

'A few years ago I met a girl,' murmured Julius in a small, dull voice. 'She was one from my native village. I have known her all my life.'

'And so?' A lightness overcame me, as if the precipice on which I was perching had revealed itself much shallower, less forbidding than I had feared.

'You must tell her. Confess what you have done.' Anthony's tone sounded absurdly serious.

'I have a son. He is three years old.'

An immense relief swept over me.

'Is that all?'

Julius looked up, and his moist eyes held an appeal. But through this, to my dismay, I read an overwhelming terror, as of a haunted animal running blindly off in the night.

'I have received this.'

He offered a crumpled sheet of paper, which blossomed in his open palm slowly, unfolding like a crushed moon flower. Words crawled over it, scribbled in pencil in gangly, uneven letters, oddly repulsive, like a dance of spiders.

'I can't read Kikuyu.'

'It is a threat.' His voice broke in a sob. 'They have put a spell on me. They do not want me to leave. If I go, I will die.'

A chill drifted through my western room, ugly with sneering masks and unmentionable rituals, slaughtered black goats, smeared entrails on muddied feathers, beating night drums, guttural songs and young boys' fears. For only a moment its power hit me, the unease prevailed. For that moment I could believe anything, I accepted that anything could happen. Once again I knew that this world I had chosen was not just red sunsets, migrating herds, sunny savannah and bougainvillaea in bloom: I remembered the snake, the screeching of imagined brakes, the open graves, the pain, the ephemeral reality which often eluded our comprehension and mocked our bewilderment: and I realized that this, also, was Africa.

I came back to the present.

'Julius, this is 1985. You are about to go to one of the most sophisticated universities in the world. You are going to fly there in a large airplane, meet many people from all over the world, learn useful things which will, when you come back to Kenya, allow you a career that is all you have ever dreamed of. By going you are hurting no one. This is what the new Kenya is all about. They should be proud of you, back in your village.'

A thought raced quickly through my mind and I chased it off.

'Who is it? Who has written this? Who has put a spell on you?'

His face had closed like a slab of stone, and I could see I would not learn it from him. Not now. Even as I was asking I knew that he would not tell.

'They think that I will not come back. They think I will be out of their influence.'

'The girl's family? Do you care for this girl?'

Julius had no time to answer.

Anthony looked up sharply with pressed lips.

'He does not see that girl any more. It was just a mistake. It was her fault. The girl has given up any hope about him. An ignorant peasant girl. She was compensated.' He waved the shadow of the girl aside like an insignificant moth.

44

I reacted.

'However, her family may think otherwise.'

Julius looked up at me with a sudden resolution in his eyes. I read confusion, fear, hatred and resignation all at once in the look he gave me. I read something else also, deep and murky, unspeakable and terrifying, which I could not interpret.

I cleared my throat.

'You must go ahead and nothing is going to happen to you. Nobody can hate you just because you go to school to learn. Spells and *muganga* cannot hurt you if you do not believe in them.'

With immense horror, I realized he did.

A shiver of rain forest and dark huts, green smoke and voodoo passed again over the glittering crystal table. As in a Gothic tale, in my imagination the candles flickered uncertainly.

The sound was low and hoarse, it was his voice no longer. It rustled like a snake and I recoiled.

'The girl did not go to the *muganga*. It was my mother.'

★   ★   ★

Three years later.

I closed the heavy door, the chill of November behind me. The bright light caught me unprepared, blinding me for a moment. The vast room was full of people and the noise of conversation echoed from the high vaulted ceiling.

I focused on the unreal scene with wonder.

The elephants moved in their cages set in a circle, swaying their sad grey heads rhythmically from left to right and from right to left.

Waiters in white jackets and white gloves circulated through the guests offering trays of canapés and cocktails. The air was warm, humid; candles glowed trembling in silver chandeliers. I looked around recognizing some familiar faces, and then I saw him.

Holding his glass of wine, still intact, dressed in a blue suit and starched shirt, a very good silk tie impeccably knotted, Julius smiled his disarming warm smile at me across the room.

An elephant trumpeted, interrupting all chatter of conversation for a few moments. The whiff of steaming dung could not be disguised by the mixture of perfumes and cigarette smoke. It was a very weird setting for a cocktail party, the Elephant House at London Zoo.

Julius had been asked as my guest.

'Thank you for inviting me. I feel somewhat overwhelmed.'

So did I for that matter. The absurdity of the occasion stood between us like a pond to cross, and I smiled.

'These poor creatures. And all the real ones, the free ones that we have left back home.'

He scowled, the corners of his mouth turned down, betraying an undisguised nostalgia. For an instant the sadness of the exiled elephant was his same sadness.

'Anthony tells me that you took to Cambridge like a duck to water.'

He looked groomed and confident enough, very much in command in what truly was an unusual environment.

Despite — or possibly because of — the trapped miserable elephant, it was a long step from Africa.

He grimaced, waving his full glass gingerly. 'I like it there; but I still cannot drink the wine.'

I noticed that his fingers held the stem very tightly, with white knuckles. For a moment I thought he was going to snap it. A black crocodile-skin strap circled his thin wrist setting off a new gold watch.

'Are you sure you are all right, Julius? Are you looked after? Are you very homesick?'

Such a long step, I thought, from those mud huts, the thatched grass roofs, the banana clumps and the smiling girls with high breasts and singing eyes. Such a long step from his real roots. If I felt somehow out of place, how would he feel? Social superficial chatter, witty whimsical remarks, politics, the economy, the last show, what happened to those rhino in Meru, the price of ivory, the rhino horn trade, is Leakey's appointment really going to make a difference to Kenya's wildlife?

A lady in a black velvet suit, a blonde lock falling artily over one eye, took hold of Julius' elbow, swept him away effortlessly and in seconds he was lost in the crowd.

For a moment I saw him as a shipwrecked sailor taken away by the tide, never to be reached; I felt I had to rescue him; then someone attracted our attention by chiming on a crystal glass, and the speeches began. When I looked again for him, he was gone.

★ ★ ★

'Julius, Julius, how nice to have you back!'

He had grown a light moustache.

'I passed the exams at Cambridge. Now I think I will go for a Ph.D.'

He seemed thinner, taller. His accent was more polished, the words chosen slowly and with care. He was detached even when answering. I felt his laughter as a superficial way of hiding a deeper concern. There were corners of his personality where he did not allow anyone to probe; what did he have to hide? What was he afraid of? What tangled cobwebs hid behind the sunny boy's mask?

'Anthony came to fetch me at the airport.'

'Nice of him, at that hour. How is Anthony?'

He lifted his shoulder with a distant look.

'I had not seen him in months. I have a girlfriend.'

He looked me straight in the eye.

'He does not approve.'

And added, in a hiss that startled me by its concentrated spite:

'As if I cared.'

'A girlfriend, but that is great, Julius! Who is she?'

'Her name is Olinda. We live together now. I love her very much.'

To my surprise, his eyes filled suddenly with tears:

48

'She is so beautiful.' He whispered it with a longing in his voice, as if talking of a fairy which eluded him.

'You must be happy, we must celebrate. It is your life. You are in your twenties. It is perfectly normal for you to fall in love. I think it is wonderful. Anthony must accept this, of course.'

What had never been said struck me, and the time was right to finally bring it into the open.

'He loves you too,' I added gently.

'I know. But that is not the problem. I can deal with Anthony.' A far-away look. 'I have done it all my life.'

'Why are you so sad then? What is there to disturb you? Perhaps you can tell me? Perhaps I can be of some help?'

Tears were rolling down his cheeks uncontrollably. I took his hand in mine and guided him unresisting to my office.

'She is of the Luo tribe.'

The phrase fell like a stone in a still pond and even I was overwhelmed by its ripples.

A Luo girl and a Kikuyu boy!

The Luo tribe is spread around the warm shores of the great Lake Victoria, in western Kenya; the Kikuyu, as one knows, originate from the cold forest areas all around Mount Kenya's snowy slopes. Worlds apart, they have always been traditional enemies. Their people are physically and ethnically different. Language, appearance, customs, taste, habits, beliefs are totally opposite, deep-rooted. Even in this modern Kenya this was a very difficult — practically an impossible — match. Its

49

implications dumbfounded me for a moment. I brushed them off.

'It does not matter, surely? She lives here in the town, far from the lake. Her people, you say, are reasonably comfortable. She is educated. She is emancipated. What does her tribe matter if she loves you too?'

'It is my mother. She will never agree. She has told me that she will curse me for ever if I marry her. I want to marry her,' he added with a sob.

I looked at him, bewildered.

'If I do not have my mother's blessing as tradition asks, our children will be cursed for ever.'

He looked at me through his tears.

The words rose from the Middle Ages, in one stroke wiping out years of education, Cambridge, books, culture, gold watch, computers, driving licence:

'She is uncircumcised.'

And so it came out, in my tame Nairobi office filled with photographs and books, the pine panelled walls that smell of the forests on the Great Rift where the wood came from. The place high on the Kinangop where Julius' mother lives, still now.

With her memories, and perhaps with her remorse.

★ ★ ★

He found her one day, that woman who was his mother, that peasant girl who had grown old too quickly through her labour, creeping about in the Nairobi flat that he shared with Olinda.

She shrank at his sight, hissing like a lizard, her headscarf half undone, trying to hide something in her apron.

He forced open her clamped hand, and recoiled in horror.

It looked like a small, dead animal, hairy and still. A thick, repulsive tangle of curly human hair, fashioned as a doll. Two rusty pins stuck out of its tiny head, like grotesque horns.

'How did you get Olinda's hair? How did you find us? How could you come in? You have never been here before.'

He pushed her away in fury, confused, afraid, angry, yet hopelessly dependent on his mother's fierce attachment, her resilient strength, her earthy power and the magnetic eyes which had subjugated him since his childhood.

I listened without ever interrupting him. He looked up through the veil of tears.

'The problem is that I love my mother. Love is not a feeling that she understands. She was married at puberty, soon after her circumcision, in exchange for a few goats and some gourds of beer, to a much older man she did not even know. He drank. He used her and beat her up every night. All day she worked the *shamba* cutting the red soil with her *jembe* to plant beans, potatoes and maize, with me and then my brothers and sisters tied to her bent back.'

He went on.

'When the coffee was ripe after the season of the rains, she went to pick it at sunrise with the other women. They were each given a large metal

51

debe and they had to fill it with the red berries. They sang while they worked and those songs were my earliest music. She was quick and still so young, so supple, almost a child, she could fill even ten *debes* sometimes. They were paid a few coins each time. In those days the coins were made of brass and glinted like gold in the sun; many still had a hole in the middle below the portrait of King George, so the people could put a leather string through them, and hang them round their neck. No one had purses, nor pockets in those times.

'In the afternoon she chopped firewood from the forest and tied it in immense bundles, which she carried on her back: she had to strap the new baby to her chest instead, so it could nurse. She smelled of milk and sweat and wood smoke, and we felt secure in her warmth. The load was held by a leather strip tied around her forehead, and it was so heavy that it left a permanent ridge-mark over her brows. Loaded like a donkey she staggered home after dusk to cook our meal.

'We lived, cooked, ate, slept in one smoky room without a chimney. The fire's smoke choked us and gave us red eyes and sore throats; we all caught pneumonia sooner or later as the breath of the night outside was chilly, when we had to go out and relieve ourselves in the pit latrine in the bamboo thicket. She gave us a brew of honey and some bitter herbs and we were cured. But it was cosy, safe and warm inside our mud hut, like a den in the forest. There were scorpions and centipedes in the roof, sometimes black house-snakes, but it was too smoky for mosquitoes and too cold for malaria and too dark for flies. It was fine. There were only two makeshift beds. We children all shared a mattress filled with straw on a low pallet made of rough branches.'

I listened without interrupting him, fascinated.

'My father drank *changaa* until he recognized nobody. The whites of his eyes became yellow and stared unseeing. I tried not to hear their noises in the dark. But it was never really dark with those red fizzing embers. Once, when he beat her up more wildly I stood up to him. I was six years old. He knocked me off towards the wall, blinded by fury. For a few days I could not move, all my body ached. Soon after this, my father left us to marry a younger girl.'

He went on.

'My mother never accepted his second wife. There were terrible scenes and she screamed; she never cried. Tears were not something traditional for the Kikuyu girls in the old days. She was intelligent, although she could neither read nor write. As a child she had learned to sing hymns at the Mission church, she had a clear high voice and could remember sounds. She never knew what she was singing though, apart from the Kikuyu hymns. She never learned any English. I went with her. That's how I learned to sing.

'She cleaned the church for a few shillings a week. She began to spend much of that money and the coffee cents with the village *muganga*. She did spells against the other wife. She could not see the contradiction between the Christian god she served and the pagan spirits she summoned to her help.

'The *muganga* was a very old man covered in monkey skins, with long hair in matted locks. He wore bizarre ornaments of teeth, dried hoofs and bones, and he stank of coagulated blood and strange herbs. Purses hung from a leather belt, he wore sandals made of raw hides, he scowled at us with red wild eyes, and I was afraid of him. He lived alone on a hill out of the village with a few black goats, next to a large *mugumu* tree. All children were terrified of him and we ran away when he approached.

'To perform her sorceries, my mother had to procure certain items that he ordered her to find from time to time. To perpetrate a really powerful incantation a goat was always slaughtered, her bowels examined and scattered with strange rituals, potions of roots and powders boiled up and, sometimes, for a sickness or a death spell, weird dolls made to resemble the person who had to suffer. You know, people died of spells very easily. Or sometimes they went mad. They still do. Those dolls had to contain a bit of hair of the victim, or perhaps some fragment of his fingernails, a piece of material from his clothes. The puppet had to be placed secretly somewhere in the victim's house or on her or his person; a pin had to go through the part of the body where the disease was meant to appear.

'Occasionally one saw someone moving around in a trance, as if sleepwalking, with a vacant stare, and we knew that a spell had been put on them. If the *muganga* who was responsible was not found and compelled to give an antidote to neutralize the witchcraft, the person lost all interest in life, stopped eating, and went off like a candle.

'My father died a few years after. They found his mangled body in a ditch one morning. The hyena had found him first. They said he had fallen in drunk. Perhaps this was true. But he had been seen looking wild and going around in circles, and I wondered.'

'Your mother would not do that to your girlfriend. Surely not. That's evil, Julius!'

He looked up at me without answering.

Then he murmured something in a half voice, something quite unbelievable, which I was not sure I had heard correctly.

★ ★ ★

He asked me then if he could be in Laikipia for two weeks, staying in the empty house overlooking the forest at Enghelesha, far from the crowds and problems, unreachable even by his girlfriend.

He had to think, rest his soul, reflect, be alone.

I saw him a few times. He was aloof, remote more than ever, closed in a world of his own. He had lost much weight. As if he no longer cared for his appearance, he had begun to grow a beard.

I invited him for a picnic at a dam one Sunday, and he came. He did not eat. He sat on a rock at a distance, throwing pebbles in the

55

water absently, only occasionally taking part in the conversation.

'What are you doing all day?'

'I read.'

'What do you read?'

'I read Shakespeare.' And with a shadow of his old humour he added: 'It is so grand reading Shakespeare aloud looking down at the Rift Valley at sunset.'

I could not agree more.

Shakespeare, Cambridge, the *muganga*, the rural superstition, the deeply rooted beliefs, his English tutor's influence, his studies, his Luo girlfriend from the great lake, this new overwhelming love and passion that he was so unprepared to handle, his terrible mother.

I was seriously worried for Julius.

I never saw him again. It was three months after that Sunday when my phone had rung with the tragic news.

'It's Julius. He has committed suicide.'

★ ★ ★

Sitting now on my white sofa, gulping down whisky absently like one who never drinks strong alcohol and could not care less about the consequences, Anthony went on talking.

'I had seen him a few days before. I found him in his room. He sat on his bed and looked at me with empty eyes, drawn, not listening. He had grown an untidy, long beard. He looked like someone under a witchcraft spell.'

I bolted.

'He had a book of Shakespeare next to him. He was reading *Romeo and Juliet*.'

A pair of star-crossed lovers.

A pause.

'He swallowed rat poison. His mother was furious when he died.'

'Furious? Not sad? Not desperate?'

'Angry, as if something had gone wrong.'

Wrong?

What was it that Julius had said to me that day long ago, in my office? It was important that I should remember. Something about the spell. The hair. Olinda's hair. No. Not Olinda's. The spell was not for her. It was for Julius. So that he would lose interest in her, leave her. The spell went wrong. Everything now was clear.

He had lost, instead, all interest in life.

His voice came back from distances to whisper:

'It was MY hair in the doll.'

Why an Elephant?

O my America! my new-found-land.

JOHN DONNE, *Elegies, On Going to Bed*

1

'*Dear Mrs Gallmann*' — the letter said — '*Thank you for allowing us to stay in the Education Centre in memory of your late son. I wish I had met him. I loved everything, but mostly the wildlife. The first animal I saw was an elephant. I had never seen one before. It was very big, I could see him from far.*
Anne Wanjoi, Nyahururu Secondary School, Ngarua'

On the large rock set in the middle of the yard, a red hibiscus beckons in the breeze.

'Felix qui potuit rerum cognoscere causas'[1]

says the inscription from Virgil, on the brass plaque. And, underneath:

---

[1] 'Happy he who can understand the causes of things' — Virgil.

58

In Memory of Emanuele.
Venezia 1966 — Laikipia 1983.

Two acacia trees, one small, one large, the symbol of survival and of hope, are engraved below.

A short life, an entire story in a few words.

I am at the Laikipia Wilderness Education Centre, built of stones and thatch in the heart of the ranch where I live and where my son died and was buried at seventeen, one sunny day of April in 1983.

Yet, in the agony of his loss, slowly, like the secret buried seed which finds the strength to sprout, forcing its way up towards light and life, I found the key to survival. I understood that Emanuele, like Paolo before him and all the ones who had gone ahead faster than us, had simply changed dimension, and that, if I could no longer see his body, I could always feel the power of his essence, of which I was myself part. There were no boundaries.

I founded the mission to work positively for as long as I could, to justify my existence and my survival by using my opportunities to make a change.

I soon discovered that there was no end to the possibilities brought about by this new energy. Emanuele had gone to join Paolo, but the power of his love and memory, reflected in the African

59

nature that he had loved, became my inspiration to create something long-lasting, that time could not tarnish.

Walking alone on the hills and in the valleys of this place he had loved above all, I decided to open its door to other young people like him: enthusiastic, fond of the wild, with a sense of purpose, so that they might learn to understand, and so to respect, Africa.

Only two generations ago Africans knew all there was to know about their environment. They lived in harmony with their surroundings, which in turn provided them with food and medicine. They survived by hunting and fishing, collecting plants and tubers, gathering honey and wild berries, without destroying the subtle, fragile balance of their eco-system on which their very existence depended. In those days they were familiar with their roots, they had pride in their customs and traditions, they valued their world, and they knew elephants. Those days are no longer.

Unless the new generation, now converging on urban areas to be educated in alien skills imported from a far-away world, is given the chance to experience the wilderness which was their immediate ancestors' familiar domain, to be proud of their land and its unrepeatable beauty, there will be no hope for the ecology of this continent. The forests will go, and the plants and the biodiversity and then the birds and the animals, and Africa will remain a mangled landscape, ravaged by droughts and floods.

I believe that childhood impressions live in us

to guide our adult behaviour. This is the principle that guided me when I created the Wilderness Centre.

★ ★ ★

On a day like any other, sitting on the look-out built at the end of the promontory on which the school stands, on the shores of a small dam covered with clumps of papyrus and frequented by water birds, I watch a herd of impala coming gracefully down to the water to drink. Egyptian geese fly off, screaming, in a flutter of wings. Behind them, a water buck, and from the *lelechwa* shrubs, one after the other, file the elephants.

Standing on the shore, in their colourful school uniforms, a group of African children watch in awe.

2

The young man in the neat, well-cut blue suit held a card with my name, misspelled.

'It's me you are looking for.' I introduced myself, and he flashed back a frank open smile which split his pleasant dark face in a happy grin.

'I was not quite sure of the spelling. I hope you had a good flight.'

I was tired, coming in from a few days of work and promotion in Seattle, still jet-lagged, but looking forward to exploring this part of

California. The air was warm but surprisingly dry. The sun shone. From the sky Los Angeles' suburbia had looked like an arid, overcrowded third world city of endless, low, identical buildings.

I followed him through the crowd.

'Let's take my luggage and then we go.'

He took my computer case and glanced quickly at me.

'I cannot place your accent.' He was self-assured. 'Where are you from?'

I laughed.

'I am originally Italian. I thought everyone could detect my accent as soon as I open my mouth. My Italian accent has not faded after more than twenty years in Africa. I am rather proud of it, and in any case there is not much I can do to improve it.'

After all, I was once Italian.

'Oh I love Italy. I flew here with Alitalia and they said 'Signore e Signori, benvenuti a bordo'.' We laughed together. 'It sounded so nice I would have liked them to repeat it again and again. Where do you live in Italy?'

'Well, I actually no longer live there. I live in Africa.'

He stopped abruptly.

'Where, in Africa?'

For the first time I noted that his accent was not American; I had taken for granted from the beginning he was an African American. Now I looked at him better.

Slim, of medium height, intelligent eyes, small ears, regular, slightly familiar features.

'I live in Kenya.'

Even before I said it I anticipated what was going to happen, but still his joy took me by surprise.

'*Oh jambo! jambo jambo mama. Hata mimi natoka Kenya. Mimi ni Jaluo. Halla bahati mzuri sana kukutana na wewe hapa.*' I come from Kenya too. I am a Luo tribesman. What strange good luck to meet you here.

How lucky indeed. That the person sent to meet me in Los Angeles where I went because of the planned feature film based on my autobiography, *I Dreamed of Africa*, is an African and a Kenyan, and this by pure coincidence, cannot be a coincidence. It is an omen. A fantastically good omen.

That set the mood.

I am delighted; a chance to speak Swahili during this trip.

We find the luggage, he goes and gets the car. A comfortable, dark blue, normal-looking limousine, not, thank goodness, one of those over-long vulgar affairs.

★   ★   ★

We settled in and I asked him about his life. How and why did he get here?

He drove with easy assurance.

'I had a dream,' he said, 'of becoming a business administrator. I wanted to go to college in California. That's what I am doing now. I drive to help pay the fees.'

'Your family must be quite well off to send you

over here. How did you come? You must have connections.'

He grin at me in the rear mirrors. 'Not a penny. Not a single connection, apart from an older friend who was working here. I had twenty cents in my pocket when I arrived.'

I considered his new suit, a good tie, clean, perfectly ironed shirt. A certain opulence transpired from him.

'How long ago was this?'

'Three years ago. I slept on the floor in my friend's rented room for months. And, to survive, I cleaned toilets. A job no one wanted. I cleaned toilets for cash. I was not allowed to work, to start with.'

I was transfixed.

'And then?'

'And then, after months of cleaning loos, I started cleaning windows. I saved every penny.'

He looked at me in the mirror.

'From windows, I graduated to selling things in the street. Odd jobs. Whatever came up. It was not easy, but everything is possible in America.' He paused, there was pride in his voice.

'Now I have a green card. I go to college. I graduate next year.'

We were crossing many roads and finally went down the freeway towards Santa Monica. The ocean glittered, blue and turquoise, and on the white beach people jogged.

'It must have been hard to start with,' I murmured.

'Not really. I knew what I wanted to do and

64

there is no work too humble, when you do it for a purpose.'

I loved that attitude.

'I work for an insurance company too. I study mostly at night and at weekends. Life is great.'

'Your family must be very proud of you back home.'

'They are. My brothers and sisters. Back in Kisumu.'

What a step from the busy, provincial little town on the shores of Lake Victoria to this chaotic modern symbol of America's metropolis.

'Do you miss Kenya?'

'I DO in a way. Yes. But I will go back next November. I saved enough for the ticket.'

I was more and more amazed, proud of him. He achieved the practically impossible.

We had reached Santa Monica. The ocean sparkled, small waves crowned in foam, and on the beach, walkman and headphones on, a young couple ran, holding hands. A few youths dashed fast amongst them rollerskating.

'Joseph' — he reminds me of another Joseph, the same joy in his eyes — 'Did you ever see an elephant back home in Kenya?'

I had managed to surprise him. For a moment his self-confidence was out of balance.

He braked, almost swerved.

'An elephant? Why?' His eyes were round with surprise. He shrugs.

And here, in his reaction, in his bewildered answer, was the drama of Africa's environment, the loss of identity of the African people, the reason why the environment is not safe, and my major reason for being in America.

To create awareness. To ask for help.

Local people in Africa cannot afford even to see their own wildlife. As if in Italy we could not afford to enter our churches, to be inspired by our monuments, to visit our museums, to contemplate the Roman ruins, to experience the art which makes Italy great. And this is why I have built the Wilderness Centre.

'An elephant? Of course not. How could I possibly see an elephant? How could I afford to see one?'

★　★　★

I have invited Joseph to come and stay in Laikipia when he returns to Kenya in the fall, to see the sun rise on the savannah in a deafening concert of birds, to walk to the waterfalls on the edge of the Great Rift Valley amongst palms and fig trees, and to stalk his first free elephant, king of the bush, so that when he returns to Los Angeles, the memory of the pachyderm which is part of his heritage will make him walk tall.

I know well that like thousands of other youths who have visited Ol ari Nyiro, he will never be the same, because he will have seen an elephant moving majestic and free through the African bush.

One Day, in Kiwayu

A man who is not afraid of the sea
will soon be drowned, he said, for he
will be going out on a day he shouldn't.
But we do be afraid of the sea, and
we do only be drowned now and again.

J. M. SYNGE, *The Aran Islands*

The heat of the sand penetrated my tired body
and I dug my toes in it, stretching my muscles,
content, finally relaxed, conscious of having the
whole earth as my bed. The sun warmed my
back. Through half-closed lids I could see the
small waves of low tide lapping the shore. The
whiteness of the beach reflected a million hidden
crystals, minute shells, and across the bay the
island of Kiwayu was green, its lacy acacia trees
filigreed with hanging liana. The rocks encrusted
with oysters exposed by the tide were now
rimmed with foam, and a wind had begun to
rise. Clouds were gathering on the horizon:
perhaps it would rain in the evening.

Today was my birthday, June the first, in
Kenya Madaraka Day, a national holiday. We had
flown to this idyllic stretch of sand not far from
the Somali border on my return from a long
overseas trip. Here I could rest before going back
to my demanding work routine, get rid of the
jet-lag, celebrate my birthday away from

67

disturbances, thousands of kilometres far from civilization, where no telephone, no message could reach me. Even in Laikipia the problems accumulated during my absence would have been waiting for me. It had been Aidan's idea, thoughtful, caring as ever. Kiwayu was special to me.

A place full of memories of sand crabs dancing away on light legs, like my emotions, of small grey waves licking the shore, red suns melting on pearly waters, as in a floating mirror of coral and quicksilver. Of walking to the village of Mkokoni, where Paolo and I had once spent a blissful summer camping on the beach. Of Emanuele sailing out for cowries with the fishermen in the early morning, his thin arm lifted, waving goodbye. Of night picnics on the sand, sitting on large damp cushions of cotton *kangas*, smell of sea wind and long-gone youth.

I breathed the warm, balsamic sea-air deeply. Next to me, Sveva stood up.

'I have been asked to go out sailing. Can I?'

I looked at her long tanned legs, hips which had recently taken a new rounded shape, a body which seemed to have bloomed almost overnight, while I had been in America to launch my book, to talk for the Foundation, to work. She shook her heavy, honey-coloured mane of hair, one of her most striking features, and I realized with surprise that she was a child no longer. Gone was the chubby Mediterranean angel face, the fine silver gold baby-hair. Soon, any time now, she would be a woman. Soon she would be gone.

'Are you sure you know how to?'

With the sudden, resolute Paolo's look which I knew I could never fight, a determined glint in her oceanic eyes, she turned to me. A smile of full lips, Paolo's white teeth, the radiance of her glowing complexion.

'If I never try, I shall never learn. I'll be back for lunch.'

She ran off, a glimpse of youth and blonde and copper, to join her waiting friend. Only a short unease, a brief misgiving; and the tide of sleep and exhaustion, the giddiness of the jet-lag, the warmth and the rhythmic, hypnotizing sound of the ocean claimed me, and I was asleep.

I woke up slowly feeling stiff. My shoulders were burning and the sun was now over the zenith. I glanced at my watch and saw that I had been asleep for over two hours. I must get back to my thatched cottage, see how Aidan was, find Sveva. I was hungry now.

I stood and looked along the beach. A solitary figure was coming towards me, almost running.

The wind was stronger and the choppy sea looked green and murky, with large ugly waves heavy with seaweed.

I sheltered my eyes with one hand and saw that it was Aidan. His tall frame bent forward against the wind, he moved with a curious speed. There was a sort of urgency in his step which I could detect even at that distance. With a quickening in my heart I ran towards him. A greeting smile died on my lips when I saw his face.

He always came straight to the point. His

voice was more serious than ever. Its gravity added to my apprehension.

'You'd better come quick. It's Sveva. There has been an accident. I am afraid she doesn't look too good.'

Instantly, my mouth dried out and my voice with it. A silent scream rose within me, from those depths of agony I had visited before, closing my throat, carrying, like a chill breeze, the familiar sense of horror, impotence and impending loss.

Not again.

Oh no. No. Not Sveva. Not Sveva, oh gods in heaven.

In moments of despair my soul goes begging to the spirit friends I have in the world of beyond. The ones I have loved and lost. The ones who would always care for my tears and for my pain.

Paolo, oh Paolo. Emanuele, Emanuele, please. Nonna, Nonna. Please. Not Sveva, please, not her.

I stood only an instant irresolute, a painful rigidity choking me. Aidan's blue eyes were slits of worry, his forehead closed in a frown. He held me up.

' . . . Not really serious. It's her eye. Her face. She was hit . . . '

I was running. Why was the burning sand so cold at high noon that day in Kiwayu under my flying feet? Why was the distance between me and the cottage in the raffia palm grove interminable? Why was the beating of my fear like a pulsating drum which deafened any other

70

sound? And all along, in the back of my mind, the knowledge that it was now afternoon and a national holiday, that we were hours of flying from any medical help. We could never make it before dark.

Aidan could have flown in any weather, with any moon, but tonight there would be no moon at all. We could not fly in total darkness over lightless lands.

I prayed with no words to the ones who would care enough to make a difference.

Please please please Paolo, Emanuele, Nonna, per piacere aiutatemi.

The familiar, determined coolness which terror carries with it took hold of me again and I split in two. The other Kuki ran. The sun was dark and alien like a sun in the moon. *Run Kuki run.* The last rise over the last dune. A tangle of sea vines twisted around her ankle and almost tripped her over. The entrance of the room, sheltered by bright cotton *kanga*. The palm matting on the floor cool, soft under the soles of her feet. She held herself a moment against the door-frame, short of breath, and she was there. Back to the here and now, and to herself.

In the dark it took some moments for my sun-dazed eyes to adjust. Sveva lay on my bed, wrapped in a red wet *kanga*. The young man who had taken her out sailing was crouched at the bed's foot holding his head. Ignoring him, I ran to her, calling her name, and when she heard my voice she moaned.

She is alive. She is alive.

I looked.

Her wet hair was plastered to her skull. Below it, what had been her angel face was red and swollen, covered in blood. A crescent shaped open cut scarred her left cheekbone, and blood mixed with tears dribbled on my bed linen. She looked up at me through tears.

'I see two of you. I see two of everything. Mamma. Will I be all right?'

Since she was a little girl, when anything happened, a scratch, a fever, a pain of any sort, with total faith she asked me: 'Will I be all right?' and waited for the verdict with an absorbed expression of complete trust.

My heart fluttered, at her reverting to childhood in a time of pain and need. She was alive, yet she might be disfigured. She could be blinded.

She moved and tried to sit. Her eyes rolled, I held out my hand in time to help her gently back to her pillow. She was suddenly sick. I took her in my arms trying not to touch her skin, giving the others quick instructions.

In the hurry of packing a small bag after arriving yesterday from the United States, I had forgotten to take my first-aid kit. There was no mercurocrome. No antibiotic cream. Nothing really but a harsh disinfectant that I knew would cook the skin badly, and butterfly plaster stitches that I knew I had to find the courage to use. Boiled water then; ice. The delicate skin below her eye should not be disturbed. Radiocall the hospital. Ask their advice. No question of having enough daylight hours to be able to make it back to Nairobi. And tomorrow would be too late for stitches.

'I can't see. I see double. Two of you. Two beds. Two Aidans. I feel sick. Sorry.'

She was sick again.

'Mamma. Mamma, will I be all right? Will I be able to see again?'

★ ★ ★

There had been narrow escapes before. The time she had been attacked by killer bees. The time her horse had bolted when she was pursuing zebra, and she had been catapulted into the rocks. The time that she, still a toddler, had refused to board the car already packed to go back to Nairobi from Laikipia. She had stopped in her tracks, unusually stubborn, ready to throw an uncharacteristic tantrum. It was Wanjiru who had told me to humour her.

'Nyawera,' she had said, calling me by my Kikuyu nickname, '*Makena najua. Kama yeye ataki hio ngari, lazima iko na kwa sababu.*' You, The One Who Works Hard, The One Who Smiles knows. If she does not like that car, there is a reason.

Reluctantly, I had moved all the luggage to a land cruiser. I felt the absurdity of the situation, but Sveva's and Wanjiru's coalition was too powerful to fight.

Next day, when our driver Karanja drove a friend who had been staying with me in Laikipia, to Nairobi in the other car, over the Kabete escarpment it lost a wheel which we did not know was loose. Out of control, the car flew over the bank, overturned and crashed, and my guest fractured her spine. I drive much faster than Karanja. The thought of what could have happened had we been in that car, dried out my saliva. Inscrutably, with the African acceptance of the improbable, Wanjiru had nodded.

'*Asante Makena,*' was all she said. Thank you, The One Who Smiles.

There had been the time that, during an evening walk with the dogs at Paolo's dam beyond Kuti, we had wandered without realizing it into the middle of a herd of elephants. They had been so silent that in the twilight I had not seen them. Unknowingly we had ended up almost between the legs of a towering matriarch invisible in the dusk. A sudden blare of trumpeting coming from a yard or so above us, ivory tusks protruding, a huge head shaking, flared ears. And in an instant I had gathered up Sveva, a child of four or so, and had run at an angle towards the elephant, in the direction of the wind, to get out of the line of scent as soon as possible. My heart in my mouth, legs scratched by thorns, trying to avoid the remaining herd, only after a while did I realize that Sveva, bobbing up in my arms, was waving at the elephant, giggling.

And there had been, of course, the time, soon after Emanuele's death, when a little friend had pushed her by mistake into the swimming pool at Kuti, and run away in fear. She had sunk to the bottom, a baby who could not yet swim, but inexplicably she had managed to climb out alone, soaked, but safe. There had been other stories. Accident prone, as Paolo had been, there was however something unknown — or someone invisible — which saved her in potentially tragic situations, some benign force that had so far rescued her.

★ ★ ★

Now the story came amongst broken sobs, and it chilled me.

They had sailed out in the choppy sea with the irresponsibility of youth, without life jackets. Sveva thought it would be easy, thought her friend would know how. The current of the receding tide took the small craft further and further from the shore. There were no other boats to be seen. The place was about to be closed for the Long Rains season, and all craft had been taken ashore. Somehow I had been spared the horror of watching, useless witness, impotent to intervene. That would have maddened me. Sveva tried to grasp the slippery side of the boat to keep her balance. Then the wind caught the sail violently, the boom turned, hit her across the face, flung her into the water. The boat capsized. Sky the colour of fright swirled above her eyes.

Stunned and unconscious she went under water, heavy as lead, but inexplicably she did not sink and bobbed up again. The cold made her regain consciousness and miraculously she managed to keep afloat, pain burning her face, eyes blinded with blood and salty water, waves higher and higher, and no life jacket. The aquatic

Paolo streak prevailed in her as it had long ago, when she was pushed into the pool in Laikipia.

Yet again, when she could easily have drowned, she did not. The pain and the chill kept her conscious and she managed to stay afloat. Then the boy grasped a lock of her hair, floating like a bronze seaweed amongst the driftwood, and lifted her on the now righted boat, where she embraced the mast. Painstakingly, they reached the shore when Aidan, who was working at his papers in the cottage, was alerted by a boat attendant.

The afternoon drew on. Through the crackling of static, on the radio, the nurse in charge at the Casualty department at Nairobi Hospital gave us instructions, reassured us. We were to keep Sveva cool, quiet; give her pain-killers. Tomorrow we would leave at sunrise for Nairobi, and the hospital. But for today, only I could help.

I kept vigil over her agitated sleep, anxiously drying out oozing serum mixed with blood and praying that her face would be spared. When darkness fell I knew that the time had come for me to stitch the cut. It was drying out open, a gash shaped like a fan, and, unless I acted now, it would stretch her smooth skin and leave a nasty scar. Aidan held high the hurricane lamp and the young man a torch while I, conscious that it was up to me to keep her beauty, steadying my hands and biting my lips, applied the stitches to my girl's face one by one. From the swelling and pain I knew that her cheekbone was fractured. Perhaps the eye was affected. I finished finally. But she would not die.

76

Two years have gone by now and she is unblemished. The eye has finally recovered, and even if her eyesight has been slightly affected, the bone has mended and only a fine crescent shaped line, translucent like a new moon, remains below her left eye to remind us of that afternoon in Kiwayu.

The doctor next day commented that the stitches were applied perfectly; mother concern and love had guided my hands. But Sveva and I knew that it is the spirit friends who had helped again. Until next time.

★ ★ ★

Next time was a couple of years later, here in Laikipia, while she was driving with her friend Tim in a wave of music along the short cut between the Big Dam and the Wilderness Centre.

My large land cruiser climbed a steep slope too fast, landed sideways on the opposite downhill side and bounced up.

She hit the brakes, lost control, and the car rolled. She banged her head on the ceiling, and was catapulted like a rag doll stunned, unconscious, to the back of the vehicle. Driverless, the car kept going at full speed, rolled once more and landed on its roof. The front windscreen hit a jagged stump and exploded in a thousand crystals.

Shahar, the agriculturalist from Israel who had at that time just joined our team, was riding his bike towards the Centre, when he saw the car:

upside down, the engine still running, music still pouring out and no one inside. The stump of an acacia branch, pushed against the front seat, would have beheaded her, had she still been in the driver's seat.

The car roof had caved in. A death trap.

The tracks of naked feet were visible in the red dust, and Shahar followed them.

She was walking in a daze, holding Tim's hand. She had crawled out of the window, extracted and comforted him. His collar bone was broken.

She did not have a single scratch.

Then there was the night in Nairobi a couple of years ago. It was her last day of school in Kenya before leaving to study in Europe. She had gone out to the end of year party.

I went to bed early and woke up suddenly in the middle of the night.

There had been a noise.

It had been raining earlier on but it had stopped now. Water dripped from the guttering. The dogs were silent. Someone was knocking, urgently, at the downstairs door.

'Mummy, open the door.'

I shook off the sleep.

'What happened to your keys . . . it's four in the morning . . . '

'Mummy, we've been robbed. They took everything. Open the door. I'm all right.'

Soaked in rain, her long hair damp on her shoulders, Sveva stood with her friend Tim on my doorstep. Over a steaming mug of tea the story unfolded.

Their car, moving slowly in the heavy rain, had been ambushed up the hill, in Forest Road. A *panga* had gone through the half-lowered window, Tim had been yanked from the car and made to kneel on the grass at the side of the road. His face was pushed into a muddy puddle, a foot placed on his back to hold him down, while a bandit searched and robbed him. Sveva had crouched inside, invisible in the dark, protected by the fogged windows. With self-preservation she had removed from her neck her golden chain with the pendant of the two trees logo I had given her as a present. She hid it between her breasts and she got out. Caught unawares, the bandits turned. One leaped towards her, pushed her, took her purse, grabbed her blouse, began to undress her. Time stood still.

Smiling unexpectedly at angry, tense and frightened people disarms them, takes the wind from their sails, acts as a balm. It is often infallible and even this time it worked.

Standing in the night rain in deserted Forest Road, Makena bit her lip, swallowed her fear, smiled at the robbers, and joked with them in her fluent, gracious Swahili.

Could they not see that they were young, and there was nothing much they could get out of them, they had a little money, here it was, they could take her watch, here it is, take it, a good watch from Europe, and her necklace with blue lapis lazuli, it was real silver — you can always get another watch, another necklace — could they not see it was cold and they were wet, all they wanted to do was to go home?

The bandits were caught unprepared. They knew how to deal with rage, with fear, with aggression. Her calm, her words, her bright smile disarmed them.

Once again, the silent star of Makena's luck prevailed; another escape, as for Paolo, long ago. The page was turned, the time for violence gone, the robbers disappeared into the fog, like a nightmare at dawn.

The rain kept falling on the deserted road.

Looking for Sandy

In memory of Sandy Field

Great things are done when men
and mountains meet.

WILLIAM BLAKE, *Gnomic Verses, i.*

The morning of the 14th of June 1996, dark clouds gathered in the sky over Nairobi, brought by strange and invisible winds. It had been one of Kenya's weirdest rainy seasons in people's memory.

The long rains of April had been delayed, and when finally the sky darkened one afternoon and large warm tears of water fell in untidy splashes, faster and faster on the parched red soil of my garden at Gigiri, we were well into May, in fact into June, almost.

In Laikipia the cattle had grown thin, and the Centre Dam was so low that, with a few shreds of meat, we could gather a bucketful of crayfish in a few minutes just from the shore.

The buffalo I met on the road at night stood dazzled in the car headlights. Rooted on stocky legs, with bent heads, the heavy horns weighing them down, the old males' muzzles lifted towards the car. Opaque ribs showed below dusty hides, a weariness in their eyes, and lions grew alert, I knew, waiting for their chance.

81

Through the dry sparse silver grasses, windswept in the evenings on the ridge of Mugongo ya Ngurue, I could see Lake Baringo shrink, the banks emerging, brown on the jagged shores; the middle island grew larger, accentuating its sleeping dinosaur shape; hiding in the muddy shallows where fish had long disappeared, hungry crocodiles began to attack goats, and the tree frogs were thirsty and silent in the chilly nights.

In Enghelesha, the fields that Shahar, our young agriculturalist from Israel, had prepared for planting, were waiting too; clouds came and went, bypassing us, and the sound of thunder filled the sky, grumbling only from the west over the Cherengani hills. The eastern sky, from where the rains come to Laikipia, remained clear and sparkling blue like wild convolvulus.

The lawn in my garden at Kuti dried partially, and Paolo's dam was empty, the creamy chocolate clay in the bottom cracking slowly in the sun.

The elephants waited for the night to settle before approaching my garden, tempted by the still green shrubs and fresh leaves on the irrigated parts; and the askari had a hard time restraining them from getting too close to the graves. Their dung was found practically every morning, still steaming, all along my drive, and as close as Sveva's old playroom. Often buffalo and zebra droppings began to appear too, closer and closer on the murram paths, and my dogs howled their disdain at the renewed invasion of their territory, but their barks were lost in the moonless nights with the cries of plovers.

The concert of birds, converging from miles around to the bird baths and the pawpaw that we laid out on the stones for them, took over any other sound in the scorching afternoons. Hundreds, thousands of birds, covering the dogs' food bowls with an incessant flutter of feathers.

Then, from the garden taps came a gasping sound, and we knew that the water had dried out in the tanks, and we had no choice but to pump it all the way from Ol ari Nyiro springs, well over six miles away.

There was no grazing left; only below the *lelechwa* did some grass sprout still, grey with age and exhausted of life. Even my rain stick did not seem powerful enough this time to stir the clouds.

Finally, brought to despair, I decided to follow the ancient custom of the land, and hired some old *wazee* from Mutaro to perform a rain ceremony. A sheep was found, completely black, with no white markings whatsoever, and, led by Garisha, a cattleman from Meru whom we had employed on the ranch for years, the old men sang and danced below an old *mugumu* tree next to the Mukutan stream, slaughtered the sheep ceremonially, and proceeded to consume in secret, ritually but with satisfied glee, certain chosen parts.

We waited. We waited hoping to hear the sound of rain on the roof and the frogs waking up in the pond. But nothing seemed to happen.

About a week had gone by when, although no apparent change was detected in the air by us humans, bees started swarming, passing above the yellow fever trees in buzzing clouds which cast fast shadows. On the newly potted palms, on the papyrus in the fish pond, the weaver birds landed to tear off long shreds and, in a frenzy of activity, they began nesting. Soon, heavy bunches like intricate baskets festooned the acacias' branches on the west side of the wind, and my cook Simon took to looking east, with straight head and wide nostrils sniffing the air, and commenting gravely: '*Mimi nasikia arufu ya mvua.*' I can smell the rain.

Then I woke up one morning, and knew that the wind had stopped. The air had grown moist, pregnant with water, and the heavy western sky purple and black. Clouds hung, lead coloured, gathering above like a moving blanket.

Thunder and lightning shook the sky, a sudden breeze lifted, the bougainvillaea trembled, livid in the strange grey light, and the rains came.

In Laikipia the termites woke up from their secret tunnels, the earth opened, and golden clouds of living insects drifted high in the last twilight of dusk, in a nuptial frenzy of new wings, dancing dizzily upward.

They did not seem to stop. The dams filled and overflowed; the Mukutan stream became a river, hurling down the *luggas* and the gorge with a continuous roar. The Demu ya Schule had gone over the road, the gap filled with murky water widened, and the Wilderness School woke up as an island on a livid morning of more incumbent water. The staff, the following night, all standing in their nightdresses on the tables and desks, had to be rescued urgently because the level kept mounting and no one could swim. The land cruiser which went over to fetch them never got out of the water, and we had to send a tractor next day to tow it. Cars got stuck continually in the black cotton soil, and in the gluey red clay alike, and everywhere was flooded.

Crayfish became impossible to catch, now that the Centre Dam had become a mighty lake, refilled constantly by the Big Dam, and, after subsequent showers formed countless running streams, a constant flow of water ran from the overflow, to concentrate into a deafening, rumbling grey river billowing through the valley of Maji ya Nyoka. There is no mid-way in Africa: it is either drought or floods, life or death, it is the land of opposites.

All our rain-catchments were full as they had not been in years. Our sixty-two dams were unrecognizable.

The Red Dam, the Black Dam, Nagiri's Dam and Ngobithu's Dam, were fuller than they had ever been. And Mutamayo Dam, Nandi Dam, Enghelesha Dam, Corner Dam, Luoniek Dam, Ol Morani Dam, Kudu Dam and Dam ya Faru had flooded over the road; new islands had emerged everywhere, water ran into the *lelechwa*, waterbucks stood confused on the flooded shores. Even water holes were enormous.

In the kitchen at Kuti a few inches of muddied water covered the floor, where Simon waded ankle-deep and bare-footed, rolling croissants impassively, with great style.

In Nairobi, it became a problem to take off

and to land in the dense fogs; and often the airfields at Wilson were closed to any traffic for hours.

★   ★   ★

It was a morning like this, the one of June 14th. I had taken off at 12 p.m. with Benjamin Woodley, our pilot and game warden, who had come to fetch me with our plane.

The clouds hung low; a grey impenetrable curtain covered the Aberdares. We circled round the clouds, going too far south in the process, well off our north-west route. We flew very low, with no shadow, over herds of goats, which streamed away like brown and white seeds scattered on the flat savannah by a hurried hand. Masai herdsmen clad in red blankets looked up, leaning on their spears, so close I could see the colour of their beads and the knots of their *rungus*, and when, beside the cattle, I began to see giraffe and zebra, I knew that we had gone well below the Longonot crater. We circled and circled, first lower, then higher, trying to find an opening in the barrier ahead. But the sky looked ominous, closed to our probing.

We climbed finally above the clouds, so high that my fingertips became dizzy and my head too light, and I found it hard to keep my eyes open in the blinding white reflection of spun clouds and the sun, too close and too aloof to care for us daring insects. I felt unimportant and vulnerable, suspended in a man-made flying machine inadequate to compete with such powers.

Yet we managed to make it. Benjamin, skilled and cool-headed, finally located a hole in the canopy and dived through the sky as a fish into the deepest ocean; found a gap through the cliffs of Hell's Gate, and we flew very low over the siphons of hot smoking sulphur. Some large buffalo crouching on the grass looked up at us; waterbuck and eland and giraffe and zebra galloped off, but there before us Lake Naivasha glimmered, pale yellow reflections rimmed the clouds announcing tentative sunshine ahead, and we aimed towards it, past Ol Bolossad, up the escarpment.

Far on the right we left the dark Wanjohi area of deep forest and bamboo and igenia, black in a storm of rain.

I looked ahead at the familiar hills on the Great Rift. Enghelesha, Kutwa, Mugongo ya Ngurue. It was the Laikipia plateau, and with immense relief I knew we were safe.

At the same time our friend Sandy Field, piloting his Cessna 172, was disappearing to his destiny somewhere, perhaps in the bamboo and cedar forest, perhaps crashed over the waterfalls, where he may never be found again.

Sandy Field was a man of adventure and charisma, had been a gallant soldier and competent administrator. As a young man he was posted to Sudan, and spoke many local languages fluently. Brave in the bush, where he shot big game, in control and at ease at social gatherings, he had a flair for words, an amazing

87

memory and an extensive repertoire of quotations and poetry. Old fashioned, cultured, polished, slim and white-haired, with a witty smile, he was a great old gentleman, entertaining and fun to be with.

Now in his seventies, he still flew his small plane everywhere, and was regarded as a cautious, competent pilot.

On the ranch in Laikipia, without a telephone, and having neglected for a few days to listen to the sked on the Laikipia Security radio network, I did not know what had happened. I heard nothing until I flew back to Nairobi a few days later; there, at Wilson Airport in the early morning, I saw a group of Highlands friends leaning against their plane with steaming mugs in their hands, unshaven, silent, wearily eating sandwiches out of a box, sitting on one wing next to some open maps.

'Having a picnic breakfast? What's the occasion?'

The question hung in the air, and then Will answered.

'We are looking for Sandy.'

'Sandy?'

'He flew out of Wilson last Friday for Nanyuki. He never landed. Everyone who has a plane is looking. We have subdivided the area on a grid system. It is going to be tough, but we are trying to find him.'

But it was more difficult than we had all anticipated.

In any other country perhaps, finding a person missing in a storm with his airplane would have been a problem left to the authorities. But not in Kenya. Here the solidarity and friendship that unites the people of the Highlands once again prevailed, and everyone who had a plane or could hire one went looking for Sandy.

I felt I too had to do my share. I liked Sandy. I admired his intelligence, his agile mind, his wit. I respected his courage and leadership. Like his friend Wilfred Thesiger, he was one of the few remaining old soldiers of bygone days, with the soul of a poet, the manners of a gentleman. Kind, eloquent, witty, a strong personality, an addition to every party, quality and humour exuded from Sandy. His disappearance left us all bewildered.

We searched for days and then weeks. Whenever we flew, even after everyone had given up hope of finding him, I kept looking down the secret valleys, the steep walls of rock, the thickets of bamboo and cedar in the hope of finding a sign. But in vain.

All the wildest stories, the most adventurous guesses soared and subsided after a while. Sandy had flown south to Tanzania; had disappeared in the Naivasha Lake; had crashed on Mount Kenya; was alive, in Ethiopia. The last word on the radio before silence had been 'Abyssinia'. We would find him alive up Mount Meru, camped below the wing of his plane . . .

During the search, an old propeller airplane, of whose remote disappearance there was no record, was discovered on the bottom of Lake Naivasha; countless illegal charcoal kilns had been reported, and logging of the rare, precious igenia in unvisited forests, but no trace of Sandy.

Still, we looked from the plane, scanning every crag of the mountains. And then a medium from Europe declared that the plane had gone down in a certain gorge of the Aberdares next to the Wanjoi valley, and, to clear our conscience, we decided to go and look.

We left at sunrise from Laikipia, Aidan and I, on a dark morning of late June, and drove, through muddy tracks, up green hills and mountains. At the park gate we took with us a ranger who knew the way, a young Tugen from our boundary of Enghelesha, it transpired, trim and fit, well equipped with rucksack and tentage, and a very good uniform. We got stuck a few times up hill, walked in the red mud to put branches below the wheels and were astonished to see so many tracks of lions and hyena spoor. I wondered what they ate, as there seemed to be few signs of buck.

Lions were not indigenous to the Aberdares. They had been recently introduced, and — ecological tragedy — had multiplied beyond balance, almost completely destroying the rare and shy bongo antelope that feeds on the moss growing off fallen trees in the cold and rainy mountain slopes. In recent times, drawn by hunger, they had been known to attack and kill people, and I knew a scheme to control their numbers was under way.

Finally, we reached a fog-covered peak, where for short seconds when there was a break in the clouds, a sensational landscape intermittently appeared below us. We set camp at dusk, in the middle of the track, as the sides were thick with impenetrable vegetation. There was a drizzle of rain which soon grew to a mighty downpour; every inch of tent was wet and the mattress was swimming in chilled water. We ate a scalding bowl of soup, and piping hot stew to revive us, cooked on a small camping gas-stove that I had providently brought, for our campfire would not burn with wet wood, and, after a hot, sweet rum punch, we slept surprisingly well.

In the morning the search began down the crags of the land, over the slopes and inside the bamboo thickets. But it was in vain, and at night we finally returned, convinced that Sandy would never be found.

The bamboo, we knew, would have closed, resilient, over the plane and would have grown many feet in few days, obliterating it from view for ever.

Everyone knew that the forest was full of wild animals, and hyena are unkind to the wounded and weak. We hoped for a quick end, a peaceful rest in the unknown forest grave.

★ ★ ★

In *absentia cadaveris*, a memorial service was celebrated for Sandy in the church in Nanyuki, resplendent with elaborate flower arrangements by the accomplished ladies of the Gardening Club. There was all the crowd one sees at weddings and at funerals, at the polo matches of the North Kenya Polo Club, and at the Beating of the Retreat in Nanyuki, when some kilted Scottish battalion marches back and forth in the drizzle, with impeccable martial choreography, to the lament of Highland pipes. Everyone knew everyone else, all men wore identical blue blazers over ill-fitting trousers, the women assorted frocks and flowery hats. There were old settlers, farmers and retired game wardens, old timers and, finally visible, the faceless voices of the Laikipia Security Network.

Sandy's friends delivered moving eulogies, like Tony Dyer, a fellow pilot and a contemporary, and few eyes were dry. Everyone sadly agreed that we would never know where Sandy lay.

But we were wrong.

The honey gatherers found him.

They had been up in the forest slopes, smoking out bees from the old olive trees across the clumps of bamboo. They heard thunder meeting earth, and the shudder of the impact. They ran towards it, warily at first, and then, spying through the dripping leaves, they saw it, the white bird of metal that had fallen from the clouds and crashed miserably, a wounded seagull, sinking through the tall green foliage like a boat at sea.

They watched breathless for a while to see what happened, what creature would erupt from the contorted wreck. There was only silence, except for the shrill calls of invisible monkeys up on the treetops, the sound of water rushing from the bamboo.

In the impact, Sandy's life had lifted from his body and joined what was before, and after. Over the purple-ink clouds of the Great Rift, gliding along the waterfall's drops covered in moss, over the silent lakes bejewelled with flamingos, over the valleys and savannah, riding on the long necks of giraffes galloping in slow motion on the plains, or amongst trumpeting elephants in the dust, up on the mountain slopes and up to the dazzling light of the equatorial sun, like a butterfly finally hatching from its cocoon, what had been Sandy's energy, now freed from his body, exploded to blend with the Whole.

The men approached tentatively, climbed over the wing and spied inside: the *musungu* reclined on the steering wheel, his white hair visible, his forehead resting on the dashboard splintered in a thousand diamonds of exploded glass. He looked asleep, but the two men knew with the wisdom of the bushmen, from the shape of the neck, that the white man would never move again.

There was no harm, they thought, to find what he had no longer use for — clothes, watch, shoes, money perhaps? — that they could well use. It had been a bad year; life was hard on the mountain. The last honey harvest had been meagre and it looked as if the next one would be too. What if they helped themselves to what would rot anyway up the mountain?

No one would suffer and no one would find out. They cut the seat belt and dragged him out of the plane. He was light. Gently — there was no hurry — they put him on his side, and searched his clothes. They worked quickly, without talking, taking everything they could. His briefcase, all his clothes, his shoes. Then they covered the wreck of the plane with branches to hide it from the sky, for even in their ignorance they knew there would be a search. The more delayed the finding, the more chances they had of not being found. The forest animals would come. It would be easy, quick. Hyena were always pacing the game trails at night with their loping gait, sniffing for food. The forest would swallow the *musungu* man as it was now swallowing them, thick, impenetrable, keeper of secrets.

Loaded, happy they ran off, the honey search forgotten for today, to divide the loot in a safer place.

But it was not the hyena.

When the night came with its cloak of fog and drizzle up on the mountain slopes, and the night frogs woke up in a choir of life, the old leopard came out of its den under the boulder of rock, hung with fern and wild figs.

The leopard sniffed the air and moved slowly and surely through the undergrowth, towards the strange white shape in the bamboo.

And it was the leopard who carried Sandy off to the tall tree.

The forest men, months later, having learned of the reward offered for Sandy's discovery, went to report to the nearest forest station. A group of friends in the helicopter lent by Halvor Astrup went to land immediately on that spot, which no plane or car could have reached. Traces of hair on the dashboard and the cut belt told their story, and so did the leopard spoor abundant round the wreck.

Now Sandy lives in a leopard up the mountain slopes, a healthy strong lustrous leopard, and we know that he would have loved that.

The Road to Rubu

We shall not cease from exploration
And the end of all our exploring
Will be to arrive where we started
And know the place for the first time.

T. S. ELIOT, *Little Gidding*

One summer, not so long ago, we decided to go north of Kiwayu to explore, Aidan and Sveva and I. We bought a second-hand Land-rover old enough not to represent a temptation to *shiftah*,[1] but in good enough condition to carry us safely with the luggage and camping kit that we had purchased. Aidan also acquired a boat, a sturdy white plexiglass dinghy with an awning to shelter us from the sun, a good engine, and a spare engine, which had been Paolo's, kept safe in a store in my house at Kuti, where it had waited for years, for the time when again it may feel the same waters.

The plan was to drive north of Kiwayu, cutting a track along the overgrown trails to Rubu, on the north Kenya coast. This was an area which, for over a generation, no one had gone through because of the constant threat from bandits roaming the lands near the Somali border, around the frontier town of Kiunga.

---

[1] Bandits from Somalia or Ethiopia.

I had journeyed there first in the summer of 1973, when Paolo and I, young, in love and eager to explore remote corners of the country we had just chosen as our home, had travelled north with our car and a rubber dinghy, and spent two magical weeks in a tent pitched on the beach at Mkokoni.

To reach it we had driven through barren and untamed country, encountering wild animals, visiting small Muslim villages and making friends with the people. With our boat we had glided happily round the canals and climbed up steep tangled slopes, spotting wildlife on the sandy dunes covered in sea vines, and marvelling at the rare privilege of discovering that so much virgin, unspoiled land still existed, it seemed to us then, for us alone.

So it was, to some extent, to retrace our steps, that I returned twenty-three years later, and found that very little had changed.

The elephants were no longer there, belly-deep in the tidal ponds, and the blue waterlilies had died out. But we saw a cheetah the first day, and lesser kudu and dik-dik at the side of every track.

★　★　★

We drove into Mkokoni first, looking for Mote, the fisherman Paolo and I had employed that long-lost summer, more than twenty years ago.

He had been a young man then, nimble of body, quick to spot fish in the shallows, agile and ready to steer his boat through the labyrinth of

96

mangroves of which he knew every turning. In those two weeks we had shared adventures, and, with unfailing generosity, he had put himself and all his competence at the service of these two young *wasungu*, the first to come so far through dangerous and unvisited country, and to stay on.

Over the years I had not forgotten him, and I had seen him once in the late seventies during one of Emanuele's half terms, when an exclusive safari village for discerning guests had been built along our beach, and I went to find some of my memories and him.

Emanuele had loved to collect cowries in those days, and Mote promptly offered his *maho*[1] and two of the crew to sail out of the Melango at high tide and wait for the tide to go out, exposing the bank of molluscs at Oyster Bay, where, with luck, a *Cipraea Vitellum* or perhaps *Caput Serpentis* could be found, to my son's delight.

I had not seen Mote since, and was not sure if he was still alive: after all, Paolo and Emanuele had died, wiped out by an indifferent destiny, and the life of a fisherman in the Indian Ocean is not a long one: his brother had been eaten by a shark, while diving for lobster just out of the Melango.

But Mote was still there.

He came in from the beach where he had been fishing, a loincloth round his belly, a live lobster

---

[1] A smaller version of a *daho*; traditional wooden sailing boat used by fishermen in the North Coast.

glistening in his hand, still dripping wet and with the light step I remembered, small wizened face, and the slight figure of an old child. He looked up at us searchingly, and his face split almost instantly in a delighted grin.

Years ran like sand through the hourglass of his memory, and I knew he had remembered me.

'*Allah Hakbar! Mama Kuki! Kwisha rudi! Leo mimi nafra. Nashukrani kubwa sana kwa Mungu.*' May God be praised. Mama Kuki is back. I rejoice today and give thanks to God.

He intoned these words in a high-pitched voice, jubilant, and his cries soon attracted half the village. His brother Haji came out, bearded, older seemingly, fatter, greyer, resembling our Mote not at all: by another wife, I wondered?

Bajuni children and beautiful women assembled, colourful and elegant, greeting us. Soon we were sitting in the shade of Mote's house, on the Swahili beds of thatched doum-palm leaves, and were offered *tangawezi chai*,[1] with no milk. It was the full 'travellers' welcome', traditional in this strict Muslim community. Shelter, drink, food. Small sweet yellow corn cobs were produced for us, while we told of our safari and of what we wanted to do. A young man was recruited from the village, and our boat on its trailer was examined by everyone, found good enough, and accepted.

It took us three days to reach Rubu.

The village had been abandoned over twenty years ago, when constant *shiftah* incursions from

----

[1] Ginger tea.

neighbouring Somalia made it impossible for the inhabitants to stay on.

The track had become overgrown, tangled with liana, sansevieria and thorny acacia shrubs which scratched deep ridges on the car's metal, impeding our progress. But Aidan was determined, and with Mote, Ali the boatman and our young recruit, plus the drivers we had brought with us, we managed to clear a large enough gap for the vehicle to proceed slowly. We camped at night in the middle of the track — hooking mosquito nets on bushes over our mattresses — so dense was the vegetation around us that there was no room for our tents.

The bleached bones of an old elephant marked a spot, below five tall baobabs, where the entrance of Rubu had been. There were the crumbled ruins of a mosque. Small heaps of porous, decaying coral rocks indicated where houses had once stood, and disintegrating wells, made of yellow sand and lime. Arab inscriptions from the Koran, engraved on a few oval tombstones planted around with blue lilies, discovered behind a dune, indicated where the Rubu community had once laid their dead to rest. To one side, still partially functioning, was a flat *jabia*, the ingenious traditional way to collect rainwater to drink.

Sand vines and sansevieria grew everywhere, and on the slim stretch of grey beach left open by the mangroves, hundreds of fragments of broken crockery were scattered, blue and white and green and maroon, amongst pearly nautilus shells, and old elephant molars, yellowed with age and salt water: all that remained of a living community, already as ancient as millennia's old archaeological ruins. Far in the distance, over the bay, lay a long island, and the Indian Ocean glittered, breaking on the distant coral reef in sprays of white.

We cleared a patch over the sand dunes, and there we pitched our camp. The sound of the waves on the reef was unchanged.

The boat was lowered into the water next day, amongst singing, and *dahos* came over from the island to greet us; fishermen offered gifts of lobster and fish and left in a wake of songs and drums in the evening light.

Time seemed to stand still on the shores of Rubu, facing the long island which changes its names to match the names of the villages along the shore. It was a time of peace and harmony, of exploring the untouched shores where Muslim tradition had sheltered the people from the pollution of so-called progress, and lives still developed following ancient rhythms and customs.

The women were tiny, gracious, slim as girls, wrapped in bright *kangas* and with their hair plaited in smart, tight patterns; their ears were bright with red stones, the slender arms with bracelets, the small hands and feet painted with henna in floral motifs; sometimes a ruby glinted in a nostril, while barefoot children clung to their skirts.

They did not cover their faces, the Bajuni girls, like the Arab women in Lamu or Malindi, nor their heads, and I never saw them wearing a

100

buibui, the black flowing, nun-like garment of the strict Muslim ladies of the Coast.

They looked at us from the shadows of their doors, shyly returning our greetings in sing-song voices; and curly-haired little girls stood next to them, enveloped in faded European-style frocks a few sizes too large, but with shiny, eager eyes, devoured by curiosity at our foreign appearance, by the details of our clothes and hair.

I have always been conscious of the scrutiny of those young eyes in Africa, when, at remote villages, the crowd of silent, observing children approaches. Drawn by curiosity they leave the repetitive monotony of the games they have been playing in the dark shade of their homes, assemble at a distance, and finally come close to your car, almost touching it, and there they stop, girls with girls and boys with boys, barefoot, slim, staring silently, absorbing everything, examining the foreign animals we are.

We went for long trips on the boat, circling the islands and waving when we met the fishermen's *dahos* cutting the waves, loaded with biblical figures in long *shukas*, turbans loosened by the monsoon. We slid beside cliffs of steep rocks, hung about with liana and wild aloes and sansevieria, with the odd baobab suddenly appearing silver and majestic through the undergrowth; we spotted awesome sculptures of driftwood on the beaches, carved by the endless fantasy of long waves, and once, a large iguana crouched precariously on the edge of a rock, grasping a branch protruding on the canal, her black tongue flickering, her glassy eye

101

expressionless. A prehistoric encounter. We watched troupes of vervet monkeys taking over the dusk, jumping with incessant chatter amongst the baobab branches along the shore, where the small, black, left-handed crabs with one giant orange claw scurried down their holes in coordinated shifts, like dancers. We searched for oysters, with an old rusty hammer, and ate them where we were, half-submerged in the tidal ponds, squeezing a lime on their pearly flesh. We went bottom-fishing with Mote as I had once done with Paolo, and caught the same type of little round fish, silver-pink, with a black spot on the side, which Mote roasted for us on the beach on a rudimentary spit cut out of a fresh mangrove twig, and which we ate with our hands, skin and all.

While trailing with our boat in the evenings, we sometimes caught some very large red snapper and Aidan's surprised joy was like a child's, endearing in the experienced man that he is. We cooked them whole, with spices, lime juice and garlic; our camp was lovely, with large, open mess tents like verandahs, and two Lamu beds for sofas, that Mote's brother had made for us on commission, and sold us for far too much.

It was extremely hot, but there blew an evening breeze, the moon rose creating strange shadows, and we were merry.

Over those days of bliss and simplicity, far from the noise and cares of a distant world, the idea slowly formed of finding a place somewhere in that area for us to come and unwind during the busy year, and, in exchange, to start some activity to benefit that community. Something to protect the environment and to give people a way of life.

We sent messages.

So, the day came of the historical meeting of the *wazee*, who had travelled from far to hear what we had to propose.

From the beach, from the tracks overgrown with sea grapes, they began to come. They had heard from the fishermen's drums that we had opened again the old road to Rubu, these crazy *wasungu* who travelled by air, but had reached that spot by driving through harsh thorny land, and had pitched their camp on the beach, next to the mangrove bay, below the ruins of the house that had been Mohamed Mussa's.

The news had travelled at night, brought by rhythm and by song. Above the mangrove forests and clumps of doum-palms, through the tall tamarind trees and the outcrops of coral rocks overgrown with green creepers, to the pockets of people still living in clusters from Kiwayu to Kiunga, as far as Mkowe, through the fishermen's camps on the island, people listened and learned of this strange and unusual fact.

They knew that we travelled with Mote, *mzee* Mote from Mkokoni, and that we had hired Haji's son Ali. Some of them had already heard, when they were consulted for the spelling in Arabic of the word 'Rubu', painted in ocean-blue on the white side of the boat. And from Mkokoni to Kiwayu village they all could see Mote beaming with anticipation and growing in importance in his own eyes because of the

103

association with us. From his behaviour alone they had guessed some excitement and novelty lay ahead. Who were these *wasungu*?

Everyone knows that *wasungu* are slightly touched: those who can sleep in beds and sit comfortably inside, but choose incomprehensible hardship, like walking for miles in the sun following camels, without being obliged to do so, or who sleep out in the open under a mosquito net in lion-infested areas, and come all the way to this god-forsaken land, remote from man and civilization, not a *duka* for hundreds of miles, not even a road to get there. And what for?

I presume it was an irresistible curiosity to find out why, and the concern that we might have some sort of plot for Rubu: they wanted to claim the place for theirs, as it was; to show that they had first stake, that they cared what went on there, even if for thirty years none of them had taken up a *panga*, called for companions and, slashing at the vegetation, for about fifteen miles, made their way through tse tse country on the old road to Rubu. Now the track had been opened and the spell was broken.

Speculations of all sorts were born each morning and died with each sunset, to be reborn at sunrise and discussed all day long. But now they had gathered to hear from us directly.

Alerted to the arrival of the wise men, Aidan had driven to Kiunga earlier, to fetch Chief Jamal, the DO and the assistant chief.

I served everyone *bajuni* tea, and biscuits, under the awnings of blue and turquoise *kangas*, and then they all gathered under the tamarind tree below the *jabia*. After a moment's hesitation, I declined Aidan's invitation to join them because this was a Muslim world and my presence at the start would have made them uneasy: I knew women did not appear unless called. I felt that, by this show of instinctive respect of their tradition, I would myself gain in respect, and this was auspicious. As it happened, shortly after the meeting began they sent for me, and it was a prouder thing to join them at their request than to sit there uninvited at a meeting in their own land.

The meeting began with prayers to Allah. They then spoke formally in turn, welcoming us amongst them, asking what they could do for us. They had been impressed by our determination to reach that spot, and at our respectful way of proceeding; they had learned that we were looking at the land and wanted to know what we had in mind. There were some old men, and some others quite young, whose wisdom had given them seniority. They sat cross-legged on the sand, dressed in clean long *kikois* and shirts, all wearing embroidered Muslim caps, apart from the DO who was a Christian from Nandi, Mr Towett Maritim. He was still quite young, and very agreeable. Slim with an open, intelligent face, he was gifted with a positive attitude and natural leadership. He spoke very well, in excellent Swahili as they all do, in a sing-song of coastal accent, very pleasant to hear, the melodious intonation of all fishermen dialects across the world: a tone and a *cantilena* pitched to cover and pierce the sound of waves, to call from boat to boat over the oceans.

We told them of our love for that land, and of my memories of long ago; we explained our busy lives and our many commitments, but also our desire to find a place of quiet and peace, and of our intention — should they agree with our offer — to help them to rebuild and develop their village in a way that respected their old customs and their environment.

I looked at Aidan over the crowd of elders: another commitment, I could read in his eyes, with all the thousand things that already crammed our days. Yes, *wasungu* are mad, why ever start all again from the beginning, pioneering far from our known lifestyle, and our comforts?

But they listened with deep interest. We represented hope and change, adventure and challenge. Their eyes lit up, Allah was again invoked, they shook our hands repeatedly, they asked us to look around and to give them our proposed terms.

★ ★ ★

It took quite a while — like all things of worth — subsequent visits, letters, meetings in darkened offices in the old Lamu town, under palmtrees in the dusty town of Kiunga, in banks with fans whirring from ceilings of peeling plaster, and in open fields of cassava, where we managed to land to meet one more of the old people and get his blessing too: the unavoidable bureaucracy which is the other face of most dreams.

But finally, it was nearly done. Through my enthusiasm and Aidan's perseverance, his knowledge of the rules and his fairness of play.

It was for me the crowning of a dream long shared with Paolo, but which there had been no time to accomplish, to have the use of some land at the coast, and some sort of dwelling there, built to please the eye. Somewhere where the noise of the waves on the reef was the last sound at night and the first in the morning, a rhythmic, heaving sound like the beating of a large heart.

The image of Paolo kept coming back in that place he had loved most. Then we would sit and listen for the roar of lions, in the nights of those two lost weeks. And above the noise of the waves on the reef, brought by the *Kaskazi* wind from the sandy acacia-dotted savannah below the baobabs, sometimes we heard, with a shiver, the powerful deep call which is so much the sound of Africa.

Memories glided back with the tides at Rubu, when I paused on the shore, alone, to think, like waves reaching out on the grey sand between the mangrove sprouts.

Memories of Paolo.

Buffalo had enthralled him above all other African animals.

There, to his emotion, we watched a few old males coming down one evening to wet their muzzles in the semi-sweet brackish water amongst the mangrove.

Paolo.

Where was the shadow on the dunes, the tall slender shadow of the man who has gone? Why could we not say our farewells? The long wait for him to come home, his voice on the telephone, disembodied, far away, then the shade growing longer on the lawn, a gloom descending with dusk, the intuition of loss, the ultimate pain, the startling agony of bewildered, foreseen loneliness, the knowledge of nevermore. I put my hands around my stomach, felt the life I was carrying, knew the other life had gone on. I knew there would be no more holding hands, eyes gleaming with life and excitement, deeply searching mine in a quest of love.

'Farewell' — I thought — 'my Paolo, Paolo of the golden hair, Paolo the chivalrous squire.'

And Paolo had left when his time was up. His time was up and there was nothing anyone could do. Circumstances, delays, a variety of events, brought Paolo to that spot where, at the same time, the faceless lorry-driver chosen by destiny decided to turn into Hunter's Lodge. And it was at Hunter's Lodge that Paolo the hunter met the trailer, when his time was up.

I knew it with a jolt which left me breathless. An abrupt intake of breath, as if his spirit, abruptly freed from the cage of its body, had exploded with the same powerful energy of when he was physically there.

And Paolo touched my face with his fingerless hands, caressed my stomach where his hidden child curled, slowly growing into the blonde, radiant Paolo-girl he would never see. The one who was now running towards me on the beach, long-limbed, suntanned, laughing.

Memories.

Memories of running uphill, sitting on windswept rocks at the moment of sunset, when there is a chill in the breeze, shivers run from the shoulders down, and we look at the lake, at the blue Cherengani hills, at clouds with strange shapes, like dragons or fish. Of running downhill, hand in hand, eyes in the eyes, tripping on stones, and laughing.

Memories of long nights of music, the fire blazing, talking and talking.

Of other dogs sleeping on carpets, of other flowers fading away in vases.

Memories of brown, warm eyes, intelligent and old, even if young. A solitude, a far-away wisdom.

My lost child, my lost boy child.

★ ★ ★

In the months following our first visit we returned to explore with new eyes, no longer passing visitors who might never return; eager to find a good landing strip, slowly driving our boat up through the sleepy mangrove-lined canals at high tide. We discovered it at last, at a corner of the canal bordered by banks of red earth, below a hill crowned with baobabs and filigreed with porcupine tracks, the perfect landing strip. Bleached mangroves, like ancient noble bones exposed to salt and sun, lined the sides, and there Aidan landed his plane with ease.

It was late afternoon, almost sunset. Just enough time before darkness fell to pitch our tent beside the plane, gather a pile of firewood

109

and light a fire to bake bananas and to boil water for tea. Fireflies danced in the warm night and from the coastal forest came the calls of bush-babies dancing high in the baobabs.

The following morning, leaving the plane on the shore, our tent and equipment a few metres from it, we jumped into our waiting boat. Mote left us on the beach, at Ndoa, and went to have his *chai* at the fishermen's camp on the island. We walked inland, exploring, following tracks of bush-pigs, and to our amazement saw a male bush buck jumping, alert and handsome, through the tangle of sea vines.

We went down to the sea to swim and, in a grotto left open for us by the receding tide, we set our picnic.

We were eating cold fish with lime and soya, when we saw Mote sprinting towards us. He leaped over the rocks, agile and lithe like a sand crab, and he was screaming. The ocean wind took away his words, and only when he was close we heard:

'*Moshi! Ni moshi mingi kwa campi yetu. Moto! Ni moto kwbwa . . . Ndege . . . *' Smoke. A big smoke in our camp. Fire. A large fire . . . the plane . . .

We already were running before he had finished. Gathering our gear, wading into the water up to our armpits, climbing into the boat, firing the engine. With a wide circle the boat gained the entrance of the *melango*, left the ocean boiling behind, reached the lagoon where the horizon spread before us. Standing on the rolling boat and sheltering our eyes with our

110

hands, we watched in silence.

High into the sky, lifting exactly from the place we knew as Abukari — where, hidden behind the mass of green leaves, we had pitched our camp and our airplane was parked with all we had brought — over the mangrove forest, moving into the wind, ugly with the inevitable, lead-grey colour of fear, was an enormous column of smoke. No one spoke.

In the distance, running up and down the short beach at Rubu, we could see the small figure of Mohamed Mussa gesticulating towards us, urging us to hurry. The tide was out, the water low, exposing banks of white sand, and there was no way our boat could reach the bend in the canal and the airstrip. We had to walk.

We jumped into the water before reaching the beach and dashed off. Mohamed led the way. We flew uphill over the sand dunes and reached the swamp. The forest closed over our heads. The mangrove roots stood out, caked in mud, like gigantic spiders. I tripped a few times, losing my sandals. The sucking noise of crabs and raucous calls of parrots, a fish eagle taking off like hope from the treetops into a perfect sky, our steps deep in the gluey sand, the beating of my heart, my fear, my prayer.

Yes, I did pray to those who have always helped. Who have gone ahead where time means nothing, where anything can happen. I prayed with an intensity which left a dry salty taste in my mouth, tears stinging my eyes.

I prayed for the impossible to have occurred; for the random, compassionate breath of

Providence to defeat the chronology of events, and to blow away, retrospectively, the destructive fire; for the clouds to melt into rain and soak the embers.

All the time I was thinking of the aeroplane, of the tanks full of aviation fuel we had left below its wing, of our breakfast fire that had seemed too close, that we had believed extinguished; of the unbearable heat that the fire must have caused . . . was it my imagination or was a blade of fine rain falling ahead, obliquely . . . was it my imagination, or was the smoke getting lighter? No longer like a leaden column, but drifting wispily in the breeze?

The last mile was the longest. We reached the canal and plunged in, partly swimming, partly wading up to our armpits. Then we came past the bend, and we saw it.

Up to our waists in the receding tide, Aidan and Mote, Mohamed, Ali and I watched, speechless.

Along the middle of the long strip of sand fringed with mangroves, several metres wide, half a mile long and beginning at the water's edge, was a dead stretch of burned grass, of charcoal stumps still glowing, like a grey carpet unrolled by that inferno. All the firewood we had accumulated below a thorn tree had been destroyed. A scorching, choking stench of smoke remained.

No more than two inches away from the smouldering ashes, on opposite sides, incongruous, intact as we had left them, were the airplane and our tent. Only one of the tent's strings was scorched and hung limp. In the distance, smoke still rose, some shrubs still glowing, but, inexplicably, the fire had subsided on its own.

Mote was the first to climb up the beach, where he fell to his knees, arms outstretched, praising Allah. In his way he voiced our own feelings: to the day we die none of us will forget that that morning at Rubu we had witnessed what we could only call a miracle.

I looked around at the baobabs, at the bush, at the sparkling sky. I looked down at the sand as I stepped from the water. It felt right and it was like an omen. There was a large lion track, fresh from the previous night, and a buffalo, I could see, had come down to the sea shore.

Night of the Lions

A brave man is always frightened three times
by a lion: when he first sees his track,
when he first hears him roar and
when he first confronts him.

Somali Proverb, from *The Short Happy Life of
Francis Macomber* by ERNEST HEMINGWAY

It was the *askari* who brought Meave back in a
wheelbarrow, one April morning when I had
been gardening.

The bougainvillaea were a riot of purple and
needed taming. The first long rains were just due
to begin. It was the right time.

I loved the concentration, which left my mind
free to wander, thoughts forming, stories
unfolding, solutions finding shape. I liked the
sun on my face and the sudden breeze and the
call of turaco from the treetops.

From the shade of the large yellow fever tree I
saw the strange procession approaching.
Through the pepper trees, in and out of sun
blades, they came towards me. I stood, putting
down the secateurs I had been holding, and
touched the warm head of one of the dogs. There
was a weird gloom in the way they moved.

Dragging his long *kaputi*[1] on the ground, his

---

[1] Military coat worn by night watchmen.

114

cap askew, preceded by two of the other dogs and followed by a gardener, Nyaga pushed a handcart from which the matted tail of Meave, caked with blood, trailed on the grass.

The dogs approached cautiously, sniffing with lifted noses, baffled. Meave was the oldest female of my Alsatians, the leader of the pack.

Nyaga looked up at me apologetically, his normally happy face split in a thousand wrinkles:

'*Pole. Ulipata yeye kandu ya bara bara. Aliona ndamu kwa nyayo: ni Simba. Uliona mugu.*' I am sorry. I found her on the side of the road. I had seen tracks of blood on the path. I saw the footprints. It's a lion.

Nothing I could do would save Meave.

She was alive; motionless; she looked up at me with a stoic acceptance of her fate, black eyes still, ears alert, impassive and fearless as Meave could be. I looked down at her twisted body, her hindquarters seemingly dead.

I had asked my cook Simon to bring a basin of warm water and ran to fetch my first-aid box.

I washed her gently and shaved her rump. She did not whimper, as if she had become insensitive to pain. And excruciating pain there must have been because, on the bluish skin my razor exposed, were four deep gashes from which blood still poured, round deep holes spaced like the fangs of a very large lion.

Flashes of the scene darted through my imagination. There were so many possibilities. Perhaps the dogs, out on their night's escapade, had found the lion on the kill. My dogs have learned that the lion's presence means meat to scavenge. They follow the feral scent through the bush early in the morning, before sunrise. They come back panting, wildness in their eyes and a rank smell on their fur, and jump into the fish pond exhausted, before drinking noisily from their bowls.

The story of their night's encounters, of meals shared with jackals, of bones fought over with hyena, the excitement of the hunt, will remain a mystery. I could imagine a short fight, the lion's annoyance, a deep growl . . . a snarl that becomes a bite, deep, deadly, effortless. A crunching sound of fractured bones. Like a rag, Meave flew in the air, landed in silence. The dogs scattered. The lion went on eating, unaffected. Meave's back was broken. She managed to drag herself a few metres away, below a *lelechwa* bush; and there the *askari* found her.

I disinfected her wounds with red mercurochrome which mixed with her blood, blotted them dry and stitched her thick skin with the curved needle from my kit. I applied powder and bandages, I did what I could: but I saw that her spine was broken, her back legs paralysed, and knew that the lion had won. I put her on a mat, in a quiet corner near my room where I could keep an eye on her; she drank some milk, but I could see that she was incontinent, and after two days she refused food and lay there with closed eyes, barely breathing.

It was a gun shot at sunrise, at the bottom of my garden. I had asked Aidan to help do what

Paolo loved archery.

Sveva and Mote at Abukari.

Kuki and Sveva and the dogs at Kuti.

Paradise. View from The Nest.

The acacia trees on the graves at Kuti.

The pond at the springs at Lontopi; Ahmed Nyukundu
and Lwokignei Meto filling cans.

The end of the safari.

Ahmed Nyeusi at the wells at Koiya.

Outspan at Matokole; twelve miles to Koiya.

A daho off the Bajuni Islands and Sveva.

Low tide at Ndoa.

The Road to Rubu: Tim and Sveva on a *bamba* coffee tree.

The mangrove forest on the canal at Rubu.

Sveva at The Nest on Ol ari Nyiro Springs.

A pack of young lions in Ol ari Nyiro.

had to be done, but which I was incapable of facing.

She had been sedated with Nembutal and had fallen asleep, while I caressed her head. The echo resonated in the paling sky, startling the birds. A flight of starlings took off from the fever trees with a vibration of wings in the sudden silence.

It was a fresh dog grave next to many others, not far from the place where Paolo and Emanuele rest.

I went to look at the tracks that same morning and saw the lion's pug-marks in the dust. They were soft and rounded, immensely powerful and emanated danger.

Even more than a direct encounter, even before you hear his roar for the first time, it is the lion's footprint, marking the dust of a game trail, the unmistakable proof of his passing along the very path you are walking, that makes you feel that you are really in Africa.

After a time, living out in the African bush, you learn that there are animals you see and others whose presence you sense, not far from you, hidden by the undergrowth at the side of your track, the thick *lelechwa* or the clusters of euclea. Or in the night's shadows, expanding impenetrable out of your windows. In the border of darkness left outside your tent by the embers' glow of last night's campfire.

The elusive ones, whose scent only you detect, brought by a change of wind, betrayed by the cracking of a twig under a cautious paw. A powerful breathing, rasping and alien, rhythmic and implacable, like the very essence of Africa.

117

Those, the animals you never see, are the ones that give you the deepest shiver of emotion, the sharper taste of fear, the strongest longing. They are the ones you will remember.

Like the nights of the lions.

* * *

Not so long ago, in January 1997, when Sveva was about to return to school in London, she asked me if she could spend at The Nest one of her last nights in Laikipia, before returning to Europe and the cold winter ahead. She hoped to see rhino. She would go on a night picnic organized by Shahar, our young agriculturalist from Israel, at the hot springs below the Retreat at Maji ya Nyoka, and would be dropped at The Nest, where I would fetch her next morning. She brought her sleeping-bag and her hurricane lamp and of course a torch. She would have a radio handset. She had done it before. But I was uncharacteristically uneasy, and went to bed, myself, with a handset radio resting on my pillow.

Even our cook Simon seemed doubtful tonight and looked at her seriously.

'Makena,' he pleaded, 'hapana sahau radio. Chunga sana.' You, The One Who Smiles, do not forget your radio. Be very careful.

Lions had been roaring at night in Laikipia in recent days, more lions than I had heard in a very long time. At night I was often woken by my dogs' growls, by their rush of barking breathlessness as they ran for the door of my room where

118

they slept, and were quickly lost in the night. They scattered on the lawn, howling high, as they felt the lion's presence on the hills. But when lions came close, the dogs kept quiet. They cowered back to my room and lay down on my carpet, with alert ears, unsleeping.

This night was no exception. The rhythmic deep growls echoed on the hills on the side of the old Boma ya Taikunya, near the Ol Morani boundary line, and came closer. I could almost hear their padded feet on the track below Paolo's dam, along my garden, outside the guest rooms, as they moved towards the water trough of the *menanda*, where they could find buffalo, eland or zebra. I let the water overflow especially over the rim of the tank, where only elephant could reach it, so that it collects below it in a muddy hole, a delight for the buffalo. I suspected that lions and other carnivores had become increasingly attracted to the area. Landing one afternoon, I had seen a cheetah standing at the end of my airstrip, on an old anthill, checking out some young impala, undisturbed by the noise of the plane and swirls of dust; and at night I could often hear the magnified, see-saw purring of leopard: many impala went to the water.

I found it hard to sleep. Memories of danger haunted my mind. Still fresh was the memory of the recent encounter with the calf killer, in the last night of full moon.

★ ★ ★

When the moon rose I could see the cattle sitting around the *boma*, not far from the embers of the *wachungai*'s fire. They were mostly white, the cows of the breeding herd with their small calves next to them.

I was watching them through the thorny branches of the shrub I was sheltering under. My head covered in a cotton shawl rested on a double pillow, my blanket under my chin against the chill eastern wind. I was alert, and waiting. Next to me, stretched fully dressed on the mat, were Aidan with his lion rifle, Issak the headman with a spotlight and Ali the head of the *wachungai* at the *boma*.

The lion had come every night for the last two weeks, most nights taking off with one or two calves. The lion had developed a passion for newly-born calves. With any amount of young buffalo, fat zebra and tasty eland to feed upon, a lion addicted to killing cattle becomes a vermin no rancher can afford. Every week I had the cattle's *boma* moved out of the lion's territory. But the lion had followed, lured by the ease of taking tender young calves. Thirty calves had been taken, and I was left with no alternative.

Tonight, if the lion came, he would be shot.

He would come in the dark of the moon, at the time when the cold bites hardest, when the embers are greying and the men asleep. Wrapped in their *shukas*, curled around the camp fire, they would sleep without dreams until dawn, apart from the one keeping watch, fighting off sleep with scalding mugs of spiced tea, smoky with honey and milk.

The noise of cattle was in an odd way soothing, despite the snorting ruminant gurgles. The smell of fresh dung was overpowering, herby and natural in an odd way. I liked it.

I reflected that the smell had not changed in Africa over the centuries: no artificial fodder had been introduced to pollute the old ways. Cattle here lived outdoors all their lives; they wandered freely for their food and water; they were not stabled livestock, tame and safe in cosy enclosures where everything was available but freedom.

Here at the equator they got wet in the rain and walked for miles in the scorching sun to find water. They were resilient, patient animals, who knew how to survive; they recognized the song of the tick bird, the taste of new grass, they could smell a salt lick from great distances, and they knew lions.

It was as if a sudden wind had come from the *mukignei* shrubs in a short, intense burst; the same sound, like an immense, collective intake of breath. The cattle stood all at once, silent, alert, like weary ghosts.

And from the east, in stealthy, focused leaps, aiming straight for the youngest calf, came the lion.

Next to me, with astonishing speed, followed by Issak and Ali, Aidan had sprung to his feet, and while I kicked off the blanket, thankful for having kept my shoes on, and rushed for my gun, I heard the shot.

It shattered the night and echoed in the valley, with the deadly, disruptive finality of a rifle's burst. Deafened for an instant, running after the others in total silence, I heard only the drumming of my heart. A few metres away, in the dust the lion rolled, doubled up, gurgling its hollow death rattle. In a few seconds it lay still, and its eyes, no longer seeing, were a phosphorescent pale green, like dying fireflies.

Driving home later, alone at the light of the moon, trying to avoid potholes and hares on the rocky road, with the dead lion in the back of my car, I had wondered at the strange ways of my destiny and thought of other stories of lions in the night.

★ ★ ★

Sveva was alone at The Nest. The Nest is my refuge beside Ol ari Nyiro springs, a shelter of wood and stone open to suns and to moons, under a roof of thatched papyrus, with no windows or doors. It is built on a slope, overlooking a salt lick, and it holds a thousand spells.

There is the spell of the wind and that of the gentle rain. The spell of the storm, of thunder and lightning in the livid equator sky; the swallows' and swifts' spell, and the starlings' which roost on the beam above the four-poster bed made from old twisted olives and stones from the bush. At night come the fluttering bats with their special bat-spell of ancient caves, and dormice peer curious from their tiny holes, running fearlessly to pick up crumbs from my bread. Genet cats and porcupine come too, and leave their musky savannah spell, and in the night I try to guess which of them is chewing the remains of my guava. There is the spell that the orange-headed agama with the turquoise body laid on the stone under which Sveva's child hand had carved 'Paolo' and a heart of shells, and the powerful spell of the friendly cobra who sleeps underneath it.

There is the rhino spell and the elephant spell and the spell of the lone male eland. But the one that leaves me enthralled is Paolo's spell like a breath on my cheek, and Emanuele's, who had carved on to a log an acacia tree just like the one that one day would grow on his grave.

Presences of creatures and people like mysteries populated the shadows of my beloved Nest, but the strangest of all — and the one that kept me awake that night — was the one of the lion which sat on my bed.

A few weeks earlier I had visited The Nest with some guests, looking for buffalo. There had been a weird, sickening stench, the distinct feeling of a presence disturbed by our arrival, the glimpse, out of the corner of my eye, of a tawny shape dashing off down the slope, and in the sitting room, a large, evil reeking excrement, which I recognized for a lion's. Never before in Laikipia had a lion entered a house.

Narumbe, my wildlife ranger who was our escort that evening, had confirmed it:

'*Simba!*' he murmured, shaking his head in awe. '*Simba ndany ya nyumba!*' A lion in the house.

He turned his proud head round, still, like a

wooden sculpture, flared nostrils sensing the wind, his perforated lobes, pendulous at the side of his head, alert to detect a revealing noise.

The Nest is built high on the hill, a perfect spot to survey the valley and watch wildlife. A few days earlier a young eland had been killed by a lion, just down below. Now, a herd of buffalo was emerging from the *lelechwa*.

'*Yeye natega mbogo hama siruai.*' He would be stalking buffalo or eland.

We had gone in, a sense of disquiet and unease. On the printed counterpane of my large four-poster bed, a fluff of coarse yellow hair confirmed the tale.

A lion on my bed. A lion on my bed, no one would ever believe it.

That episode, and the knowledge that animals mark their territory with dung and urine, had taken some of the shine from spending nights alone at The Nest, a place all open, impossible to lock, like a verandah. Sveva had shrugged off the eventuality of another feline visit:

'It will never happen again. Really improbable. We have disinfected and cleaned everything. His scent has disappeared. He would hate the smell of antiseptic.'

She was quite right. I did not give it another thought. Not until now.

Aware that Sveva was alone at The Nest, I was disturbed, inexplicably alert and awake. I kept tossing on my pillow, resigned to a disturbed night of wakefulness.

The crackling of static that indicates that someone is fidgeting with the button of the radio

124

microphone is as ominous as a phone ringing at night.

It started suddenly but hesitantly, and, although we have many radio sets on the ranch, I thought instantly of Sveva and was immediately awake.

'Who is at the radio?' I whispered in the microphone. 'Who is calling?'

It *was* Sveva. A faint murmur, tainted with fear and urgency.

'Mummy, there are lions. Lions. Close, very close. Help. Send a car quickly. Please help.'

I was out of the bed before she had finished talking, fumbling to get the lighter and light my candle. I grasped the torch, searched wildly for my glasses, dashed for the door, at the same time mumbling into the radio urgent encouragements and reassurances, suggestions of what to do.

'Take your hurricane lamp, ready to throw it if they come in, scare them off at the last moment, plan to startle them, do not panic, do not run. Whatever happens, do not run. It's going to be all right, I'm on my way.'

I was running. My heart beat in my mouth, I could not afford to lose time. I had run that corridor before, in a time of terror. In my nightdress, barefoot, I ran again on the bare stones, wet with night dew, over the wet cold grass, my dogs puzzled around me. I could still hear lion roaring down in the valley. The *askari* caught up with me as I fired the engine of the first car I reached, the large land cruiser we use for going around with the guests. I told him to stay near the radio in case I needed help.

'Simba!' I called out as the car moved off in a swirl of dust. *'Makena, na itua mimi. Simba na-ingia Nyumba ya Mukutan. Unaenda kusaidia.'* It is The One Who Smiles. A lion is getting into the hut on the Mukutan. I am going to help.

My voice sounded shrill, high-pitched, strangled. I was thinking about lions.

Lions are curious creatures, lazy, they fear practically nothing. In Laikipia I saw them countless times, mostly at dusk or returning home to Kuti at night, in my headlights. They stand, undaunted, in the middle of the tracks or beside them. They move away slowly with an easy muscular roll of the powerful shoulders, yellow and tawny, in and out of the undergrowth of sage bush and acacia shrubs. They sit down abruptly, with sudden abandon, attentive but not wary, yawning unhurried, never moving their inscrutable eyes from the car.

They often follow if I slow down, intrigued, unthreatening. But their indolence is never to be mistaken for friendliness, for wild lions are unpredictable to say the least. This is what I feared, their curiosity, the potent, careless, deadly playfulness of cats.

Never before were eight kilometres covered in less time. I was racing. Through the shrubs, into potholes, over stones and gullies. Up the hills, down the slopes. Zebra scattered. Then the *lelechwa* thickened, the track turned sharply left where an old twisted olive grew, the narrow trail climbed a rise, descended again: I was there. In the headlights my familiar Nest stood ghostly

126

and grey like Dracula's castle in a Gothic tale. The wind blew sinister, sending shivers through the bleached wild sage. The night behind it held dangers and nameless threats. Where was my baby?

I hooted, frantically, with every blast of the horn scaring off my monsters. Sveva emerged tousled, frightened but intact, folding her sleeping-bag about her, holding out a tremulous hurricane lamp which looked so diminutive that, on second thought, no lion could possibly have been deterred by it.

She had, characteristically, recovered.

'So sorry, Mummy. It was horrible. He was so close I could have touched him. I didn't know what to do.' She gave me a half Makena-smile.

'How did you make it so quickly?'

She shook her hair. In her Paolo-blue eyes I noticed a sudden glint.

'But don't make so much noise. You'll scare the rhino.' I knew she was fine.

Memories gather in the night more easily, associations come naturally. It was when I was crossing the junction to the research camp, with Sveva sleepy in the car, that my thoughts went to another night, well over twenty years ago, more or less on that very same spot.

A story of other lions, in other times.

★ ★ ★

I had left Rocky and Colin Francombe's house — the managers in those days — with Emanuele, my mother and Gordon my dog. It was seven in the evening, dark already. It was the rainy season.

'Let's choose the middle track to Kuti,' I said to Emanuele. 'It is little used, mysterious, and there's more chance of seeing wildlife there.' I looked up at the darkening sky:

'It may rain later. The road shouldn't be too wet.'

In upcountry Africa one lives out of doors, and one notices the quality and the colours of the soil. There are endless varieties, and in Laikipia one could find samples of most of them. It is the yellow sandy dust of the savannah, or the marvellous grainy orange murram of the Niuykundu Dam; the fat, almost purple ochre of *mlima ndongo*; the brown forest earth of Enghelesha, fertile with humus; the grey volcanic gravel of the northern plains, and the light orange or white powder leading to Mawe ya Paulo, which penetrates everywhere, covering the leaves at the roadside with a sticky film. And, of course, the feared black cotton soil of *damu ya tope* and *maji ya faru*, which a shower of rain transforms into a messy glue which clings to shoes and feet and tyres until one gets hopelessly stuck.

There was a humidity in the air, a feeling of impending clouds, but the night was still clear enough after the day's downpour.

A buffalo crossed the track a few metres ahead, head high, wet muzzle towards us, and stood there watching us unafraid. I slowed down to avoid him.

'A big male. I must tell Paolo.'

128

His hind legs were encrusted with mud. The grey horns spread wide, heavy, worn in the middle with deep ridges, a sign of age. When the car was a few inches from him, almost touching his hide, he shook his head and turned on his hooves with the unexpected, lethal agility of old buffalo. In seconds he was gone through the *lelechwa*, splashing long spurts of brown mud.

The bottom of the ditch was flooded, and by now my car was too slow to negotiate the rise. Even in a four-wheel drive I felt the tyres struggling to grip the slippery bottom, skidding, burying deeper into the sticking clay at each burst of accelerator. It did not take me more than a few seconds to realize I could not get out until it dried out.

I went through the usual moves. Low ratio, reverse; I got out, wading in the mud and, helped by the others, put branches beneath the wheels; I tried again a few times but I was hopelessly stuck.

The light was fading fast. We had no radio. I quickly realized that Paolo, believing that we were having a drink with Colin and Rocky, would not think of looking for us for at least a couple of hours. Often Rocky would ask us to stay on for a bowl of soup and a glass of sherry and I would accept. Her cook Atipa boasted an endless repertoire of excellent soups, and I liked their company. Paolo would think we were having a good time. He might join us later. Only then would he realize that something had happened. In those days we had no internal radio network — and no way to communicate.

I looked up at the sky which was already dark, but with a luminescence at the horizon edge; I remembered that there would be an almost full moon tonight. The moon would rise in an hour, and even with the clouds there would be enough light to see my way back to Kuti. I would go with Gordon.

'I'm going to walk home; it's six kilometres from here to Kuti, I know my way; you stay where you are, keep each other company; I'll be back with Paolo in less than two hours. It will be fine. Cosy in the car.'

My words fell into silence. My mother looked at me, then at Emanuele. Nine years old, he was in Laikipia for half-term. He faced me, looking me straight in the eye, and even in the dark I sensed his determination.

'You are not going alone. I'm coming with you. Nonna can stay here.'

'If you go, I'm coming too.'

My mother sounded adamant. This was Africa after dark, a place full of wildlife. Perhaps she did not realize the danger or perhaps she did, only too well. My academic mother, used to museums and libraries, university lectures and hours writing at her desk in Venice. She did not want to miss out and had to be part of the adventure. If there was danger to face, she wanted to share it with us. I looked at her with new respect.

I argued for a few moments, but knew that I could not convince them to stay if they chose not to. Finally I surrendered. There was no time to lose.

'I will go ahead. You follow. Do not talk, do not make any noise. Stop if I stop. If anything comes too close don't run.' I looked at my mother's shoes and repeated: 'More than anything, do not run. Be quiet. Be still.'

I slid a pullover over my head. It would be cold. I nodded at Ema and moved on.

We were lighthearted to begin with, elated by the absurdity of the adventure. Gordon went ahead, sniffing, his tail erect like a banner. He turned to check on me now and again, came back to be patted on the nose, ran off again. Unlike the mad runs of our daytime walks, he kept close to us. We could still vaguely distinguish the silhouettes of the trees and the hills.

But I could sense my mother's justified concern and Emanuele's excitement. I felt the responsibility, and a mixture of comfort at not being alone and worry at having to plan for three of us, should we have an encounter with something large and unfriendly.

The inhabitants of the night were about.

It is amazing how the silence of the night in Africa becomes quickly animated with presences and noises, as everywhere creatures wake up and take over; from the valleys they come, from the thickets of euclea and rhus, from the crags, the savannah and the plains. Around and ahead and behind us we become aware of creatures moving. And yet, in their presence they are silent, betrayed only by a deep breathing, a stomach gurgle, the swish of leaves opening and closing as a large shape passes through. Sometimes it is the

131

elephant: a snapped branch falling, splintered by a strong proboscis. A far-away hyena, crying to the moon from the hills; a whining jackal's chorus, a lion's roar, the see-saw of the leopard; but mostly it is the tree frogs and the crickets and unknown insects singing incessantly in the background; and starlings when the moon is full.

So I walked, listening to the familiar sounds of the African night.

Sound of steps on cracking twigs. A disturbed guinea fowl getting excited in a burst of protest.

We followed the narrow road, little more than a track. I could just make it out. In places the bush on either side was impenetrable and too close for comfort. Then the bush opened out and I noticed a change in Gordon. He stopped abruptly in front of me, a paw in the air, ears pricked, listening; his nose had caught a scent; a low growl formed in his throat, and I stopped in my tracks; Emanuele and my mother stopped with me. Gordon moved his head to one side, still growling, as if he could see and smell what we could not. Then the scent was caught by a breeze and Gordon relaxed and moved again ahead. We followed warily.

I heard sounds of buffalo ahead, a large herd grazing; the distinct noise of many mouths crunching on strawy grass filled the darkness, belching and shuffling, stones rolling under heavy hooves, a warmth of many bodies and green manure. They blocked the way ahead and stretched in all directions. They surrounded us. Gordon took charge. He struck a pointing pose, rigid, and attacked the darkness.

We all stopped, braced for a stampede, which happened, blissfully, in the opposite direction. The night became rocks rolling, shrubs crashing, loud mooing and running buffalo. Soon only their warm, acrid smell remained.

At Kati Kati tank there were elephant drinking. I had anticipated this, and the danger of unknowingly cutting across the path of a heard of elephant or buffalo going to drink. Gordon was silent and circumspect, cautiously moving ahead. I knew the wind was on our side. We managed to move on unnoticed.

There were about two and a half kilometres to go; I felt relieved; but Gordon's behaviour had changed again; he did not walk ahead any more; he stayed close to my legs, as trained dogs do, a strange show of politeness; when I touched his head a few times I felt his tension and the hair stiffly risen on his back, like a hyena.

The night seemed much more silent than before; I could hear our steps magnified in this silence and felt exposed, very vulnerable, three generations of my family returning in the dark to our home in Africa.

Even the frogs and crickets had lost their voice. I found mine. To disperse the eerie feeling, I chose to break the rules. I started singing.

It was a song of snow and marching soldiers on desert sands and mountain tops, a song I had learned from my father as a child and that Emanuele had loved years ago, when I sang it to him as a lullaby. Soon he joined me.

Lungo le dune del deserto infinito,
lungo le sponde accarezzate dal mar,
oh quante volte insieme a te ho camminato,
senza riposar.[1]

My mother, now beyond bewilderment, sang with us too. A strange procession.

Finally we reached the spray race at Kuti and the familiar *menanda* looked ghostly in the moonlight; there were a few impala there. Startled at our appearance and uncertain whether to jump, they stood, fawn coloured and handsome, long-lashed beauties. Then suddenly they leaped high and fled into the night.

We entered the garden from the northern gate, and the other dogs ran to meet us, barking their welcome in a flurry of tails. We were safe.

Paolo, as expected, was reading in a room full of music, drinking his whisky on the rocks, and smoking like every night. When we came in, it took him a few moments to notice that we were covered in mud, still unchanged for dinner, with an air of excitement, like people who have just run a race and reached a goal. We told him the story and he laughed in approval. He would have done the same; he expected no less from me.

'Any encounters?' I told him of the buffalo, of the elephant. Of Gordon's sudden meekness, the silence of the night . . . he raised a brow, did not comment.

---

[1] 'Along the dunes of the infinite desert/along the shores caressed by the sea/oh how often have I marched with you/without a pause of rest.'

Next morning before breakfast he came towards me grinning. He took my hand and guided me out of the garden, along the path we had taken. There, very distinguishable in the drying clay, were our three tracks, my large ones, Emanuele's child feet, my mother's small prints; Gordon's paw marks following close to mine. And a few steps behind us, neat, all along the way, coming from a shrubbery after the middle tank, the rounded pug-prints of two very large lions.

'They followed you all the way, up to our gate.'

The tracks continued alone towards the bush.

Part Two

Only Dust, at Arba Jahan

*For Aidan, and to the memory
of Osman and of Ibrahim Ahmed*

Oh, I could live with thee in the wilderness
Where human foot hath never won a way;
With thee, my city and my solitude
Light of my night, sweet rest
from cares of day.

SIR RICHARD BURTON,
Wandering in West Africa

Return to Moyale

Our camels sniff the evening, and are glad.

FLETCHER, *The Golden Road to Samarkand*

The airplane circled low over the tin roofs of the small frontier town built in Arabic style, headed towards the airstrip, and landed in a cloud of dust, hardly disturbing the camels. They looked up from the thorn-shrubs they had been browsing, totally unaffected. I noted how very white they were, like ghosts of camels.

It was a morning of September 1997. We had come to Moyale, in the extreme north of Kenya, on the frontier with Ethiopia. I was curious to return, for happy and poignant memories tied me to this remote and god-forsaken land.

★ ★ ★

The first time I visited Moyale was with Aidan, in 1990, in preparation for a camel trek. The purpose had been to make arrangements to purchase, and, the following year, to bring a herd of breeding Somali camels to the Laikipia region.

The itinerary would cover just over 300 miles across Kenya's Northern Frontier district, from Moyale to a place called Lolokwe in Samburu district, next to the *lugga* of Il baa Okut, and

139

eventually to Ol Penguan, Aidan's ranch in the savannah of the western Laikipia plateau.

For the first 200 miles, until the wells of Koiya, there would be no water. To take advantage of the cooler temperature of the night, the march was planned around the time of the full moon in September 1991. There were reasons for such a feat of endurance.

Aidan's passion for and understanding of camels was deep rooted. The original African livestock, adapted to the harshest conditions, to desolate places with scarce water, sparse forage and scorching heat, camels are far kinder to the ecology of the land than cattle. Their soft, padded feet do not erode the soil; they browse discriminately from tall shrubs beyond the reach of goats, thus never overgrazing the meagre pasture of Africa's most arid regions. Their dense, slightly sour milk is extremely nutritious and constitutes the largest part of the diet of most of the nomadic tribes of northern Kenya, whose lives completely depend on these animals. Unlike cattle, camels do not need to drink daily; they cover vast distances effortlessly, carry loads and are immensely adaptable.

It is clearly desirable to introduce camels in areas of Africa where they are not indigenous, but where conditions are suitable, as an environmentally friendly alternative to conventional livestock. They are also an attractive and decorative substitute for horses for tourist treks.

But a true passion is seldom born of reasoning; what most appealed to Aidan's noble, nomadic soul was the romantic aura surrounding these haughty, stately creatures, 'the ships of the desert', dignified, aristocratic, resilient, indispensable companions to any explorer of the Africa Unknown.

Another of Aidan's deep interests was collecting rare and often undescribed plant specimens, particularly bizarre subspecies of succulents like euphorbia, caraluma, aloe or aechinopsis, which still grow undiscovered in isolated, almost inaccessible gorges and peaks, weeks away from any beaten track. Most of his botanical expeditions would have been impossible without his camels.

When breeding livestock it is essential to periodically introduce new blood. This was the main reason for the scheme. The other one was, of course, the challenge of the difficulty, the beauty of the land, the danger of going through uncharted territory with just the basic essentials.

Purchasing dozens of camels, and in such a remote location, is a complex operation that cannot be accomplished in a few days, and much thought and planning went into organizing the expedition. Aidan was familiar with the procedure and knew the people without whom such a plan would have been impossible.

So I flew to Moyale with him, to meet his friend Haji Roba, an old dignitary quite prominent in that small Muslim community and a crucial figure in his plan. He would be entrusted with a substantial amount of cash. He would keep it in his rusty old safe, in the back room, cool with thick, whitewashed walls, separated from his front parlour by a yellow muslin curtain embroidered with red roses. He would hand out money over the following weeks and months to Aidan's man Ibrahim Mohamed, who was already on his way by road and would be based in Moyale for however long it would take to purchase a hundred camels.

Camels were brought to the market in Moyale from across the border, tall Ethiopian camels of illustrious breeding, the females good for milking, the males bred to walk tirelessly and carry loads. One day there would be five, another perhaps ten, and some other day none at all good enough to be purchased. They would be bought after long bargaining — the dealers sitting on mats strewn on the dusty gravel in the shade of an old tamarind, next to the *sokho* and not far from the mosque, just out of reach of the omnipresent goats — after drinking endless cups of tea with cardamom and comforting glasses of smoky-sweet *susha* curd.

It would be a man's world, in Muslim tradition, a world of business and trade, of caravans and mules, and talk of *shiftah*.

Shiftah.

Shiftah is the Somali name for 'bandits'. They are highwaymen belonging to various ethnic clans, who continuously encroach from Ethiopia and Somalia to raid the borders of Kenya. They take advantage of the mountainous territory, inaccessible to administration, where they can easily disappear and escape capture.

Not a day would go by without *shiftah*-related incidents being reported: sometimes it would be only stealing a mob of camels, never without a lot of shooting, but in most cases there were serious casualties.

Shiftah would kill for livestock, but also for clothes, for shoes, for a watch, for the sake of killing. *Shiftah* were wild, brutal, unpredictable, and without mercy; often high on local drugs, they would raid *manyattas*, beat and rape women, slaughter children. They were not brave and gallant warriors, but bands of desperados with no honour, who, strong in numbers and weapons — they never attacked alone — would pounce on a solitary traveller and cut his throat for a few shillings' loot, or just because he belonged to the wrong clan. They would gallop in on fast horses, shouting and spraying bullets. *Shiftah* were no joke, and the only way to win was to stay clear of them.

Vehicles were no longer allowed to go on the murram road from Isiolo to Moyale without an armed police escort.

I remembered that first day in Moyale, and the secluded courtyard of our host, his lavish, generous hospitality, the shy beautiful little girl in the purple veil — his younger daughter, whose name was Rehema — slim and charming, with liquid, intelligent eyes, still little more than a child, who held a copy of the Koran, written in Arabic. She greeted me first by kissing my hand, then she moved to Aidan and lowered her head so that he could place his hand in sign of blessing; and when he did, she turned gently and gracefully kissed his hand before running back to the dark doorway, amongst the other scuttling small children. I noticed that now and again she raised her hand to her ear, twisting her neck, as if in pain.

To enter Haji Roba's house we climbed tall steps. In the shady room, we were greeted by some of his elder sons and, amid exclamations of welcome and commiseration for our long journey, made to sit on a long sofa upholstered in brown synthetic leather, before which was a coffee table covered in lace and adorned with a colourful arrangement of plastic flowers. From a charcoal brazier a pleasant resinous smoke of incense rose to the pale blue ceiling.

Soon the room was filled with other young men, other sons, and finally Mumina, his second wife, who was pregnant again, peeped from the door.

In the room with yellow cotton curtains, bright with bead-embroidered flowers, I waited for the time to pass, while the men spoke of their business.

Then it was time for breakfast — although it was more like lunch-time — and they showed me to a Turkish-type toilet built next to the kitchen where the women, squatting on the beaten earth floor, were deftly cooking delicious-smelling food on a small fire over three stones and singing.

A basin was brought, and a towel and a piece of soap, and we all washed our hands. Then platter after platter of food came, enamel dishes heaped with rice and goat stew and roast goat and goat entrails fried with onion; and *chapati* and lentils and banana fritters and sour camel milk with sugar and cardamom.

144

Ravenous, intrigued by foreign flavours, I ate more than I should have. Then Mumina came in and shyly embraced me, kissing me twice as is customary amongst Muslim women friends, and offered me a parcel, in which a fine Somali shawl was wrapped, red and yellow and white, woven of a very fine muslin. I draped it around my head and made a mental note to send back a present as soon as I could.

Haji Roba had organized for us to go into Ethiopia later for lunch, to meet a man who had heard of our arrival and wanted to meet Aidan. We boarded a rickety old Land-rover, borrowed from some merchant neighbour, and crossed the border without passport or any other document.

Everyone seemed to know Haji Roba; they waved at him from the side of the road and, to my amazement, quite a few people in that unfamiliar land greeted Aidan like an old friend.

We drove to a dilapidated hotel, squalidly decorated with rickety, cheap furniture, where we sat waiting for the man. He was the local government representative, a type of warlord, quite high up in the country official politics. His name was Godana.

I looked at the hotel with curiosity since it was here, seven years earlier, that Aidan had been kept prisoner for a month, when, on a botanical expedition for the herbarium, having been dropped alone in the middle of nowhere by an airplane, he had been found by the local Garreh troops. Wandering the countryside with maps and compass in his rucksack, but no documents, he had been mistaken, with some logic, for a spy:

no one could quite believe that all he wanted was to climb some unexplored mountain and collect rare plant specimens. *Wasungu* are all crazy.

Barely sustained by a monotonous diet of overcooked spaghetti of infamous quality, grainy coffee (dubious inheritance of Italian colonial days) and small bananas from a nearby grove, he was left there to ponder on his destiny, the door guarded by a sentinel who went with him even to the loo, until his rescue was organized.

Finally, the Ethiopian man arrived; with him came a polite, shy youth with eager eyes and sleeked-back hair, his son, Wako. So it transpired that university in the States was the young man's dream, an impossible dream, like journeying to a distant galaxy and we were the one bridge to that unknown. Feeling strongly for the boy, in subsequent months I did all I could to help. Years later the phone rang in Nairobi from the States, and there was Wako's jubilant voice, from far away, he who had made it after all.

★ ★ ★

We returned, making plans for the journey. Once the camels were purchased, we would fly in with Aidan's brother-in-law's airplane, a large, wonderfully old-fashioned de Havilland Beaver which could carry our bulky load. Our ambitious itinerary was dangerous, for the area was known to be riddled with *shiftah* bandits from Ethiopia. A large caravan with two Europeans would attract much attention, and we would have to avoid all known trails, and the crowded water

146

holes for the first and major part of our trek to avoid being ambushed. The march was planned across dry savannah, deserts, lava stretches and seasonal swamps, with no roads or villages, and reachable only on foot. There would be no way of communicating once we had started our safari. The time of satellite telephones was yet to come. I would bring as comprehensive a first-aid kit as I could, and would hope for the best. With no refrigeration, there was no point in taking snake serum.

We would carry all the water we needed for drinking and cooking; we would wash only after reaching the wells of Koiya. Aidan would bring his rifle and the best camel men from his ranch: the two Ahmeds, distinguished with the nick-names of Nyukundu (red) and Nyeusi (black). I would bring two of my security rangers, with their guns, for protection. I would choose one who could speak the Adjuran language. We would employ some more camel handlers in Moyale.

Their leader would be Osman.

I heard that day, for the first time, his amazing story.

The Story of Osman

But one man loved the pilgrim soul in you,
And loved the sorrows of your changing face.

W. B. YEATS, *When You Are Old*

There was a little man who looked after camels, and his name was Osman Nguyu Dupa.

He was of slight build, with frail, bird-like bones but knobbly knees and large feet, like the animals he tended. He wore a long, cotton checkered *kikoi* and a loose turban, tied a few times around his grey hair, in the Boran style. He came from the Northern Frontier, close to Ethiopia, the land of sands and deserts, of lava rocks and unforgiving sun. His skin was dark and shiny, stretched over wide and prominent cheekbones on a haggard thin face with chiselled features, like the naïve black Christs painted on Coptic icons. His eyes were bright, mobile, used to scanning elusive horizons of trembling mirages for a sign of water, which means life; of endless dunes, for a sudden movement which may mean *shiftah*, and death.

His existence was of a biblical simplicity, timed to the camels' life and to their needs. Sunrise and sunset prayers began and ended every one of his days. He looked after the camels with brisk efficiency, singing to them, calling and herding them with his camel stick, walking

148

tirelessly amongst them, behind them and ahead of them, by the end of the day covering easily ten times more miles than they had. He worked for Aidan as his head camel herdman.

Over the years they had shared many adventures. Safaris in the northern lands, walking for months through unexplored territories. They had shared star-studded skies in windy nights around the same campfire, and drunk from the same wells. Together they had risked their lives. Discovered once wandering illegally well into Ethiopia with their camels, Osman and Aidan had been taken prisoners by a local Garreh tribe, and held in their *manyatta* as spies. The local Ethiopian garrison, alerted by a runner, reached them on foot days later. After a summary trial under the scanty shade of the sparse thorn trees, they were finally freed. Small things, nuances, were responsible for their release: the women, maintained Aidan, had been instrumental in such leniency, appreciative of Aidan's help in lending the camels to help them carry their water from miles away; the men's curiosity about Aidan's rifle, and their gratitude for the penicillin he offered to cure the rampant venereal diseases.

A deep mutual respect had grown over the years between Osman and Aidan, rooted in the common love and understanding of camels, the invaluable creatures without which no desert can be crossed on foot.

It was therefore with great dismay that Aidan realized one day that something was very wrong with Osman. He could not touch food, complained of a terrible pain in his stomach and seemed to lose weight almost by the minute. Finally, when he was reduced to a light bundle of skin and bones, Aidan had carried him in his arms to his airplane, and had flown him off to the Italian missionary doctors at the hospital in Wamba.

Wamba is in the territory of the Samburu, a landmark of eroded dry red earth scorched for miles around this extraordinary hospital in the middle of nowhere, where dedicated doctors minister daily to all imaginable diseases.

In the X-ray slide, an ugly, opaque mass occupied most of Osman's stomach. The tests confirmed that a malignant cancer in its final stages had expanded to extreme conditions, and that operating would be impossible. The kindest thing was for Osman to go back to his family and die there in peace.

One sunny morning, in a deep blue sky, Aidan flew him off to faraway Moyale, a corpse almost, and left him there in the shade of one of the rare thorn trees, his wife and children gathered around him in a silent circle, mourning already the inevitable loss. Alone over lava deserts, flying the long hours back to his ranch, Aidan felt with a heavy heart that he had seen the last of Osman.

Then, soon afterwards, Aidan heard news of a famous faith-healer who came periodically to visit terminally ill people in Gilgil, and of the amazing results of his ministrations.

In this land of the inexplicable, where most believe in magic, and where anything can happen, Aidan decided to give his old friend another chance. He booked an appointment,

150

jumped into his plane, flew three hours due north, located the camel camp and Osman's *boma* from the air, circled twice and landed on the track in a cloud of white dust. Then, leaving behind a small bewildered crowd of people, camels and goats looking up in amazement from the remote strip of sand, he brought Osman in hope and glory back to Gilgil.

Again, he carried in his strong good arms his dying friend wrapped in a threadbare blanket.

It was a quiet, pleasant room with a few stools, a house plant or two, a table with a jug of milk, a pot of tea and some pink sugar-coated cake set on a tray. In the middle were placed a bench and a narrow bed. And there he laid him gently.

For many of the Africans, still unpolluted by western complexities, quaintly coexist, without conflicting, a total respect for their tribal witchcraft, and an almost unlimited faith in the capacity of European medicine to achieve the impossible.

Moreover Osman was a Muslim, a man of God, and there was in him a complete belief in Aidan's omnipotence: his companion of many adventures, the man who walked alone, who knew camels and could shoot straight, the kind, serious giant who was known to master the bird of metal with unparalleled skill, and had appeared from nowhere in the merciless northern sky to save him, was surrounded in people's tales, and in his heart, by an ineffable mystique. It was perfectly easy for him to accept that Aidan and the healer of the *musungu* God by the white hands would help him where everything else seemed to have failed. And it is on unquestioning trust and confidence that faith-healing is based.

They calmly explained to Osman what would happen. The doctor would put his hands on Osman's stomach, gently probing the swollen mass. Perhaps some heat would be felt. Perhaps nothing. Perhaps, if God was looking, the pain would ease, the evil ball would dissolve and Osman, if God wanted, would survive. *Inshallah.*

He was so weak that he was past caring. For weeks now his only food had been a few sips of camel milk, swallowed with difficulty. For months his constant companion had been an agony of pain. He had come to wish for an end to his misery, whatever this end might be. Death, the great forgiver, shrouded in white veils, would have been merciful. He closed his eyes, exhausted, dizzy with throbbing pain, ready for miracles.

The healing hands lightly touched Osman's tummy and a dry heat radiated all through it. How long it lasted he could not tell later; perhaps half an hour? But when the holy hands were lifted and the weary doctor wiped his forehead, Osman opened his eyes. He looked up and around, scanning the room with a new interest, focused hungrily on the dish of tea and the pink cake, pointed a bony finger and looked at Aidan.

'*Chai. Mimi nataka chai na sukari minghi. Na kipande ya keki, kubwa sana. Kwisha pona. Mimi ni sawa sasa. Allah Akbar.*' Tea. I want a

152

cup of tea with lots of sugar; and a big piece of cake. I am cured. Allah is great.

He spoke with no surprise, accepting the inevitability of the miracle, Aidan's power, and the doctor's magic all at once.

The conventional doctors in Wamba were disconcerted. The foul cancer mass was no longer visible. The X-rays were clear. Incredible as that might be, Osman had completely recovered.

They flew back to Moyale once more, this strange couple, the tall silent man in shorts and the small African in his *shuka*, landing again in the dust of the livestock trail. Again the children ran towards the shadow of the airplane, and, huddled together around the veiled tall woman who was their mother, waited in anxious silence for the plane to come to a halt skidding in the dust.

Even the cicadas had stopped singing.

The door opened, and in that silence Osman jumped out alone.

A collective intake of breath ran through the small crowd like the shiver of a sudden wind. Then the joyous whining began, the suffocated giggles, the lilting sing-song, the querulous talking all together.

'Get your strength back,' said Aidan in his farewell, 'and when you are fit again I'll send for you, and you must be ready. We will buy new tall Dogadia and Adjuran camels at the market in Moyale, and when we have enough I will return. You will come back with me to herd them. We'll walk them back together.'

As it happened, I walked them back too.

The Story of the Abagatha

He was a man, take him for all in all,
I shall not look upon his like again.

SHAKESPEARE, *Hamlet*

The pilot nodded to me and to John Wachira, the doctor from A M R E F[1] with whom I was coming to visit the hospital.

'Here we are. I'll pick you up on Monday.'

So there I was, back in Moyale, looking forward to the adventure. A different type of adventure from the last time I was here. I had agreed to help the Flying Doctors of Africa to raise awareness for their Outreach programme, and this was a fact-finding mission to familiarize myself with what was happening in the remote corners of Kenya where they fly in regularly to administer all types of specialized surgery and medical care, a daring, complex, romantic and desperately needed undertaking. I would write a story for them. I would stay in a hotel in the Ethiopian part of the town, and spend the day at the hospital, where a room had been set apart for me, so that I could write in peace.

★　★　★

---

[1] African Medical Research Foundation.

154

I stepped out of the plane and blinked in the harsh sunlight. The airstrip stretched dusty and unvisited; a shredded wind-sock hung limp for lack of any breeze. A few long-robed women, their heads covered in bright veils, stood on one side. Children came running, materializing from everywhere and nowhere. A Land-rover approached and people got out to greet us. Amongst them, I recognized Haji Roba. Tall and distinguished, a white Muslim cap on his head, khaki trousers, a coat and his stick. He came towards me smiling, holding my proffered hand in both of his, exuding genuine pleasure to see me. Having heard of my arrival, he wanted to find out if there was anything I needed. He asked me to go and have breakfast at his house next day, see again his wife, his children.

We drove off.

The town was as busy and dusty as I remembered, crowded with people moving in all directions and talking in excited, gesticulating groups. Slender ladies, clad in bracelets and muslin veils of red and blue and white, moved around, effortlessly balancing large bundles and enormous gourds on their heads. Goats foraged on heaps of old cabbage. Donkeys dozed wearily in the sun, and tall camels, tended by noisy leaders, ambled to the *sokho* carrying loads of merchandise from the Ethiopian side of the town. Dressed in flowing *kikois*, their bearded heads wrapped in *shammahs*, dignitaries conferred below the tamarind trees. The hot, still air smelled of dust and spices.

My return to Moyale was studded with novelty

and unforgettable incidents, glimmers of another simpler and ancient world. I shall remember the hospital where young, bright Doctor Mohamed attended to a hundred horrific emergencies with calm simplicity; the hopeful patients crowding the corridors like biblical figures in their casually elegant robes. The hotel where I slept in the Ethiopian town, a paw paw tree growing just outside my door, and huge cockroaches hiding under my bed. The eyes of the bossy little girl in charge of the shop where I purchased an embroidered white *shuka*, her sudden disarming smile when she said farewell in Italian. The young beggar with the gangrenous leg. The smell of the first sudden shower of rain on the dust, and the colourful market where, after much bargaining, I bought Sveva a red shawl. The woman pounding coffee grains with a long stick in a wooden pot, singing. The flavour of *gored gored*, the spiced stews, served in an array of *sufurias* set on the hospital floor outside the theatre at lunch time, when I joined the weary surgeon for a short break between operations. The muezzin's song from the mosque, merging with the prayers of the Coptic priest from the orthodox church.

But, mostly, the brief encounter with the Abagatha of the Borana, and the story of the *muganga* who cured Rehema.

Haji Roba disclosed that there was great anticipation amongst the Boran clan — a major proportion of the town's inhabitants — as news had come of the visit next day of their Abagatha. The Abagatha is the Boran's traditional leader, something between a tribal king and an elected president, and the highest authority of this noble tribe. He was sick, had heard of the flying doctor who had come to Moyale, and was being driven three hundred miles from their tribal domains to come and see him.

'Being driven?'

'Yes, the Ethiopian Government will give him a car,' revealed Haji Roba. 'The Abagatha of the Boran does not have his own vehicle. Boran ride horses.'

He explained to me about the Boran clan, to which he belonged. It is the largest Ethiopian clan, with several millions of people. They stretch from Ethiopia to Kenya and though they are citizens of the countries where they live, their ultimate loyalty is to their clan leader, the Abagatha. They follow their tribal law strictly, a fact acknowledged since the times of the British Colony, and accepted by the governments of the two countries.

The Borana are generally peaceful, but immensely powerful. Their traditions are deeply rooted. Their Abagatha is chosen from one of the families which have already produced other Abagatha, usually but not necessarily when still a child. He undergoes a complex education in their law, customs and secret, sacred ceremonies. He is recognized as the religious and political leader at the same time. He will be the Abagatha for eight years, when another trained youth will take his place.

Although most of them are now Muslim, traditionally Borana are neither Muslim nor

157

Christian. They pray to God in the morning and to God in the evening, and have their rituals, but no specific place of worship. They can take as many wives as they choose. They are horsemen, warriors, livestock people, brave, gallant. Their Abagatha moves from camp to camp and so gets close to his tribe and their problems. His word is law, but he is known to be fair. He travels around with a retinue of advisers.

Naturally I was intrigued and extremely eager to meet this charismatic and mysterious character.

When we arrived at the hospital on the second day I knew instantly that the Abagatha was already there. An official-looking Land-rover with Ethiopian number plates was parked below a dusty palm tree, and groups of people stood expectantly at corners. From the silence and austerity prevailing I imagined that the patient would be a grand, dignified old man.

I was unprepared for the young person in long white robes and sandals, a type of round, rigid turban on his proud, handsome head with chiselled features, adorned by a lustrous beard. Obviously in pain, he sat on a bench and looked up at me searchingly with burning, intelligent black eyes. The ailment appeared to be an old calcified hydatic cyst in his liver, caused by a dangerous local parasite that becomes embedded in the body and grows into grotesque swellings, infiltrating every organ until the patient dies.

The medicines were not available at the hospital, and I offered to get them in Nairobi and dispatch them in the army airplane which

158

brings supplies to Moyale every Wednesday. On learning this, the Abagatha sent an old man to tell me that he wanted to thank me personally. Soon he entered the small office they had given me, followed by all his escort, but without any special ceremony. He sat there on a narrow bench, communicating through an interpreter. He asked where I came from, and what was my occupation; he assumed I was a doctor, too, and looked at my computer with curiosity. On learning I was a farmer, he wanted to know if the rains had been good, if the grass was long and the grazing abundant, my camels fat and my cattle healthy; how many children I had. His penetrating eyes never left my face while the interpreter translated from Borana to Swahili. When he heard of Emanuele's death from snakebite he winced once.

From his concentrated gaze I could see something was puzzling him, and finally the most important question came, and it startled me. He wanted to know about my hair, which is quite long and streaked with blond. He explained that he had never seen hair which looked like a lion's mane before. Was it real hair? He moved a bony hand, its long sensitive fingers adorned by silver rings, to touch a lock on my forehead, and laughed suddenly, with white gleaming teeth like fresh matched almonds. I realized that I was possibly the first white woman he had ever seen, and certainly spoken to.

So it was that I was invited by the Abagatha of the Borana to be his guest, to stay at his camps, and share his food at his campfire, on the hills over the desert from where they can see the blue plains, where the nights are chilly and the days hot and dry; where they keep hundreds of horses, sleep in tents made of hides and time does not matter. I accepted immediately, of course. We shall decide on a date and this will be, I know, the ultimate adventure and another story to tell.

★ ★ ★

Haji Roba came back later that day as promised, to bring me first to the market — where, fiercely and jovially, he did all the bargaining on my behalf — and then to his house for breakfast.

I had brought a present for his wife Mumina, an ornate golden thermos for her *chai*, incense sticks and a large box of sweets for his children.

In the internal courtyard I met his two new boys, all dressed in their lacy best clothes, who ran to greet me with lowered heads so I could put my hand on them in blessing, and a baby girl of a few months carried by a maid, all born to Mumina in the last six years. Mumina was older, rounder, but still graciously, maturely handsome, and the liquid, kind eyes glinted in welcome as she embraced me.

The house had not changed much. The curtains were now a pale green and the sofa covered with a synthetic type of leopard print. The walls were freshly varnished, deep green and white, and I noticed with surprise that the gold pendulum clock I had donated to one of Mumina's baby boys six years earlier, at the time

160

of the camel trek, was still working, taking pride of place in the middle of a wall.

For breakfast I was served roast and boiled goat, fried rice, *chapati* and *samousas* and a good sponge cake with tea.

Haji Roba sat with me, eating sparsely with his hands, urging me to help myself, and narrating all the news of the past few years, slowly, with a wealth of details.

His adult sons had died. One had been ambushed by *shiftah* on the road to Isiolo. Everyone in the lorry was shot, including the armed escort. The other two were both wiped out during the epidemic of *dengi* fever in 1994.

As he spoke of heart-rending sorrows, of graves dug in the sand amongst the grey salt bushes, guarded by marabou storks, his genial face bore a mask of melancholy, and once again I marvelled at the acceptance of death of the African people.

And what became of Rehema? I had a vivid memory of the beautiful little girl who had served our food and could read the Koran, clearly a favourite child.

His face lit up and the wrinkles disappeared. Rehema was at a boarding school in Meru. She was doing well with her studies, and she had recovered physically, cured in the most curious of ways of the recurring ailment that had defeated all doctors, a chronic infection in her ear, which — as I would remember — had kept her in agony since childhood. Did I not know the story?

The Story of Rehema

For my part, I have ever believed,
and I know that there are witches.

SIR THOMAS BROWNE, *Oh Altitudo!*

After the last doctor in Nairobi, the Indian specialist at the Aga Khan Hospital, declared that there was nothing he could do to cure Rehema's ear, Haji Roba heard news of a *muganga* from Ethiopia who could heal practically anything.

He was a wild fellow from the tribe of the Surma, uncouth and untamed, with a savage reputation. He lived in primitive conditions in a tent of uncured hides set in the bush, and never wore clothes, an incomprehensible custom for a conservative Muslim.

After much pondering, they finally sent for him, and when Mumina saw this naked man with oiled limbs in her clean parlour, she covered her face with her shawl, and immediately dispatched a servant to buy some clothes for the *muganga* to wear before she could meet him again.

The man took the clothes, spat on the floor, and wrapped them around his dreadlocks in a bulky turban, remaining naked, apart from the tiniest shred of material covering his genitals.

A reluctant, terrified Rehema was eventually brought to the room where the *muganga* crouched in a corner like an animal. He approached her, crawling, breathing noisily like a wild creature. He smelled her body from head to toe, stopping finally at the back of her head, still sniffing. Then he extracted some short sticks from his leather pouch and confirmed his diagnosis by passing them over her head and limbs. When the sticks began to vibrate, seemingly on their own, near her neck, behind her ear, there was no doubt. With a small knife the man made an incision behind Rehema's right ear which was, indeed, the one which hurt. Then he applied his big lips to the incision and started sucking. Poor, petrified Rehema cried and whimpered, trying to struggle away, but, undaunted, the man sucked and sucked, until — lo and behold — two squirming, white, fat worms wriggled out from the incision along with two small cockroaches which the man spat out in triumph, showing them to the revolted audience with a devilish grin.

I was disgusted. Haji Roba went on.

A goat was brought into the yard and slaughtered, her dark blood spilled on the dust like a prayer, and collected in a small gourd cured with ashes. The man smeared the still hot blood on his hair and face, and liberally doused the barely breathing Rehema. She was then, mercifully, sent to bed, where she tossed and cried for a few hours before falling into a fitful sleep, populated by the monsters of her nightmare.

When she woke up she was washed, more blood was smudged all over her head, and the foul man again applied his greedy, obscene lips to her tender neck.

By now the man's mouth had been inspected by the entire family, scrubbed and rinsed with a toothbrush to ensure there could be no trick, until they were satisfied that it was empty. So, when another worm appeared and three more cockroaches were spat out in the basin, everyone caught their breath and prayed to Allah in awe and revulsion. Rehema was again sent to her room to sleep.

When she woke up next morning she was fresh and rested, the earache had gone and it never came back.

Haji Roba asked the *muganga* his price: ten Ethiopian birrs was all he asked, less than one English pound.

The man eventually returned to his wilderness, but not before Mumina's mother, an aunt and an array of sufferers had emerged to be cured. He extracted some hot, wet stones from a deformed foot, and some small snakes from someone's stomach, and disappeared in glory, naked as he had come.

★ ★ ★

Haji Roba adjusted his embroidered cap and smiled his crafty and humorous grin, and I never quite knew if he, a true Muslim, really believed the pagan ritual that he had described.

'*Rehema kwisha pona*,' he beamed, shrugging. Rehema is cured.

And this was all that mattered.

164

★ ★ ★

Haji Roba looked assessingly at me, and asked about the camels we had brought from Moyale in 1991, and how they were. Around my neck I still wore a small leather pouch he had given me all those years ago, which contained a page of the Koran, a priceless amulet to protect me during my travels. He shook his head a few times, shrugging off indulgently our European eccentricity, and told me that he had been quite impressed when he heard that we had actually made it, crossing the deserts on foot, avoiding *shiftah*, in such harsh conditions, because I was a woman, did not look that fit, and that journey was a true hardship and a thing for men only.

★ ★ ★

The camel journey had been a feat of perseverance, with no pauses for leisure, for washing, for resting. But the exhaustion brought by the long marches in the scorching sun; the dust, heat, swollen feet, blisters, sweat, thirst and ticks; the constant watch for predators and rustlers; the fear of losing the way; the fatigue of keeping up with the brisk, unrelenting pace of the camels; the worry for their safety, health and feed; the need to reach the watering wells within the limits of their and our endurance: all this had been tempered and made tolerable by the heady elation of moving through unbelievably beautiful, wild and unvisited country, and for me, by the awareness that such a rare and unrepeatable

165

adventure was the fulfilment of a long cherished dream. I had, in my early twenties, been crippled in a tragic car accident. An invalid for a few years, unable to walk without crutches, I had dreamed of being able to march on healthy legs over the African savannah.

It had seemed impossible. It was happening now.

I wrote a diary of the trek every day, either at night by the light of the campfire or when we outspanned in the heat of the day beneath sparse, skeletal shades. It was an exercise book bound in black cardboard, with curled up pages discoloured by sun and rain, in which I wrote in pencil.

It was still fresh in my memory. Before returning to Moyale with the flying doctors I had read again the account of that glorious, unforgettable journey, my journal of 1991.

And here it is.

But was there only dust, at Arba Jahan?

The Camel Trek

Where my caravan has rested
Flowers I leave you on the grass.

EDWARD TESCHEMACHER,
Where my caravan has rested

*Journal of a camel trek from Moyale to Lolokwe,
via Il baa Okut: September/October 1991* with:
Osman Nguyu Dupa, Ibrahim Mohamed, Ahmed Salat
(Nyukundu), Ahmed Ibrahim Adan (Nyeusi), Mamhood,
Gedi, Ibrahim Ahmed, Lwokignei Meto

Dololo Nure, 19 September 1991
Fujiyanyota — Dololo Chaka

The De Havilland Beaver flown by Tony Dyer
landed at Kuti yesterday, at about 9.30 a.m.

We are ready.

Yesterday Aidan flew in late. He was still not
completely well. The virus which has swept
through Kenya and which has affected us both,
has settled in my ear and affected his liver: what
rotten luck. Because of this we had to delay our
departure a couple of days, but we have finally
resolved to go anyway, as everything is ready, our
hearts are set on the adventure ahead, and we
have to take advantage of the full moon.

We packed the night before to have all ready in
the morning. As ever, I have more food than I

167

can fit in the camel boxes. I have to rearrange tins and packets several times before I am satisfied, and much has to be left behind. Shame about the salmon and artichoke hearts, but I manage to smuggle in a chocolate dessert.

★   ★   ★

I bring two of my security rangers with me, a gun each, Ibrahim Ahmed and Lwokignei Meto. The latter is a young Turkana, while Ibrahim is of the Adjuran tribe, as are most of Aidan's camel people, and they know the main language of the areas we shall cross. We are unlikely to encounter anyone, but should we meet people we shall need interpreters.

So we take off on the bright blue morning of 19 September, bound for Moyale and our adventure.

Laikipia looks green from the air, but I know that leafy shrubs, streams and shady glades will soon become memories made of the substance of mirages.

We are bound for the desert.

We fly high over our itinerary: mighty and partially desolate from the air. Chains of mountains and dry *luggas*, open arid plains with not a sign of water, deserts, rocks of lava, the straight lines of abandoned oil-survey tracks, seemingly unending, diminished by a parched horizon of sand, dust and desiccated shrubs apparently empty of all forms of life.

Some ostriches and three oryx are all the animals I spot from the air; camels, a few head of cattle — or perhaps goats — and limitless dunes and barren sands.

Dried out trees like bony skeletons, greyed by the sun.

Haji Roba expects us for lunch: he wants to give us a formal send-off in Muslim style. So I have to dress appropriately, with a skirt to cover my legs, while Aidan wears long trousers which had belonged to his father. I pack away my khakis and wear a new brick-red tricot ensemble, some jewels and a shawl. During the flight, engine oil spills on to me and stains my skirt.

Haji Roba is waiting at the landing strip, composed as ever, with a grin splitting his pleasant Boran face under the Muslim cap. We drive first a few miles in his rattling borrowed Land-rover to take our men and gear to join the rest of the team and the waiting camels.

From a clump of thorny shrubs filmed with white dust in the area where he has been guarding his camels for weeks now, emerges Osman; I have heard his story and I am eager to meet him. He is an exquisite old chap with a slim, wiry body and intelligent, mobile brown eyes. Quite short, but straight, and thin as only Somali can be. He looks fit and sprightly.

It is hard to believe that a few years back, this same man, reduced to a skeleton, was dying of advanced cancer of the stomach. He was cured by a faith healer and in a few days, he was back to look after his camels. The mission doctor, who had, with his own eyes, seen in the X-rays the lacerated remains of the stomach devoured by the spreading cancer, and left the moribund man to a sure grave, was rather shaken when he heard the news.

Otherwise, nobody made much of a fuss about it. As this is Africa where one accepts the inexplicable.

I like Osman instantly. Nimble, on crooked thin legs, he comes forward to shake my hand.

'*Jambo, memsaabu.*' He greets me in a flash of white teeth. I notice, startled, that he has the deep voice of a much taller man.

His liquid eyes scrutinize me attentively and I wonder if I have passed the test. The trek we are about to embark upon is a feat of endurance not really fit for a woman, an immense challenge. Two hundred and eighty miles without any water, in *shiftah* territory. Aidan, a former cripple, and eight men, one of whom is Osman.

Osman. After his amazing recovery, Aidan tells me, Osman bought a new young wife and went off to dig for gold in the Ethiopian hills. He found an insignificant amount of gold after several months and much labour; and when the danger dawned on him that he might be forcibly recruited into fighting the Eritrean insurrection to which he saw many of his companions being taken away in chains, he wisely went back to Moyale and to his camels, his true passion.

'Can you help me?' He points to his head, where I now see a long swollen cut, from which red thick blood is still oozing. He hit it on a sharp stump, trying to restrain a camel when all of them fled, startled by a hyena last night. Apart from two which haven't been seen again, all the camels have been found miraculously, taking

170

advantage of the full moon.

The blood looks startlingly bright and shiny on his close cropped hair, and I minister to him with hemostatic cotton from my first-aid box.

Haji Roba offers us the usual choice of roast and stewed goat, large bowls of steaming rice and meat, dates, *chapati*, bananas in chunks and, to drink, *susha*, the smoky yoghurt made with camel's milk, spices and sugar, cardamom tea and sodas. I choose a Coke, the last one for a long time.

I offer my gift of an ornate gilt clock to Haji Roba's young second wife Mumina, who has just given birth to a son. She embraces me warmly. My daughter Sveva has sent two glittery 'diamond and gold' bracelets to their eldest daughter Rehema, that delightful graceful little woman of a little girl, perhaps ten or eleven, who serves us with immense serious concentration, balancing plates on one hand like a dancer.

Haji Roba offers me his gift: a tiny leather pouch stitched by hand, which contains a page of the Holy Koran, a precious amulet to protect me on my travels; he looks me over pensively, as if trying to work out if I will make it, on foot, through the deserts.

We finally disengage ourselves from our warm hosts, and leave Tony at the Beaver, at the airstrip; it is rather late for his flight back to Timau.

As a parting gift Tony hands me two cartons of sun-dried raisins from his vineyards: the symbol of a European world so far removed from the reality we have chosen. He tips his hat, chivalrous as ever, climbs in and takes off in the dust while I hurry to change behind a malodorous, well-used outdoor loo.

Watching his airplane disappearing in the afternoon sun, I think that the last link with our world has now gone. We are on our own: we can only walk back over that forbidding torrid territory.

★　★　★

Ages before, when I was crippled in hospital, I had dreamed of just this: to be wandering in Africa, through savannah teeming with wildlife, with a romantic figure of a man — who belongs to that Africa — for my guide and companion. My dream of Africa had kept me going, yet I had no reason at all then to imagine that it would materialize.

I met this man when tragedy, upheaval and solitude prevailed; and now, in the ripe midday of my life, my physical wounds healed, but with more scars engraved in my soul, like the story of a surviving tree written with cuts and marks on its scorched bark — I am here, facing the challenge of the unknown.

I look at Aidan: his rugged face burned by many seasons of sun and rain; his noble head with its classic masculine features, his eyes of deep blue, familiar with deserts and mountains, prairies and drifting clouds; his long muscled legs and his slender figure made for effortless walking. He came into my life in days past, he went away and he has come back at my side.

172

That he asked me to join him in this adventure is a great honour to me: not only has he offered to share his solitude: he thinks I can make it.

Flying over the land we plan to walk through, I have some doubts: the landscapes look unforgiving, the distances immense. Will I be able to do it? Do I presume too much? Do I detect a doubt in Tony's eyes? Is the plan too ambitious? Even though my crippled leg healed long ago I am conscious that I have not regained total flexibility in my knee, and there are signs, almost twenty years after the final operation, that my leg is becoming shorter.

Whatever it is, I am taking a risk. I have now no option, and I am determined to try and live up to Aidan's expectations.

It is happening now.

★ ★ ★

I wear my clothes: new 'soft' (I thought! I was wrong) walking shoes, baggy trousers and a khaki shirt.

Our camels are waiting at Fujiyanyota, already laden by an efficient Osman, on whose head the hemostatic cotton has dried the blood, and sticks, startlingly yellow, like the feather of an exotic bird.

I admire the new camels. By the time of the full moon, Ibrahim managed to buy only eighty, not a hundred as we had hoped. Now seventy-eight remain: two escaped, when the hyena scattered them a few nights ago. Nine large impressive males, and a herd of superb looking young heifers, with dignified, graceful bearing, and startlingly white coats. I learn that this is Nature helping them to adapt to the extreme temperature. Darker coats would attract the sun, make the heat unbearable.

We leave Fujiyanyota about 5.30 p.m. Already a feeling of impending night in the reddening sky.

Ibrahim Ahmed cuts me a new camel stick from a special flexible shrub which grows at the side of the track. He de-barks it with easy strokes of his knife, and hands it over with a shy, chivalrous grin. I know that I will come to regard this stick as a friend. A camel stick to put across my shoulders, on which to hang my tiredness, clinging to it with dry hands, delivering to it all the weight of my upper body. A camel stick to love and to cherish.

We march and march, through sandy, parched country dotted with skeletal black bushes, along a deserted track.

Finally, I overtake the group of females.

I prefer walking ahead, with the feeling of choosing my own path, rather than following behind, trying to catch up with an ever advancing herd in the dust.

An hour or so after we start one of the pack camels walking in the rear, alarmed who knows by what infinitesimal disturbance, perhaps not used to carrying a load, bolts, a strap securing his load snaps, and his burden falls off.

The females, startled, go into a frenzied trot. I see them all bearing down on me, heads high, nostrils flaring. The earth trembles under their drumming hooves. Insecure about what is

174

happening, I just dive for the surrounding thickets, to avoid being trampled.

The load is put back, with some labour; all the bundles have been scattered.

We go on and on, still fresh; the sun sets in a blood-red sky behind the spidery shrubs, and it is night. The moon is high, and casts a white-green light on the ghostly shapes.

A pungent, not unpleasant, dry smell of camel in dry country, dung, dust, aromatic plants. Strangely, I think, like the smell of raw tobacco.

Finally, my feet start aching. My knees and joints are painful, numb, unaccustomed to walking for hours without stopping for a moment — camels do not stop.

We walk for five hours without interruption. We outspan finally before a stretch of lava ('*bule*' in Swahili), at Dololo Chaka. The men cut a *boma* of shrubs, built a fire, and we are each given a steamy mug of tea.

My legs feel like wooden posts, and the feet are agony. I fall exhausted on to my camel mattress, on which Aidan has spread a sheepskin. Looking at me with concern, he arranges a heavy blanket over me. I cover my head with a Somali shawl, drenched with aromatic sage oil to help my breathing, and sleep immediately, despite the chattering Somali.

I wake up with a pounding headache to a cold moon overhead. My watch says 1.30 a.m. I swallow two aspirins with water from my tin bottle, and manage to sleep only one hour before rising just after 4 a.m. Aidan is already up, and has gone to rouse the others.

175

20 September 1991
Dololo Chaka — Laga Mudama

We leave just after six. The sky is pink, the air still, heralding a hot day. It takes a long time to load the camels. The morning smells of resin and hidden things.

We walk on and on, following the track, passing a lava stretch and then a plain, then another long stretch of lava rocks. The road is dusty, with many tracks, mostly of hyena, Grant gazelle, giraffe, and many, many very large lion prints. I expect to see a lion any minute.

We outspan at 10 a.m. having walked for four hours. We have covered over twenty-two miles since 5 p.m. the day before — was it only yesterday? — in nine hours altogether.

Not a bad beginning.

Hot, dusty when we stop. So tired. Eat hot consommé, sardines straight from the tin and one orange.

Sleep a bit. Write the first part of my journal.

The place is Dololo Nure, under the hill of Kubi Maradab.

We leave again at 4.30 p.m.

Aidan rides for a time one of the pack camels.

My leg is aching.

We walk for four-and-a-half hours until 9 p.m., and outspan at a *lugga* called Laga Mudama. I eat an orange, drink almost a bottle of water, and sleep immediately, totally knocked out.

Garsa, 21 September 1991
Laga Mudama — Choichuff

Wake at 5 a.m.

Slept very deeply. Headache. I guess I must get used to the heat and to marches without a pause. After my sedentary year at the desk, finishing my book, it will take a while. My leg is hurting. But I HAVE to make it. There is no going back, anyway, and I have dreamed so much of all this.

An orange. Water.

★ ★ ★

On our way at quarter to six in the morning.

Lovely overcast weather. After the first two hours I accept Aidan's suggestion and ride. Tall, tall that camel was. Comfortable, funny, undulating movement: I fall asleep twice. Wake up with a start, afraid of falling from my saddle.

Wonderful country dotted with trees. Cool and windy.

See two giraffe trotting along, Grant gazelle. Guinea fowls and francolins everywhere, but too fast for Aidan to get them.

The idea is to shoot what we want to eat until we reach the dangerous *shiftah* country where a gunshot would advertise our presence. People have been killed up here for less than a watch. Our shoes, even, could cost us our lives.

Aidan walks ahead for four hours, carrying his gun across his shoulder. He looks very tired. The flu we both suffered from has taken its toll on him too.

It rains suddenly, bliss, soaking us to the bone with tiny penetrating needles of water. Letting the warm drops run down my face and licking the rain off my hands. Soaked in a few moments. The clothes dry on me in no time, leaving me refreshed.

* * *

We outspan at 10 a.m. after four hours' march, in a lovely greenish plain with trees, called Garsa, where I can now write my diary: how I would love to have the time to just leave the track, and SEE those trees, explore at leisure, stop in their shade, discover some secret creature and magic corners. Places we shall never again have the chance to pass through, and we cannot really say we have seen them at all, but gazed at them with desire from a distance. There is a pace to poetry, creativity and contemplation, and it must be harmony of body and soul. A restful quiet. A pause.

The slaves who built pyramids wrote no poems.

But I always knew that this was going to be no easy relaxed safari. This is a feat of endurance. Am I good enough, I wonder? I would hate to let Aidan down. He trusts me and has faith in my capacity to walk on for ever and to tolerate hardship. I must live up to his expectation. Damn the blisters.

Eat a heavy oxtail soup with onions made by Osman. Not the best cook this side of the equator, but he tries. Strange how hot food is welcome in the heat. Short vision of a chilled glass of white wine, the glass beaded with droplets, tinkling ice. No, we do not need it and I should not miss it.

Now, Aidan is asleep under an acacia tree.

I am enjoying this, actually. I have already grown to love and appreciate the camels.

The plain of Arba Jahan, 23 September 1991
Choichuff — Baji — Arba Jahan

(I did not write on 22 September; too tired.)

Off again on the afternoon of the 21st.

I walk, Aidan rides to start with. I suspect he does it to please me, so I do not feel that, when I do, I am being weak. He watches me. I know he is concerned about my bad leg.

I walk ahead grinding my teeth. Lovely country, and all the time we are accompanied by a haunting concert of whistling thorns. Eerie noise of the wind through the branches.

A few scattered Grant or Peter's gazelles; a flock of vulturine guinea fowls, necks adorned with blue feathers like lace collars, in the middle of the road track. HUGE lion spoor everywhere, hyena, honey badger, jackals and oryx tracks. An eagle-buzzard, huge, watching me from a dry tree stump; a deep blood-red sunset. Silence.

I walk ahead on the sand, glad to be here, proud of having dared.

Aidan insists that I ride and two hours later I accept.

My camel's name is Racub. A large mellow white Adjuran male. Rough saddle; hard; after the morning ride my legs are tender, my crotch painful. A strong breeze, kind to my burning face.

Curious, watching these patient, resilient camels from the top of one of them. Their strange, attentive eyes, long lashed, scrutinizing the soil they tread on with soft and gentle feet.

And miles of land unvisited and still, around and ahead.

* * *

At dusk we hit a lava patch, which goes on and on.

I have walked from 4 to 6 p.m. and end up riding until 10 p.m., for four hours.

Finally outspan just after this unending lava. We find an old *boma* in the dust, where we set our mattresses, too close to the camels snorting and chewing their cud, and to the people, talking around the fire.

A fierce moon, almost full on my face.

I do not sleep very well, but ravenously eat some delicious Italian tinned meat and pickled onions, welcome delicacy here at the equator.

On 22 September, today, we wake at 4.45 a.m.; still dark. Millions of jewelled stars. Smell of dust, camel dung, heat to come. We manage to leave at ten minutes to six, a record so far. An orange for my breakfast. Bless these oranges for as long as they last. Juicy, fresh, thirst-quenching.

An orange is a luxury, a delight, a treasure to behold.

A lava stretch. Brown-black lava rocks, like burnished bronze, become almost red hot in the noon sun, burning through the soles of our shoes, a torment to the camels. Varied landscapes.

Soon, the round dark stones of lava give way to *acacia tortilis* country, soil of deep brown, with scattered limestone, startlingly white. The feeling of walking on a huge chocolate log studded with hazelnuts and almonds. Wildlife everywhere, and many tracks.

Peter's gazelles.

Two giraffe.

An oryx, like a cave painting.

Lion tracks.

Porcupine tracks, and scattered striped quills which I keep collecting and putting into my pocket, giggling all the way.

★ ★ ★

The resilience of these people.

Gedi and Mamhood, the kind Adjuran camel herders employed in Moyale, are tireless.

Gedi wears a loose, long checkered Somali *kikoi*, turquoise and blue, and a flowing white *shuka* on his shoulder. It is all he owns and he does not seem concerned. He is unconsciously attractive and naturally elegant like a camel or an antelope. The thought strikes me that nothing has changed in the look and clothes they wear, these Somali, since the time when the Three

Kings from the Orient brought gifts of gold, incense and myrrh to the just-born Jesus of Nazareth.

Camel tracks, round, soft and gentle on the sand.

Having marched four and a quarter hours, I agree to ride again for three hours, and at 10 a.m. we outspan in the hottest place, Choichuff, and are instantly assaulted by ticks of all descriptions.

A very hot siesta; flies.

★ ★ ★

Ibrahim Ahmed damaged his nail, caught and crushed it while unloading, hanging red and yellow like a bloodied claw. I treat it to stop him from pulling it out there and then, the definitive solution he is ready to apply. It must be bloody painful as it is. I apply antibiotic cream, and wind a sterile stiff bandage around it to keep off the dirt. A strange sadness in Ibrahim's eyes even when he smiles.

'Ah. *Wewe doktary khabisa!*' (Oh, you are a real doctor), he praises me happily, the pain already seemingly overcome. They all appear impressed by my comprehensive supply of medicine and first aid.

They look good, my two Laikipia men, dressed in identical green shorts and military shirts, with their safari army gear and their guns. I notice that Lwokignei often asks Mamhood to carry his gun, but I prefer to ignore this unorthodoxy: in the middle of nowhere some rules can be relaxed, others must be kept firm.

If anything happened here, a serious wound, a terminal illness, a snake bite, there would be nothing or nobody to appeal to but our resourcefulness. No way of communicating with the rest of the world, and so far we have met not a soul.

★ ★ ★

We leave at 4.15 p.m. on September 22nd, still extremely hot. Aidan rides the first one and a half hours. My pillow is put beneath the saddle, which is now much more comfortable.

Blessed by a breeze.

I ride for three and a half hours, until 10 p.m., when we outspan on a dusty place in an area called Baji, a dry water hole.

Sitting in the dark next to the fire I take off my shoes and, looking at the blisters on my feet and the scratches and cuts that a few days of walking wild have engraved on my body, I think once again how much I have dreamed of this during the long months and years. I massage my leg where the long scars left by several operations remain. Aidan is watching:

'It is amazing that you can walk at all. That Swiss surgeon performed an absolute miracle. What was his name? Ah yes, Professor Müller. He would be proud of you if he could see you now.' He smiles at me. 'You should write to him; thank him; send him a photograph.'

'Professor Muller: I wonder where he is now . . . over twenty years ago . . . he may be dead.'

Aidan pokes the fire, adds a log, stretches comfortably on his mattress. He crosses his hands behind his head and looks up at the sky. His dark blue eyes seem almost black. His resemblance to Paolo strikes me once again.

'Tell me about him. I like to hear your stories.'

Holding a hot mug of soup, gathering a shawl about me, under a sky bejewelled with stars, listening to jackals far away, I close my eyes. From the treasure chest where my past sleeps, a face emerges, images of places long unvisited, train journeys, hospital smells, birds pecking at my window, the impression of a smile over a small moustache, twinkling brown eyes, strong hands, my bandaged leg. Hopes, fears, pain, trust . . . and memories unfold.

★ ★ ★

'Walk. Walk up and down the room.' There was a lilting authority in his strong accent, but kindness in his voice. 'No. Without crutches.'

He removed the long metal sticks I had grown used to regarding as part of my anatomy. I looked at him appealingly: without crutches I felt vulnerable, inadequate.

'Walk.'

I limped like a lame duck, hobbling on the shorter leg, biting my lip in concentration. When I turned, he was frowning. Once more he held the X-rays against the light. He had of course already studied them carefully, before agreeing to see me. Complex cases intrigued him.

I realized that — like a sculptor who dreams of

184

the statue he will mould from a mess of clay, or an architect planning a complex restoration of a damaged building — he knew exactly what he was going to achieve, what problems he could encounter, and how he would deal with them.

I looked at him with total confidence. He was my only remaining hope of ever walking normally again.

Professor Müller, the legendary orthopaedic surgeon in Bern, architect of miracles, was the best surgeon for the sort of fracture I had suffered in the tragic car crash in which Paolo's wife had died; the only one who could reverse the mess of past operations and heavy plasters that had gone wrong, who could repair my shrunken and crooked leg and make me walk again.

He looked at me intently.

'You'll need three, possibly four operations.'

He paused to see the effect his words had on me. I swallowed. After one year of plaster and two painful operations, four more operations, and the time in between, sounded like for ever. Like hell. I had been crippled for over a year now. The thought of more hospitals, exercises, anaesthetics, was unbearable. I said nothing.

He looked at me, cleared his throat.

'It can be done. It will not be easy. It will take time. You must help me. You are too young to be a cripple.'

Too young. I had just turned twenty-six, Emanuele was four years old, and I felt as if I was awakening from a long sleep to the possibility of being an invalid for life.

I simply could not afford not to be able to walk. There was Paolo. There was my dream. I wanted to live in Africa. Only that mattered. If it had to take four more operations, then so be it.

I looked back at him, and I managed to smile. 'Thank you,' was all I could say.

*　*　*

The lights overhead blinded me. I blinked. Already, the wave of numbness induced by the pre-anaesthesia was claiming me. I looked up. The kind, intelligent face smiled down on me. Brown, mobile eyes. The surgeon's mask hid his short dark moustache. He took my hand, squeezed it. I marvelled, vaguely, at the strength of that small hand.

'You will be all right. See?' The lilting Swiss accent in his polished French. He waved a sort of measuring tape. 'Your leg is going to be exactly of the same length as the other.'

The brown eyes twinkled. A needle in my arm.

'*Maintenant, contez avec moi. Jusqu'à six. Un, deux . . .*' I breathed deeply and repeated with him ' *. . . trois, quatre, cinq . . .*' I never said six.

I woke up in my bed, a few hours of my life gone for ever from my consciousness. My leg felt heavy, loaded but not really painful.

My mother, who had come from Italy to help me, looked at me with concern.

'A much longer operation than he thought, he had to combine two in one. Four hours.'

The door of my room opened gently and he

came in. Still dressed in his operating outfit, he marched to my bed. After the formal pomposity of the Italian dons, who arrived escorted by bowing assistants and a retinue of nurses, his simplicity took me by surprise.

'*Ma chère amie . . . ça va?* Stand up and show me how you walk.'

Incredulity, uncertainty, fear of falling. Standing and walking immediately after such an operation seemed impossible. He helped me up, fixed the drain from my wound to the belt of my hospital gown. He held my hand. I stood.

On the grey linoleum floor of that white-and-steel hospital room of the Lindenhof, with a dancing heart one afternoon of late July, I moved the first tentative step of my new life, no longer a cripple, the first step on my way to Africa. It would, one day, be the grassy plains of the savannah, the coral barrier of the Indian Ocean, the Great Rift Valley slopes, and now, the sand of remote deserts, the lava rocks of the North Frontier tracks. I owed much of my life to him. I blessed Professor Muller when I had to run fast from a wild beast, to climb a tree.

★ ★ ★

Professor Muller. I smile at Aidan. An extraordinary man, an inventor and a wizard. I wrote about him in my first book, just to thank him; I doubt if he ever read it. I wonder if he still works, if he is still alive. He seemed to me old then. I don't think I will ever see him again. It was all so long ago.

187

I lie down on my camel mattress, covered with a bed sheet and blanket. The sheet is a luxury which makes all the difference to my aching limbs.

The past is past, and this is my reality.

Far from the noise of the camels and the *boma* — thank you, Aidan — I spend the best night so far.

★ ★ ★

Wake up very early.

We manage to leave by 5.30, a record. Hot and very dusty track. I am determined to walk, the camels make me lazy.

Yesterday I made up many stories for my next book; I find this helps to distract me from the tiredness and weariness of walking in near silence for hours. Yesterday I imagined 'The Bull Shark of Vuma' and 'Fifty Guineas' Pike', and completed 'The Full Moon Island'. Would they ever be written? Am I creating a new book, here in these desert sands?

Today I did 'The story of Nungu Nungu'; as Aidan likes it and suggested I should write it, I shall dedicate it to him. I completed 'Emanuele's Chameleons', and I began in my head 'Only Dust at Arba Jahan'. This last one is prompted by the ever pervading dust. It could be the title of this safari's chronicle.

★ ★ ★

But how gently the camels walk. If they were cattle the cloud of dust from their hooves would be totally unbearable.

Long, long march, as we finally turn due south-west, on the long, unending desert track after Arba Jahan. We have to be careful to avoid the wells. *Shiftah* will be lurking there.

I admire Aidan's proficiency with his old brass compass, how he takes our bearings: it seems impossible that we shall ever get out of here.

We meet today the first man since we left, four days only — but they feel like four months, time has lost its meaning — a friendly camel herder of the Adjuran, sturdy-looking, carrying a curious leaf-pointed spear. He wants to sell us a camel, even on credit.

We outspan at the Arba Jahan plains, a windswept open area dotted with rare trees. Grassy straw. All the camels decide to come and feed from the tree we have chosen for our noon rest, one of two only, and far from each other, in a vast waterless plain. I am now writing here, having changed to a fresh blue caftan, closely observed by ruminating camels.

A blessed breeze: otherwise the heat would be unbearable. A few herds of camels file away in the heat waves and the distance, like mirages, silhouettes in a biblical scene; they must see us as we see them, but they make no move to approach us. They must be heading for the water hole at Arba Jahan, over ten miles due east, which we avoid as we have heard that it may well be dry, and full of desperate livestock, and starving Somali.

They will find only dust, at Arba Jahan.

Our valuable camels and our daring plan must

be kept to ourselves. We do not want to advertise our presence. Ahead is *shiftah* territory.

This tree, a Salvadorensis, underneath which I am writing, is possibly one of the last trees for days. At this time, if he is not too exhausted, Aidan usually takes our bearings with his instruments and compass.

It is an old brass compass which I gave him, found in an antique shop in Nairobi, and which surely has a story of explorations in wild lands. I wonder where it has been and what were the eyes of the man who owned it like? What did he think, how did his voice sound, and was his woman fair?

Now, in the far distance, a ghostly evanescent mountain shape may be Marsabit. Aidan shows me a gaping void in the map, marked with lava symbols, a desert we must cross. I can see he is worried, he asks our people to fetch and load *kuni* on the camels, so that we can light a fire in the day — days? — to come, for our tea and their evening *posho*.

No trees mean no firewood ahead.

Dust, heat, thorns, a seemingly unending old livestock track, and finally the desert, lie beyond.

Just enough water to the wells of Koiya?

24 September 1991
Arba Jahan

We started walking at 4.30 p.m., yesterday afternoon, leaving behind the last yellow-grassed plains of Arba Jahan. Arba Jahan means 'Three

Elephants', but there are no elephants left in the arid and cracked soil of this unwelcoming landscape. We have promised Tony Dyer to note any sign of elephant in our route, but so far we have seen none.

I like this place, however, its space, its silence, the feeling of walking on high land.

I am glad that we changed route. I feel like holding my head up and sniffing deeply, sensing the breeze, as the camels do.

Dark and dusty terrain, cracks covered in straw, full of the white, conical shells of ground snails, which crawl in vast numbers out of their holes in the rains. Thousands of squirming, slimy snails. Revolting thought. I have always loathed snails.

*　★　★

We walk for two hours on the plains, where Aidan sees a cheetah with two cubs in the distance through his field glasses. But when I look, it has vanished. Mirages are part of the landscape here and encounters are glimpses, mysterious and evanescent, they escape long scrutiny.

I walk rather than ride, as I had in the morning, and feel in great shape.

At 6 p.m. Aidan shoots a Peter's gazelle, a young male, for the *watu*'s meal. A last treat before the desert.

It happens so fast. We spot a small group of gazelles in the distance, watching us with high necks, as still as statues. Without pausing a moment Aidan nods to me and gives me his hat to keep so that we can get on walking without changing pace, not to alarm the gazelles. There are about eight in a small herd, perhaps half a mile away. He pulls out his .22 without altering the rhythm of his step, quickly and precisely, with fluid movements, as a hunter must. We hear just one shot, quick as a whiplash. Then I see Osman leap high like a grasshopper and dash through the plains with a young hare's sprint towards the creature, to cut its throat as Muslim custom demands. Without this *halal*[1] practice they cannot eat it.

Young Gedi, one of the two junior camel herders, runs after him with incredible speed, *shuka* flapping in the wind.

The horizon seems close and far away at the same time, and there they are profiled on it. I move towards them across the immensity of the plain.

The gazelle dies instantly, hit through the heart. Just enough time for Osman to slit its throat with Aidan's knife. They cut off its head, and in the dusty pupils, opaque and open in the twilight dusk, I can detect no pain. The memory of other dead dark eyes in the sun.

Jubilation, as meat equals a feast to all Africans. They throw the dead gazelle across the saddle of one of the pack camels and we move on.

We march and march for five hours through lava, and finally outspan at 9.45 p.m. in the

---

[1] Slaughtered according to the Koran rules.

middle of the track, the only possible place free of rocks.

A full moon, whining jackals and wild dogs and hyenas filling the night with prayers to the sky.

A lion roars at 12.30 p.m.

Wake up at 4.45 with an orange to wash my mouth of sleep, and leave before sunrise.

★ ★ ★

When the sun rises we watch it.

The desert lies ahead inexorable, forbidding, simmering in the distance. We cannot see its end. The sky is salmon pink. We stop a few moments to consider the challenge before beginning our march through it. Aidan turns up to me, our eyes meet and hold, and I nod. Just that.

'*Oho, galla*,' he prompts them. The camels snort and we move on.

I only walk for two and a half hours, my feet are aching so much after last night's five-hour march and the five hours in the previous morning. I do not think I could have continued to walk this time. The heat is scorching. The lava rocks burn through the soles of my shoes like live coals; Aidan's shirt sticks to his back, its green colour already faded and discoloured.

I agree to ride. All the men are silent.

★ ★ ★

My camel's name is Racub; quiet fellow. I ride, with drizzling dreams, falling asleep in the saddle, for three and a half hours. Aidan walks, showing no sign of tiredness. This desert seems to stretch over the horizon for ever. The swelter lifting from the stones at noon is extraordinary. Heat waves like mirages of water tremble on the horizon, trees appear in the distance, dark, with promise of shade, but we can never reach them. They are illusions of the fever of the heat, substance of dreams or hallucinations.

The sides of the track are burned by some exhausted fire; ashes and carbonized tree stumps add to the inferno feeling. Surprisingly, strange oblong nests of invisible birds festoon the majority of the skeletal shrubs like hope, transforming them to ghostly Christmas trees.

Where are the birds I wonder, and what can they eat or drink? Not even insects can survive in this heat.

In my head I write 'The Secret Cove', a story of ocean, water and of long-lost days.

Driven by the fear of being held in that hell, we make it much faster than we thought: time loses any meaning when walking through endless, monotonous stretches of desert like this one.

We outspan finally in a god-forsaken lava stretch, after crossing another desert of burned grass and whistling thorns. The sun is high on the horizon, unforgiving.

The camels stand silently next to us, with bowed heads, without eating, searching for a sparse shadow, and elusive moisture. We make an illusory shelter, tying my green canvas *tandarua* to a low dried-out shrub and to the handles of our food boxes. We slide under it, no more than a foot or so, on the stained camel mattresses, and Aidan is suddenly asleep.

25 September 1991

I walk the first two hours, having left the desolate lava stretch at 4.20 p.m. I am getting used to walking.

The camels take a very fast trot, and the men sing and whistle in high spirits, galloping along as fast as them, and probing them now and then with their camel sticks.

Although I feel really well, I just cannot keep up and finally have to ride. It is a painful ride, as I am sore and hot.

Beautiful country, though, open, wild, with yellow grass.

Is the rest of the world still there?

* * *

Outspan at 10.30 p.m. on a pleasant enough open area, with tall dry grass.

The camels begin to suffer from thirst and too much heat. They are splendid creatures, and I am full of admiration and respect.

We are treated to the classic dish of liver, kidney from the gazelle and onions, cooked by Osman: but it is inedible, too salty, strong and gamy. A powerful after-taste of urea.

The men sing and laugh late into the night around their fire.

Outspan in the heat of noon below an acacia tree facing silent hills, live with wandering insects.

Leave this morning, 25 September 1991, at 5.10 a.m., having woken at 4 a.m. The camels doze nearby, nibbling from sparse shrubs in the stillness.

Aidan looks preoccupied while consulting his maps and searching the horizon for landmarks. A far chain of unknown hills is all we see. Where is water? Will we make it to it? Will the camels survive?

We have apparently taken the wrong track, and will have to cut across country, a thought I relish, as this will free us from the monotony of following a marked line, however faint.

But what if we get lost?

Aidan finally sights the lava ridge which is our landmark to Koiya and water.

We should reach it in two days, but I do not dare to hope it.

26 September 1991

Walk through much nicer land, seasonal swamps, not easy for camels as the dry shiny grey swamp-grass is slippery and hides some dangerous holes.

Aidan knows we have missed our track and is anxious about losing precious time, concerned about the difficult terrain ahead. Tall tangles of thorns and spiky shrubs reach the camels' shoulders and are practically impenetrable, dangerous as they could hide deep cavities and the camels could break a leg. Vicious little hooks dig scratches through our torn shirts.

But we must go ahead without delay. Water is the key. What will we do if we cannot find the wells? Aidan's mouth is set in a grim line. But I am in much better spirits, as the landscape is so lovely and African and the pace much slower so I can easily walk. I secretly rejoice at our involuntary mistake.

Suddenly, on a straight stretch amidst tall acacia and thick silvery swamp grass, in a glade of afternoon light there stands a magnificent animal, unafraid and graceful, a male gerenuk. A fairy-elf of the savannah, who can only bring us luck. We watch each other for a while, then he leaves at his own pace, in elegant, unhurried leaps.

An unforgettable sight.

⋆ ⋆ ⋆

We leave the main track to cut across country. Luckily the landscape has changed, open now, with no more twisted shaggy bushes to impede the camels' progress: thanks, Emanuele! I always appeal to him when I am in trouble. Aidan has been so worried that I have to cheer him up. I just know it will be all right. The camels, patient, wise, gracefully bear their burden in long strides. My optimism is rewarded: a good lesson.

And then, in answer to my silent prayers and to make Aidan happy, we come to red sandy soil, dotted with acacia and comiphera. Totally wonderful walking through this terrain, resilient and solid soil allowing a bouncing step. My spirits lift as they have not in days. We outspan on a vast *mbogani* and light our own fire for the first time, while the men cut the usual *boma* of thorny bushes which will confine the camels for the night. Darkness falls on my happiness at having left the dreary straight line. The moon rises white and silent.

Then Aidan grimly announces that thirty camels are lost, and the herders are following them. They kept on by the light of the moon when we stopped, aiming towards far hills, which to them perhaps meant water. Like ghosts in the silvery light, they moved on, drawn by inexplicable instinct. There is nothing we can do but hope that our skilled people will catch up with them in time.

I try to cheer Aidan. If the herders can find the tracks by moonlight, they will follow them and we will wait here for a day. Not a bad thought, relaxing in this lovely country. Aidan is pessimistic. I reason that we are far from water holes and the confusing footprints of other camels, and that it will be easier for our skilled herders to follow the pale silvery tracks in the moonlight. But if the camels decide to go at a brisk trot, looking for water, it will be hard to catch up with them. They could be found by *shiftah* and stolen easily. It has happened before. And if the large lion whose footprints we detected on the track decides to ambush them, as is quite likely, they will gallop off in terror and we shall never see them again.

We go to bed early, having spilled the water, the salt, the muesli and the pasta!

But we underestimated our people; at about 10.45 p.m. we hear calls, whistles and screams. The night is full of activity. And we know they have found the camels.

⋆   ⋆   ⋆

We leave at sunrise on the 26th, happy, carefree, in excellent mood, through attractive pale yellow grass plains, rusty sandy soil. Compact and easy to walk on. Reach the lava boulders.

Outspan in a sandy *lugga*, under a clump of *Salvadoria* trees, a delightful refuge, and I feel happy. Ahmed offers me a special twig he has cut out of the tree's fibrous root, a valued original toothbrush to chew on. I am happy. Alive.

Aidan has learned the value of drinking water liberally during this safari, and although he is not at all well, he certainly has improved enormously. But he has blisters on his back, legs and his poor *sedere*. Bad suppurating tropical sores from scratches gone septic, which make walking painful with the chafing and the heat. I wash them with half a cup of warm water and apply antibiotic cream from my kit. I have convinced him to wear a loose *kikoi* rather than trousers, as our Somali do. He looks great in it, long-limbed as he is; and I feel in superb shape.

⋆   ⋆   ⋆

Matokole, 27 September 1991
Still twelve miles to Koiya

Last evening, having outspanned on a plain before dark, Aidan shot a francolin which we devoured, grilled on an open fire, impaled on a rough wooden spit, and spread with salt. A feast.

At bedtime, as I lower my head on to my mattress on the ground, I glimpse a quick movement, like a flutter, by my face. I have learned, after years of Africa, that instant reaction can save your life. Without thinking, I instantly sit up: a large pale yellow scorpion, the lethal *Sole Fugens*, disturbed by my gesture, his poison-laden tail arched, runs out of his stone, straight into the fire, where he sizzles to death in a few seconds.

We walk through the most beautiful country this morning: no sign of livestock or men because there is no water. But full of game. Grant — or Peter's — gazelles, oryx, giraffe, a landscape of tall fantastic acacia, open red-gold sands, a divine place. Walk for seven miles, between two lava ridges, of outstanding stark beauty. Must be wet seasonally, as there are signs of old livestock and M A N Y lion tracks.

Aidan tries to shoot some guinea fowl and francolins, but they are far too clever and fly off.

We take some photographs of the camels moving through acacia; then Aidan discovers that his camera has been empty all along! Tough luck. I have some good shots in mine, I hope. Now outspan on a sandy *lugga* of large acacia not far from Koiya. A disturbing feeling of people around. Although they are invisible, it seems that we can hear livestock bells.

The camels are all around me, lying in a circle and observing all we do. They nudge my head. They placidly guard me while I write. I wonder if they know how close water is: but is it?

Koiya, 28 September 1991

KOIYA!!!!!!!!!!

Water at last, and T W O days ahead of schedule.

Clean, fresh, abundant, sweet water at Koiya.

We marched yesterday evening along a lovely, grand sandy *lugga*, Matokole: difficult walking, and I refined the skill of finding the hard bits of sand — usually a darker grey crust — on which to walk without sinking.

We meet four youngsters from the tribe of Rendille in bright beaded ornaments and red *shukas* — the first people, after that Adjuran herdsman. Then, their scrawny white cattle, in clouds of dust.

Lion tracks — these omnipresent but invisible lions — gerenuk, but incredibly attractive banks along the river, with trees and palms, huge acacia and enamel-green bushes. I wish we could stop below them, but we have to go on.

Instead, we spend the night on a small rise of white pebbles and grey soil; Aidan shoots two francolins in the *lugga* — and two for the men, who rush to cut their skinny throats — and we roast them on a basic spit on an open fire, a royal meal, plus half an orange each and hot cocoa.

Wake up at 11 p.m. with a fat tick stuck on my shoulder, gorged with my blood, little swine; amazingly, the first tick to bite me, in this tick-infested country, and we always sleeping on the camel mattress thrown on the bare soil.

Sleep soundly thereafter until 4.30.

Leave at 5.45 a.m. on the 28th September.

★ ★ ★

The camel bells tinkling away like birds in the noonday sun, we proceed, following countless livestock trails, all converging on this famous place, the only water in miles and miles, but the herds are always ahead and never to be met.

At 7 a.m. we come across a Rendille *boma*, tiny, with goats still crouching. A sleepy, cheeky young Rendille wrapped in a red *shuka* is milking them with lazy strokes, the sun already high, to Aidan's indignation. He cheerfully greets us with no curiosity as to how the hell we could materialize, two Europeans and eight Africans carrying guns, with our seventy-eight camels, in the middle of nowhere.

Koiya appears at 8.15.

We stand for a time in silence, overwhelmed, to watch the target of our unforgiving progress.

A far outpost of the government. A group of *mabati* rondavels scattered on a rise, goats, a tiny *duka*, some round huts from whose dark doors people watch in silence. Luscious doum-palms on a *lugga* and clumps of tall acacia trees advertise the wells, like the oasis in the Sahara I

202

remember visiting once with my father. That is it. We have made it to Koiya, after all.

From clumps of rounded dwellings that look like the yellow cocoons of giant insects, a thin figure in long robes comes to meet us, holding a ceremonial stick. He is a kind old fellow called Hassan, the councillor who — guess what! — knows our friends Jasper Evans and Maurizio Dioli, and buys camels for Jasper.

In Muslim tradition, he greets us with deference as weary travellers, and accords us the courtesy our status demands. In no time — and with some fuss — he organizes his well for us, and a secluded patch of trees to outspan under.

The well has been dug in the sand, the opening lined with round borders of a pale compacted clay, and the water is transparent and yellow like a topaz, incredibly inviting and, for me, forbidden.

The camels drink in disciplined shifts of four at a time, waiting patiently for their turn in the shade of the acacia, while we watch and the two Ahmeds sing the haunting Song of Water. This is an antique hypnotic tune of celebration, evocative and melodious, which is sung whenever camels are approaching water: for the camels it means drinking, and, obedient, they perform accordingly. If camels could laugh, the air would resonate with their nasal whines of jubilation.

I really admire the control and dignity of these creatures, thirsty as they are, who let their companions drink their fill before they move forward. They curve their gracious white necks and drink rhythmically, unhurriedly from the troughs carved out of hollowed tree trunks. Their caved-in stomachs inflate gradually before our eyes; the bony ribs disappear, and those haggard tired beasts are transformed once more into handsome, fit young camels ready to start the endless march again. They begin to feed instantly, peeling small leaves off branches with spongy lips.

Aidan buys our people a goat, assisted by Hassan who does the bargaining, and we shall feast on it tonight. Osman is busy frying oil in a pan.

Liver and kidneys and onions and rice will once again be our spartan/glorious meal.

Aidan goes up to his waist into the yellow tempting water, helping to fill the troughs, and I envy the men's freedom in the Muslim world which does not allow women to bathe at the wells, for fear of defiling them.

Now: the first bath in eight days any second, any amount of water, and I shall wash the dust off my hair, behind a charming screen Aidan is building for me, a perfect retreat, sheltered from people's eyes. Now and again he smiles at me. His beard has grown and gives him the patriarchal look of some biblical prophet.

I love him.

Torngong, 29 September 1991
Koiya — Torngong

We spend a blissful entire day and night at Koiya.

204

We set up our little den by a clump of trees, under a mosquito net, the first private and comfortable bed since we left. The men sing low and hoarse songs of love — of war? — around their fire.

Earlier I noticed, in an abandoned seasonal *manyatta*, curious contraptions of tall scaffolding made from branches; Aidan explains that they are suspended beds, to protect people from mosquito, which do not fly that high.

So I suspect the night will be disturbed, but in the event, not a single mosquito is heard. Too dry at this time of the year for them.

Soon after settling down and arranging our camping gear, the Rendille come with their amazingly skinny goats, but they soon pass on, discreet and unbothered by our presence, and Koiya is all for us.

I observe these goats and the most rachitic looking sheep, nibbling at invisible morsels of food, never lifting their patient, bent heads from the dust: they seem to eat just that dust, but Aidan informs me that in fact they feed on fallen acacia flowers, so small and inconspicuous as to be like powder. Extraordinary survival skills.

A girl comes over and I give her a sweet. She takes it shyly, runs away, and soon three more girls are there, waiting in silence. I give them a handful of peppermints each, and they go off together, giggling like tinkling bells.

★ ★ ★

I sleep, write, take it easy. Wash my hair and all my body, luxuriously, lazily and happily, with plenty of water. Change into a clean caftan; walk down to the wells to see the camels drink, and generally regain my human condition.

Leave at 5.45 a.m., having woken up at 4.30 a.m. after a disturbed night as the camels — too close — never stop thumping, and the men have forgotten to muffle the wooden camel bells with handfuls of hay.

Walk at a steady pace to the lovely hill of Sepi, boulders of quartz with trees in the smouldering heat.

I pour water, now fairly abundant in our jerricans, all over myself and my shirt and trousers, and I feel renewed. I am dry in a few minutes.

Soon on our way to reach . . . Kairu?

★ ★ ★

Now, on the evening of 30 September, sitting out on a plateau overlooking the hills. Hills like a stage, empty of actors. Close to an old *manyatta*. I write in the last light before dark, while the men are cutting a *boma* to enclose the camels. Lions are about and we could have a stampede.

30 September 1991
Torngong — Lontopi

Lions roared continuously last night at Torngong, very close to us, ready to attack; the night resonated with their hunting growls. The camels stayed awake, nervous in the dark, ready to stand and scatter in all directions. We had to build a stronger *boma* and the men slept in turns, with fires all around. I lay staring at the stars overhead, sensing danger, and sleep fled.

In the morning their pug tracks mark the dust around the *boma*. We leave at 5.50 a.m., and walk only three hours and a quarter. It is on this track that we find the first unmistakable footprints of *shiftah*: three people walking alone, with no livestock, wearing the characteristic rubber sandals, fashioned from old tyres, that they are known to favour. The men become quiet and wary. Aidan loads his rifle. We all keep looking around, uneasy at the silent, enigmatic hills approaching Lontopi.

Despite our concern, when we stop Aidan builds a shelter for me on the side of a reddish *lugga*, and I wash again with great relish while he keeps guard. My hair dries in minutes.

Lontopi, 1 October 1991

This is the idyllic place called Lontopi, in Samburu land where there are ponds among the rocks; where there are springs and palms and shady trees along the hills; where in the sun one can wash, and let emotion prevail.

On our way to Kairu, back on schedule now: not many miles — just over twenty — covered in the last two days, as the terrain is uneven and rocky and lion tracks are everywhere.

We shall now have to work hard, walk more, to keep up with our plan. But it was worth this rest and indulgence from 9 a.m., and the memory which will not fade.

These large camels, I observe, love to feed on the most improbable grey, desiccated weeds — *Indigophera Spinosa* — which must be powerfully nutritious, but look like cobweb. I watch them nibbling at these frail delicate grasses with their prehensile lips, chewing them again and again patiently for hours to extract any nutriment they may have.

They munch away in great content all morning, and drink at the springs at Lontopi, while I watch them, perched on a rock like a baboon.

A beautiful mountain ahead, with great boulders and some doum-palms in the vast pink sand *lugga*.

Shiftah hide on these hills to survey the land around for their quarry. We could be that quarry, in fact. An eerie feeling, possibly being observed by cruel, invisible eyes, narrowed below lowered turbans. Images of cowboys in a Western movie being ambushed by impassive Apaches sitting on ponies from hilltops.

Everyone is alert and the men hold their guns carefully.

I try not to think of their AK47s and the long curved knives they use to cut their prisoners' throats. Osman, his eyes like slits, comes and talks to Aidan in hushed tones. They turn to look at me and I understand that I am the topic of their conversation.

The night is throbbing with crickets and strange unknown insects singing their diverse songs of life. I write by the light of my little diary cover, fitted out with battery and bulb, bought in a camping store one May morning in Washington DC, when I wore an Armani suit and had an appointment with a senator: days impossibly far removed from this reality. I notice that Osman has placed himself closer to us on my other side. Aidan is next to me, his loaded rifle at hand.

The night vibrates with tension.

I wake up early, stiff and covered in dew. I see Osman's eyes on me, in the livid light before dawn, and know he has not slept.

I sit to finish my diary, while he revives the fire for tea.

For as long as I live I shall remember images of this unusual and unrepeatable safari — which has gone almost, already, in a soft haze of days. Places unvisited by man, reachable only on foot. Far from roads, miles and miles behind hills and *luggas* and waterless plains; lava hills and quartz sands, stones glittering with green and coral fire.

Patient camels, resilient, trustworthy, wise with the timeless instinct of survival in the harsh forbidding lands where they belong.

I shall remember oryx trotting off up hills, black tails flickering; the gerenuk surprised in the swamp, in the narrow path of grey silvery cane-grasses. The Song of Water at Koiya, exultant, melodious, and the jutting, darting walk of the wild Rendille warriors clad in red, with their fine faces and lithe bodies, muscular elves of the sand *luggas*; the starving goats and sheep searching for invisible particles of food amongst their own pellets; the gentle rhythm of the camel bells; the methodical unhurried chewing of their cud; their eyes, fringed with long wise eyelashes, their way of kneeling on the dust, sudden, complying. The funny shape of their sturdy tails, like huge silverfish; the way they urinate, backward, letting their brown gummy urine with its aromatic penetrating smell of unknown herbs trickle down their back legs to evaporate and cool them; the oily sap of the spicy *ginau*, the balsamic plant tasting of mango and turpentine; the colour of the rising sun in skies of red, the silhouettes of the camels against the horizon; the morning light on the pale yellow grass streaked with silver; the dust and twigs in the eye of the dead Peter's gazelle; a little natural shelter on the Arba Jahan plain, below a *Salvadorensis* tree, surrounded by the camels browsing on its leaves. The quest for Koiya and the elation, the sense of achievement, at reaching it ahead of time; the colour of the first water in the well, topaz yellow and transparent, so good to drink and fresh on my sunburned skin.

The Rendille girls, heads small, circled by bead ornaments, rusty red peplums over brown leather beaded skirts.

Our fires in the silence of the night.

The emotion of the pond at Lontopi.

The long ride on the endless desert.

Walking, step by step, in Aidan's tracks, the pattern of the soles of his shoes, familiar round marks on brown rubber.

The lion's roar with the moon. Its pug marks

printed in the dust. Its feral smell brought by the breeze.

The ever present fear of invisible *shiftah*. The taste of adrenalin when we see their tracks.

Osman's eyes, coloured by his courage.

★ ★ ★

Tonight I am writing lying on the sheepskin on the camel mattress; the fire smoulders. A quiet intermittent touch of camel bells; songs of nocturnal insects. The sound of my breathing.

A breeze, like waves through the palm trees. The flavour of wonder.

Aidan, asleep at my side.

2 October 1991
Lontopi — Il baa Okut

At Il baa Okut, our second to last night in the bush.

Walk through Samburu land, across the Kairu *lugga*: huge expanse of white sand, doum-palms in large clusters and an almost dry well circled with tangles of thorns.

We meet two Samburu women and one donkey going for water. A biblical scene. Then a little boy in a red *shuka* herding surprisingly fat calves.

Hot, hot and very aching feet. Amazing views of the Ndoto mountains and Lolokwe in the distance, our target tomorrow, and the end of our journey, where Karanja will be waiting.

3 October 1991
Il baa Okut — Lolokwe

We walk along the pink quartz sand *lugga* of Il baa Okut, extraordinary old trees with hanging roots, on the banks among tall hills made of red granite boulders, emerging from a sea of green bushes. Osman walks ahead leading Racub, a youthful spring in his step. He turns to smile at me with true liking, and I am touched. I can well see why Aidan, who has been here before, so much loves this place.

The surprise of a lesser kudu, motionless, watching us from the middle of the *lugga*; a grey monkey, darting agile across, and up a tree.

Tracks of cattle ahead, but we never seem to reach them.

I have grown to dislike cattle during this safari. Their total unsuitability to this land, and what they do to it: a lifeless, desolate landscape of dust and dried dung, flies, ticks, hoof marks and torn shrubs. The camels on the other hand, majestic and solemn, sail on disdainfully, leaving only their soft print, which does not raise dust, docile camels who know their names and people's voices, noble creatures. I am totally sold on camels this trip.

Now, waiting under a tree just before the rendezvous, where my driver Karanja should be already, with water, milk, *posho*, vegetables . . . but is not, so we send the two Ibrahims ahead to guide him here.

Aidan builds yet another bathroom for me, the last, the most charming of all, with my

212

green screen and stones for the shower's floor, and I wash my hair, soap in bubbles, and I feel fresh, civilized. I wear a red caftan for happiness.

The camels are grazing quietly nearby, watched by those tireless herders, Gedi and Mamhood. Osman silently brings me a mug of sweet strong tea with ginger. We wait for the car from Laikipia.

We have today, at 10.45 a.m. completed 280 miles in thirteen days. Twenty miles a day average, though in the first six days of the safari we averaged twenty-seven miles a day; we slowed down when we stopped walking at night and left the track. It seems impossible to believe, but I actually made it.

⋆ ⋆ ⋆

The noise of an engine.
Karanja has arrived with my Toyota.
And this, then, is the end of the safari.

⋆ ⋆ ⋆

Later we send Karanja with Aidan's Samburu guide, and Ibrahim, to buy a goat in a nearby *manyatta* of Samburu Moran.

Tonight a last celebration. Then, Laikipia. The camels will proceed to Aidan's ranch with the staff: the remaining itinerary is not so intriguing, because it is not new to us, and we shall go ahead with the car. Karanja says there has been trouble with the government, and possibly

Saturday there might be more unrest. It seems so far away and pointless.

4 October 1991

We feasted last night on the goat, with rice and fresh cabbage, and fresh milk with which I made Aidan a surprise treat of a chocolate mousse, having smuggled a packet in my saddle bag and saved it for the last meal.

Extraordinary how just a few hours of rest make one regain one's human condition, and the pleasure of appreciating the gift of wilderness. How one looks at things and savours them again. Our people have been great. Their prompt smiles, their hot teas, their morning songs.

Osman, a born leader, knowledgeable and wise, loyal to the end. Gedi and Mamhood, the two Ahmeds, Ibrahim and Lwokignei, my good Laikipia men, to whom I must give new watches as souvenirs of the trek. I do not think they have ever owned one.

Finished now. Yes, I am sorry it has ended so soon.

I only wish there had been more time, at least after Koiya, just to look around, to pause and perceive the magic of our surroundings. But the camels do not stop. One has to follow, otherwise one is quickly left behind. And camels are of course the only means of transport through desert lands, and the only chance to arrive here. So, there is no time to ponder on a bird or a tree, the gracious curve of a bank, a sudden view of hills and the shape of those oryx in the distance. An unhurried hurry is essential, inexorable and leaving no quarter. No chance to treasure the fleeing moment in the 'here and now', as the 'here and now' goes too fast, like a speeded-up film.

Like a marvellous book of complex and fine drawings, each leaf of which would be worth the pause of the attention, but the pages flick by too rapidly, without allowing the time to be observed, absorbed, and known.

Were it not for this scanty diary, scribbled in exhaustion in noons too hot for wisdom, in nights of distant jackals at the light of fading embers, perhaps I would not remember all the pauses, the views, some fugitive landscape already left behind by our unforgiving progress.

Yet I shall remember what I have not written too, as so complex and resourceful is the mind. And the colours and sounds and lights will come back unexpectedly years from now. I shall value these memories, and I know that when I am old and grey I shall look at my camel stick, shiny with wear, with deep nostalgia. And wherever I am, I will smell the resin and dust of the plains at Arba Jahan.

I am waiting for a welcome sound, the tinkling of his camel bell.

Isobel Burton, letter to Lady Paget

I turn the last page. There are other, more recent pages written in ink.

Laikipia, 30 November 1991

He survived the camel trek through lava deserts
and we managed to avoid *shiftah* at the water
holes, all the way up to Il baa Okut. We never
met the bandits. But they caught him when he
went home on leave, to rest. It was the time of
the tribal clashes between the Dogadia and the
Adjuran clans.

Shiftah ambushed Ibrahim Ahmed on his way
to his *boma*, not so far from Moyale, and they
slit his throat. I never saw him again.

They stole his new watch.

Laikipia, 24 December 1991

Aidan flew low over the house this morning and
landed at Kuti before lunch.

'Can we take the car?' He smiled. 'There is
something I would like you to see. Over the
Corner Dam. I'll drive with you. Bring Sveva.'

We drive off in the late morning sun, leaving
my house where the aroma of roast turkey and
tortellini announces Christmas dinner. Even
after twenty-five years, I never got used to a hot
sunny Christmas, whose traditional tinsel deco-
rations, made for grey snowy afternoons, look so
totally out of place.

We meet a herd of impala and some zebra and
eland and elephant coming to water. But on
reaching the last stretch of carissa shrubs I see
them, and am totally caught unaware.

A grinning Osman, leaning on his camel stick;

216

Gedi and Ahmed Nyeusi, smiling, loosened turbans on their proud heads held high; and behind them, the camels.

Tall graceful Adjuran female camels, led by Racub.

With a lump in my throat I turn to Aidan. I always thought those camels were for him.

'I had no idea . . . '

He is watching me. His serious, intent eyes hold a smile:

'The breeding females were always meant for you. And Racub. Sorry I can't wrap your present. Happy Christmas.'

He hands me an envelope. There is a card. A photo of myself at the wells at Koiya, with the camels drinking in the background in that blinding white light.

On the other side is written:

'Christmas 1991. For my love, fifty camels.'

Postscript

Osman, The End

One evening, in early February 1998, Osman
Nguyu Dupa flew into Ol ari Nyiro with Aidan.
He spent the night with Issak Ngolicha, our
cattle headman, to whose clan he belonged and
whose friend he was.

I saw him next morning at Kuti.

He had come to greet me. He carried a camel
stick shiny and noble with wear. His traditional
dress made him look taller: a long Somali *kikoi*,
a shirt, a dark jacket, open sandals. A white
turban of light cotton muslin was knotted a few
times loosely round his head. I noticed that the
hair showing beneath it was black, as if the grey I
recalled had disappeared somehow, and he
looked younger than I remembered him.

He was uncharacteristically cheerful, more
talkative than ever before. He asked after Sveva,
about what I was doing. I told him that I was
completing a book — this book — and that the
story of our camel trek of 1991 would be part of
it.

He seemed extremely pleased.

He took my hand in his and shook it a few
times vigorously:

'*Asante sana. Kukumbuka ni mzuri. Asante*

219

sana.' Thank you, it is a good thing to remember.

He repeated this again with his deep, solemn voice. His serious, sorrowful eyes shone with a rare smile which spread over his ancient face with such luminous intensity that its memory still haunts me.

He was going on leave, to Moyale, for two months. Things were bad there. There had been lots of *shiftah* incidents in recent months. Many people had been murdered and a killer strain of malaria was rampant after the El Nino rains. All the same, he was looking forward to seeing his children. His teeth were startlingly white when he smiled.

It was the last time I saw Osman.

The news came to me from Aidan, one day in early March 1998, after sunset. He told me on the internal radio network, on the eve of my departure for London to visit my daughter and bring this manuscript.

Osman had been taken by *shiftah* and was believed dead.

The communications with Moyale were interrupted and telephones did not work. Because of the floods all roads were cut off. It was over ten days before one of my staff returned from leave with accurate news.

The Ethiopian clan of the Garreh has for some time been in the pay of the Tigre Government of Ethiopia, in order to report on the rebel Oromo clan, a related tribe, Borana-connected and speaking the same dialect. The Oromo rebels have been retaliating. Cattle and camel raids are the order of the day. People are killed. The

Oromo *shiftah* have guns and knives and they know how to use them.

One morning, during Osman's leave, in full daylight, the sky seemed to explode, detonating with screams and shots and cattle's and camels' cries. The Oromo *shiftah* were attacking the *manyatta* where Osman kept his livestock.

He was a few miles away and heard the commotion. Immediately he realized what was happening he ran to help. They tried to restrain him and failed. With him went a woman whose son, for whose safety she was concerned, was staying at the *boma*.

They were on the road to the *manyatta* when they were ambushed. The woman was savagely beaten and left for dead, and the *shiftah* dragged Osman with them to the hills.

There, they cut his throat.

News came of his severed arm, sent to the village as a warning of what would happen to others if they spied. The rest of his body was never found: no doubt it was left for the hyena that roam each night the barren Ethiopian hills.

At the time of writing, Aidan is flying to Moyale to find out more and to help and comfort his family.

When I return to Kenya, and we have obtained the necessary passes, we will go back together to look for Osman's remains. Almost certainly, it will be impossible to find them. But we owe it to Osman to try.

As a faithful Muslim, he must be buried with his head towards Mecca. Perhaps, this will be the time that I will call in my favour to the Abagatha of the Borana people. His support and protection will be invaluable in that harsh land, riddled with rebels, where human life has no value at all.

I shall write that account in due course. Now is the time to mourn. Sadness descends on us when we remember our companion in adventure, and reflect on the meaning of his violent and barbarous death. Our consolation is that Osman died bravely, and for one of his faith this represents certainty to be in the paradise of Allah, in the company of heroes.

As it is written.

London, March 1998

We do hope that you have enjoyed reading this large print book.

Did you know that all of our titles are available for purchase?

We publish a wide range of high quality large print books including:
Romances, Mysteries, Classics
General Fiction
Non Fiction and Westerns

Special interest titles available in large print are:
The Little Oxford Dictionary
Music Book
Song Book
Hymn Book
Service Book

Also available from us courtesy of Oxford University Press:
Young Readers' Dictionary
(large print edition)
Young Readers' Thesaurus
(large print edition)

For further information or a free brochure, please contact us at:
Ulverscroft Large Print Books Ltd.,
The Green, Bradgate Road, Anstey,
Leicester, LE7 7FU, England.
Tel: (00 44) 0116 236 4325
Fax: (00 44) 0116 234 0205

Other titles in the
Charnwood Library Series:

LOVE ME OR LEAVE ME

Josephine Cox

Beautiful Eva Bereton has only three friends in the world: Patsy, who she looks upon as a sister; Bill, her adopted cousin, and her mother, to whom she is devoted. With Eva's father increasingly angry about life as a cripple, she and her mother support each other, keeping their spirits high despite the abuse. So when a tragic accident robs Eva of both parents, Patsy, a loveable Irish rogue, is the only one left to support her. Tragedy strikes yet again when Eva's uncle comes to reclaim the farm that Eva had always believed belonged to her parents. Together with Patsy, Eva has no choice but to start a new life far away . . .

COLDITZ: THE GERMAN STORY

Reinhold Eggers

This is the story of the famous German prison camp Colditz — as the German guards saw it. It was a place where every man felt that in spite of the personal tragedy of imprisonment, it was his duty to overcome. The book vividly describes the constant battle of wits between guards and prisoners, the tunnelling, bribery, impersonations, forgery and trickery of all kinds by which brave men sought to return to the war.

THE POPPY PATH

T. R. Wilson

It's 1920 and, the years of wartime rationing over, the inhabitants of the seaside resort of Shipden are turning again to the good things of life. The hottest news is that a new doctor has arrived in town: a handsome young man who would sweep any one of Shipden's many hopeful females off their feet. So when James Blanchard decides to marry pretty Rose Jordan the community is both shocked and outraged. Like many of the 'war widows' around her, Rose is an attractive, highly intelligent, single mother. But the scandalous difference is that Alec Taverner — the father of her four-year-old daughter — is still very much alive.

FALSE PRETENCES

Margaret Yorke

When her goddaughter is arrested during an anti-roads protest, Isabel Vernon is startled to discover that the fair-haired child of her memory has become a shaven-headed environmentalist and that Isabel herself is now regarded as Emily Frost's next of kin. Emily, released on bail to the Vernons, takes up a job as home help to a local family and forms an instant attachment to Rowena, the four-year-old girl in her charge. Emily's presence in the Vernons' house proves troubling, and is deepening the profound tensions within Isabel's marriage when the arrival of someone else threatens the safety of both Emily and the child, Rowena.

TREVOR McDONALD FAVOURITE POEMS

Trevor McDonald

Trevor McDonald, popular newscaster and also Chairman of the Campaign for Better Use of the English Language, has now compiled an anthology of his favourite poetry from across the ages. The collection is based on material published in his regular Anthology column in the *Daily Telegraph*. It is a comprehensive introduction to the poetry of the English language, from Milton to Ted Hughes, from Britain and abroad. He has included both perennial favourites and less familiar but accessible poetry. Each poet is introduced with a concise history of their work and there is something to suit all tastes and moods.